Advar [illegible]

"*Dissonance* is a courageou [illegible]
trauma, and how it reverberates into adulthood with devastating after-shocks. Farison has transmuted her pain into an exquisitely told story that depicts, with great precision, the grooming process that allowed an exploitative teacher to forge a bond of diabolical dependence, holding her emotionally hostage for years. This unforgettable book is a must-read for those who cannot imagine the web of bewilderment, guilt, and helplessness that ensnares victims—and it will inspire survivors who long to reclaim their lives."

—Stephen Mills, author of *Chosen: A Memoir of Stolen Boyhood*

"Bridging the divide between past and present, consent and exploitation, Megan Farison invites the reader into a powerful story of redemption and healing."

—Dr. Ingrid Clayton, PhD, author of *Believing Me*

". . . a knothole into an Escher-like depiction of how grooming erodes our foundational understanding of trustworthy connection. Megan reveals the disorienting impact of child sexual abuse and the enduring confusion while simultaneously illustrating a love of family and self-compassion too often absent in a survivor's narrative. Through her authentic writing, Megan emphasizes that, while abuse is a piece of her history, love is the heart of this book."

—Anna Sonoda,
author of *Duck Duck Groom: How a Child Becomes a Target*

"As an educator who has worked in the field of sexual abuse prevention . . . as a mother, daughter, woman . . . as a human who lives in a world where adults use their positions of power to take advantage of the children they have vowed to protect, I can say with absolute confidence: *Dissonance* is a must-read."

—Mackenzie Bufis, co-founder of The Elephant Alliance

"Every voice that speaks up is one more voice in the battle against sexual abuse. Megan tells her story bravely and selflessly, and in doing so brings society one step closer to quashing the stigmas that seek to silence us."

—Cara Kizer, classical musician and survivor

"Compelling, timely, honest, and necessary."

—Anna Schechter, head coach at First Book Coaching, MA Victorian Literature, University of Oxford

"As band directors, music teacher educators, and leaders, we have a responsibility to bear witness to these stories to better recognize and respond to signs of abuse within our profession. In *Dissonance,* Megan bravely confronts her childhood trauma with the clear purpose of protecting others from the pain she endured. The future of music education is safer because of her."

—Hannah Greer-Young, music educator and researcher, author of "The Call is Coming from Inside the House, Sexual Misconduct in U.S. Band Programs"

"I saw myself in Megan's words . . . Her bravery paves a path for those who have not yet spoken."

—Sara Bigge, survivor

"Dissonance intricately explores the ripple effects of trauma on personal relationships, self, identity, and the struggle for healing and redemption."

—Kori Orlowski, trauma survivor

"History, despite its wrenching pain, cannot be unlived, but if faced with courage, need not be lived again."
— Maya Angelou

Dissonance

Randi,
I'm still so grateful for that day we met up at the crepe place. Thank you for always being so kind and supportive.

Dissonance

A MEMOIR

MEGAN FARISON

GIVE HER THE PEN

Dissonance is a work of nonfiction.
Some names and identifying details have been changed.

Published in the United States.

ISBN:979-8-9918867-0-3
Application to United States Library of Congress in progress.

Cover design by Victoria Heath
Interior Design by Danielle Szabreath

meganfarison.com
giveherthepen.com

For Dan, who said,
"Do whatever it takes to heal."

And for You . . . wherever you are.

"As long as you keep secrets and suppress information,
you are fundamentally at war with yourself . . .
The critical issue is allowing yourself to know what you know.
That takes an enormous amount of courage."

—Bessel A. van der Kolk
The Body Keeps the Score: Brain, Mind, and Body in the Healing of Trauma

"I suppose that I did for myself what psychoanalysts do for their patients.
I expressed some very long felt and deeply felt emotion.
And in expressing it, I explained it and then laid it to rest."

—Virginia Woolf

AUTHOR'S NOTE

I've often read the advice, *wait until you're fully healed to write your story*. I disagree. If we all waited, most of our stories would never get written, and those who need our stories most would never hear them. As Dr. Brené Brown once said, "Shame cannot survive being spoken." So, I will speak.

If you've ever lived in fear of what you've done
or what's been done to you.
If you've ever struggled to separate the two . . .
you are not alone.

Prologue

Monday, November 25th, 2019
6:13 P.M.

It was as if the house and I were grieving together. I looked around me and all I could see was *loss*. In shadowed corners, tables and countertops suffocated under stacks of unopened mail. The kitchen sink drowned in crusted weeks-old dishes. Cardboard boxes laid in corners, slumped, their dusty heads collapsing under the weight of neglect.

Except for a mid-century lamp that hung in the dining room, every light in the house was off. The lamp cast a sick, yellowy glow across a nearby wall that held the history of a love story, told in framed photos of family and friends, babies and school pictures, cherished pets that had long since been buried in backyards. Through my sore, swollen eyes, I narrowed in on a particular image—older than the rest—of a starry-eyed teenage girl with long sandy blonde hair, lanky limbs, and under her hazel eyes the permanent dark circles she inherited from her grandmother. She's standing behind a birthday cake and smiling. She's happy.

Of course she is. She doesn't know.

Into the adjacent living room I dragged two chairs and positioned them in front of the sprawling brick fireplace mantle. I turned the chairs to face each other, then stepped back to measure the distance between them. I made slight adjustments to one, then the other. Again and again. As if it would make a difference. Still, it was something I had control over, and that was enough to stay the course. Once everything was in place, I waded through the thick twists of wool beneath me, the remains of a shag carpet that would soon be gone. Pieces of it had already been ripped out, revealing patches of worn subfloor that for decades had been hidden from sight.

When I reached the center of the living room, I realized there was nothing left to do but wait. I glanced back at the girl in the photo as if to say, *I'm sorry.* I imagined what I'd do if I could magically climb into the photo, back into my old kitchen. I'd wrap my arms around her and tell her everything. But what would she do? She's just a child.

The distant rumbling of an engine drew my gaze back to the front window and its view of the driveway, which sat dark and empty. It wouldn't be empty for much longer.

I checked my phone.

6:31.

Oh God.

As the engine grew louder, the beating inside me grew faster and heavier. My chest tightened, like someone had double-knotted a shoestring around my heart, the painful and persistent thud marking time with each passing second.

Oh God. God, please. Please help me.

Panic shot up as two beams of ghostly light darted across the dining room wall. I turned my head and saw the truck pulling into the drive, its headlights growing larger and more threatening as it inched its way closer to the house. With clenched fists, I held my breath and braced for impact.

This is it. Any moment he'll walk through that door. He'll know what's happened, and our marriage will be over.

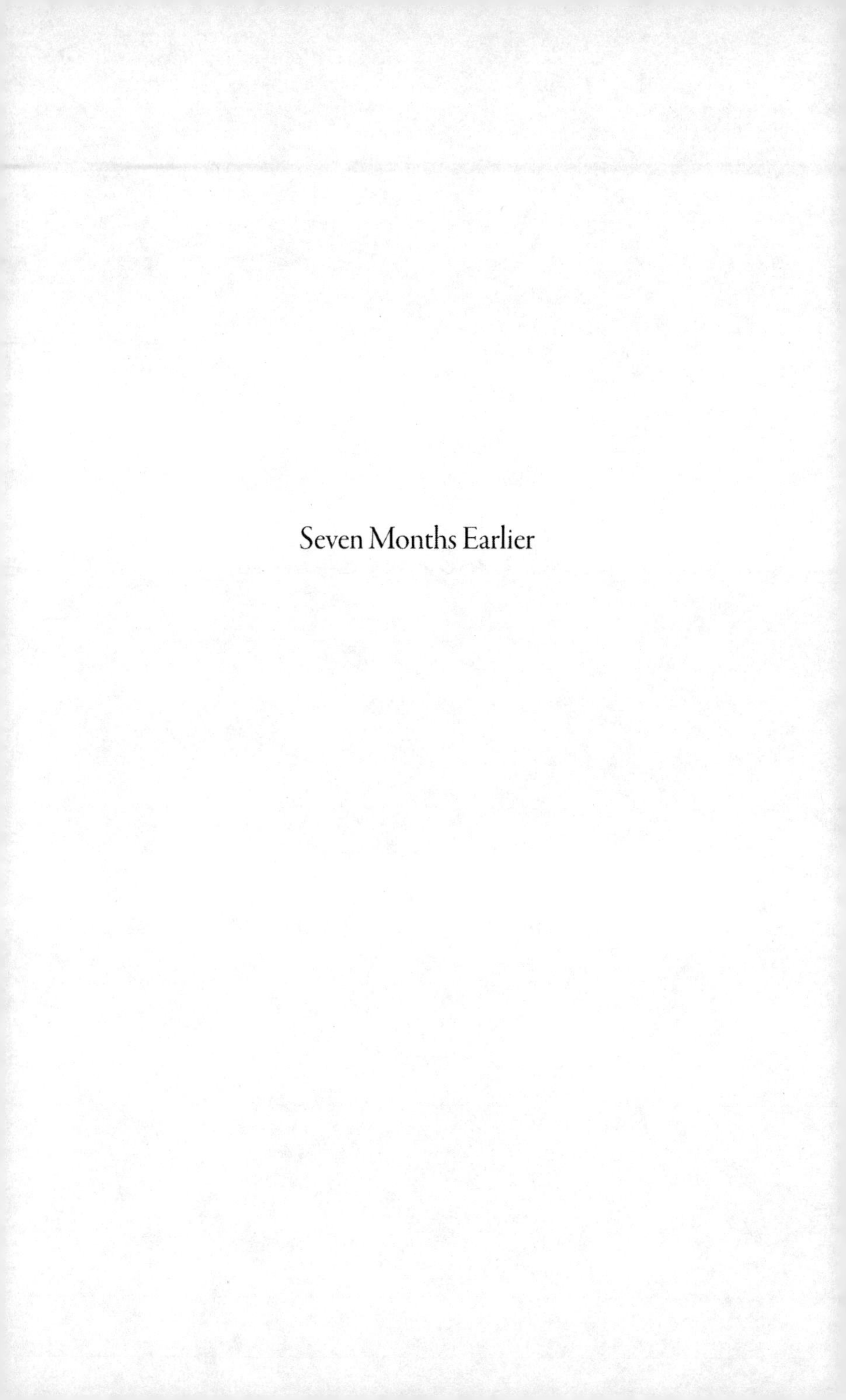

Seven Months Earlier

April 8th, 2019

Today is going to be a great day. That was my first conscious thought that morning. Most days I'd wake to a head full of chatter, a relentless monologue of dos and don'ts: *make breakfast, pack lunches, load the dishwasher, sign the field trip permission slip, reschedule the dentist appointment, pick the boys up from school, take them to piano lessons, find the motivation to cook dinner instead of grabbing McDonalds again*. But that morning, as my gaze drifted across the bedroom ceiling, my mind was quiet. My body at ease. I wasn't worried about work or my weight or my kids. I didn't even feel guilty for drinking half a lowball of bourbon the night before, even though I had promised myself all day that *this* was the day I would avoid the liquor cabinet.

Lazily, I rolled over to find Ian on his back, the tip of his nose pointed at his phone screen. "Reading anything exciting?" I said.

"The usual," Ian said, yawning. "The world's a mess."

I reached over to the bedside table and checked my phone. "It's past seven. You gotta get up," I said, rubbing his shoulder. "Just think. Only two months of school left."

His eyes shifted toward me. He looked unamused. "Easy for you to say."

I was in the kitchen packing lunches when Ian grabbed a light jacket from the closet. I watched as he hurried past me to the sliding glass door that led to the three-season breezeway. "Excuse me," I said, playing coy. "You're just going to leave without kissing your wife goodbye?"

Ian made a quick about-face and hurried back to the kitchen. "Sorry, I've got a lot on my mind." With a sharp, stilted gesture that was almost marionette-like, he leaned forward, eyes open, lips puckered. I threw my arms around his neck, pressed my mouth to his, and waited eagerly for him to press back. When his lips didn't budge, I felt a familiar ache in my gut. "I mean, a *real* kiss," I said.

Ian's sturdy frame softened. He stared down at me, shaking his head and smiling. "That *was* a real kiss."

I had seen this look before, many times—an expression that fell somewhere between fondness and frustration. It seemed to say, *What do you want from me? Don't you know I love you?*

Of course I knew he loved me. I just wanted to *feel* it at that particular moment.

Breaking Ian's gaze, I turned back to the counter and patted the blue vinyl lunch box. "Don't forget to take this."

"*Right.*" Ian grabbed the lunchbox, along with the lanyard that held his work keys. As he was getting ready to leave a second time, footsteps appeared, padding across the floor above. Ian turned back in my direction, his eyes assuring me, *Don't worry. I'll wait.*

Before long, our nine-year-old, Evan, was standing at the bottom of the stairs in his Spiderman pajama set, rubbing sleep out of his eyes. "Bye, Daddy," he cooed.

Ian bent down. He pushed back the thick tuft of dark hair Evan had donned since birth, gazed lovingly into Evan's brown eyes (a perfect color match to Ian's) then kissed him on the forehead. "Love you, buddy."

From a distant room, a high-pitched voice cried out, "Wait! Daddy!" followed by a *thump, thump, thump,* zooming across the floor and down the steps. Like a wild animal, our six-year-old, Eli, jumped at Ian, who caught him with a guttural *oof!* Ian threw his head back in laughter, gave Eli a kiss that made him tickle-squirm, then carefully lowered him until his bare feet were safely on the ground.

"I've got to go," Ian said, his words picking up speed. "Be good at school." He opened the glass slider and stepped into the breezeway, passing the metropolis of boxes that still needed unpacking from the move.

As he disappeared from sight, I called out to him one last time, "Love you!" His voice echoed back to me, followed by the thud of the garage door.

When it was time for school, the boys and I meandered out the door to our white minivan, which sported over 225,000 miles and a growing coat of rust. It was paid-off, though, and the engine still ran, that's what mattered—one less bill to pay. Evan yanked the sliding door open and hoisted himself into the booster seat. I checked Eli to make sure his seatbelt was laced securely into the red safety clip, then I walked around the van and climbed into the driver's seat. "What's our pump-up song for the day?" I asked. It was Evan's turn to pick.

Before Evan could speak—"'Old Town Road'!" Eli hollered, his legs kicking excitedly.

Evan rolled his eyes. "You always want that song. How about 'High Hopes,' Mumma?"

I peered into the rearview mirror and gave Evan an approving look. "Good choice, buddy."

It was never Ian's dream to live in the city. He had always groaned about "city living" and "city people," said there was nothing worse than someone practically living in your backyard, telling you what you can and can't do with your property. Ian grew up in a rural area outside of Midland, Michigan, on seven acres of mostly wooded land. It was a far cry from my upbringing in Flint, one of the largest cities in the state and, at one time, one of the most prosperous, until General Motors closed up its factories in the '80s.

Before I turned three, my mom and I moved in with my stepdad, Randy, who sold used cars for a living. The house Randy owned sat directly on the car lot, a fact I wore like a medallion because it set me apart from other kids. Whenever I told friends or classmates where I lived, their eyes would widen with disbelief. They'd say, *You live on a car lot?!* And I'd smile back and say, *Yes, I really do live on a car lot.*

A child of the '90s, I was raised on Disney princess films and boy bands. I dreamed of getting married and moving into one of those white picket fence colonial-style houses in made-for-TV movies: yellow birch trees lining the sidewalks, couples walking dogs, neighbors hosting cookouts, the cranking of wheels and sharp ringing of bells as children ride by on their bicycles.

Ian, on the other hand, cared little for suburbia. His dream was a reincarnation of the life he'd had as a child: wide open spaces to plant gardens and raise livestock, a pole barn to fix vehicles and tinker with old trucks. When he and I got married, I happily made his dream my own. What mattered most to me was that we were in love and we were on a journey together. Besides, it was easy to romanticize country living—the quiet pastures and porch swings, late-night bonfires and peaceful walks in the woods. A simple life against a picture-perfect backdrop. Since neither of us came from money and both of us wanted to be teachers, Ian and I knew we would never be wealthy, but we always thought we'd make enough to live comfortably and provide a good life for our family.

Things didn't exactly go according to plan. In 2016, after eight years of marriage and teaching, we were finally able to afford a home with some acreage. We were living in the country, but we weren't living the simple, country life we had hoped for. There was too little time and not enough money. Ian and I were both working full-time as choir directors in the same school district—Ian on one side of town and me on the other—leading high school and middle school choral programs in addition to teaching multiple classes of elementary music each week. We led after-school ensembles and musical rehearsals, organized concerts and community events. Every day, one of us would drop Evan and Eli off two hours before their school day started, and one of us would pick them up two hours after their school day ended. To help with bills and paying off student loan debt, Ian worked as a wedding DJ most Saturdays from May through October.

It was nearly impossible to keep up with the demands of work and personal life. When I wasn't at work, I was still working, or I was thinking about work, which left little time or energy for anything else. I didn't want to give up teaching, but I was drowning mentally, emotionally, and physically. I needed more freedom to take care of myself and my family. So I started praying for a way out.

In the summer of 2018, a full-time music director position opened up at a prominent church in town, a unicorn of a job that paid a teacher's salary but offered a more flexible schedule. When I got the job, I felt lighter than I had in a decade. I had forgotten what it was like to be present—truly present—with my children, to have enough free space inside my head to read stories and play make-believe with them.

The church job improved our lives significantly, but it was still a full-time job with evening and weekend commitments. Meanwhile, Ian's teaching responsibilities were expanding and the boys' schedules were growing busier. Since our daily routines revolved around work, school, and church, Ian and I discussed moving into town as a way to make our lives easier. The discussion was never too serious, at least, not for Ian. I knew he wanted desperately to stay where we were. I knew he would bend and twist himself into whatever shape life demanded, carry whatever load was necessary so we wouldn't have to surrender what we had worked so hard to attain.

In October, Ian surprised me with pictures he'd found online of a 1960s mid-century ranch. "That is the only house I will move into town for," he said.

I didn't see the appeal right away. It certainly wasn't the two-story colonial I'd been dreaming of since I was a child. But when Ian described how he saw it, the house magically transformed into a charming vintage time capsule. He *oohed* and *aahed* over the craftsmanship of the cabinets and the built-in shelves, marveled at the living room's sprawling fireplace hearth.

I pointed at the picture of the living room, my face squinted. "Lime-green shag carpet? Are you serious?"

He laughed. "I like it! This is the neighborhood where engineers and doctors used to live in the '60s and '70s. This house reminds me of simpler times."

We moved in on March 1st, 2019.

It seemed too good to be true. I had a job that gave me room to breathe and, as a bonus, provided a wonderful church home for my family. I was living in a beautiful house in town, tucked inside a picture-perfect neighborhood. Everything was falling into place, and I couldn't imagine wanting anything more.

Not long after I started working at the church, a visiting pastor and I were having a casual conversation following the Sunday worship service. We were seated at a circular table, one of many scattered throughout the brightly lit fellowship hall where churchgoers gathered every week for coffee and donuts.

"How old are you?" he asked, sipping from his glass of water.

I wondered why this question was relevant. Did he think I looked too young to be the church's music director? He wouldn't have been the first. "Thirty-three," I said.

His eyes brightened. "*Ah*. The Jesus Year."

I'd been attending church my whole life, and I'd never heard anyone use that phrase. "What's that?" I asked.

The pastor leaned in, his expression sharpening. "The most significant events of Jesus' life occurred when he was thirty-three. His growing ministry, his death, and his resurrection." He nodded, gesturing toward me. "This is *your* Jesus year. It's going to be a significant one."

• • •

After dropping the boys off at school, I stopped by my favorite coffee shop just down the street from work. Tea latte in hand, I circled the block toward the church parking lot. It was empty when I pulled in just before 8:30. I strolled through the lobby and down a hallway to the last door on the right. Once inside my office, I slid the dimmer switch to a half-lit position and turned on my corner floor lamp, saturating the cozy rectangular room in a warm glow. I relaxed into my office chair and began tackling my to-do list for the day.

It was ten o'clock and I'd just finished an email to the worship band. I was flying through each task, reveling in my productivity, when the phone rang.

It was Ian. "Hey, honey. How's it going?"

"Really great," I said. "I'm getting a lot done."

"That's great. Can I stop by and see you?"

He didn't typically visit me during the workday. I figured he must've been on a short break, traveling between school buildings, and missing me. "I'd love that," I said.

"Okay, I'll be there soon." He paused. "I love you."

Ten minutes later, Ian came through my office door. I hopped up from the desk and threw my arms around his sturdy center, squeezing him. He squeezed back, but when he let go and took a step back, his posture weakened. He looked as if he'd just taken a beating in a boxing match—shoulders slumped, head hung low.

A series of questions raced through my head. *Did someone die? Was there an accident? Is someone sick? Are the boys okay?* "What's wrong?" I said.

He lifted his head, a film of water now present in his eyes. "I wanted us to be together when you saw this."

I followed Ian's gaze down to his phone. He was holding it to his chest, clinging to it tightly. When he moved to hold it out in front of him, his hands were trembling, his fingers hovering hesitantly over the black mirror below. He drew in a labored breath, tapped on the phone to unlock it, and turned the screen to face me.

In my narrowed vision was a photo—*No, a mugshot?*—of a man who, all at once, was intimately familiar and painfully unrecognizable. Above the man's face were big blocky letters, a headline of some sort. The words "Band Director" and "Underage" hooked into my consciousness.

Everything stopped.

I couldn't move. I couldn't speak. I couldn't think. I just stood there, eyes frozen to the screen. Disoriented. Numb. Like my insides had been sucked out and spit back in. The minute I could move again, I grabbed onto Ian's arms and pulled myself into him, leaning my cheek against his shoulder, inhaling the familiar scent of his sweater. "It's okay, honey," I exhaled into his chest. "This doesn't affect us."

I believed what I said. Of course this didn't affect us, I'd forgotten this man even existed. He had absolutely nothing to do with our lives.

Ian straightened his posture and wiped away the tear gathered in the outside corner of his eye. "You need to read the article," he said, holding the phone out for me to take.

I had no desire to know what was in the article. Perhaps my brain had already formulated a story. Something familiar. Something I could make sense of. I wanted to tell Ian, *This has nothing to do with me. Whoever this article is about, I'm sure she's fine, too. He's the one who has to deal with the consequences.* But I did as Ian asked. I took the phone and sat back down in my office chair.

For the first time, the title of the article came into clear focus: "BREAKING NEWS: WINTER PARK HIGH SCHOOL BAND DIRECTOR ACCUSED OF RECORDING SEX ACTS WITH UNDERAGE STUDENT." The page looked like a bunch of jumbled up meaningless words. I felt nothing, like I was reading air. I moved on to the first paragraph.

"Winter Park High School's band director, Christopher Blackmer, was arrested after a video surfaced of him and a juvenile engaging in sexual acts . . . ."

The word "video" was a blow to the side of my head. *What video? Whose video?*

". . . The investigation started after an anonymous witness contacted the Orange County Police Department on January 28 regarding inappropriate messages between Blackmer and a former Winter Park High School student . . . . After Blackmer's car and several personal items were seized, a search of Blackmer's phone revealed a video of Blackmer and a male victim engaging in sexual acts."

Male.

I read the word again to make sure I hadn't imagined it. It flashed repeatedly, like a glitch in my brain. *Male. Male. Male. Male.*

My eyes shot up from the phone screen. "What is this?"

Something started to gnaw at me, like a dull-toothed rodent burrowing and chewing its way through the top of my head, making its way down, down, down into my chest and my stomach until it had consumed the very core of me. I unraveled into violent muscle spasms, jerking and shivering uncontrollably. Tears poured down my cheeks and onto my blouse, my body wringing itself out in long, angry twists. This wasn't an arrest article, it was an obituary. The man I knew had died, swallowed up into a black abyss, and in his place was this imposter.

Out of my hollowed chest, an unfamiliar voice spoke: *He's gone. I'm never going to see him again.*

A second voice broke in, this one more recognizable: *Why does that matter? You had never planned on seeing him again.*

Five minutes earlier, thoughts of Chris were an ocean away. He was a long-forgotten relic left on some desolate island of memory. But now, the only thing I wanted was to be in his presence, to know he was okay, that he was *alive,* for him to assure me that these terrible things were not true.

Ian watched helplessly as I continued to convulse and purge. When at last I had no energy left to hold my head above my shoulders, I stared blankly at the surface of my desk, fixated on the tiny imperfections, the discoloration of the faux-wood patterns.

"Did you read the part about talking to the police?" Ian's voice was tender, as if one word could shatter me into a million pieces.

"Yes."

He nodded, his eyes expectant. "They said, if you have any information . . . ."

"I know."

Ian paused. "What do you think you'll do?"

I had no time to process what was happening. All I knew was, that morning, I thought my life was normal, and in an abrupt flash, nothing was. I never knew I had information the police would want, and now I couldn't *unknow* it. They were asking for help, and I had the power to help them.

"I have to contact them," I said.

Ian checked his watch, then shook his head in apology. "I'm sorry, but I have to go back to work. Are you going to be okay?"

I lifted my hand. "Yes. I'll be fine."

"There's something else I want you to think about . . . ." His eyes shifted, uncomfortably. "I think you should consider talking to a therapist."

I nodded in silent agreement. Nothing in my life had ever been too much for me to handle. Nothing so bad I couldn't fix it. But this was different. This felt bigger than I was.

Ian came around the table and placed a gentle hand on my shoulder. "Call me if you need me." I watched him trudge across the room, slowly turn the handle, then disappear.

Alone again, I took my phone and pulled up the article Ian had just shown me. I stared at Chris's picture and thought about the last time I'd seen his face, six years earlier, when a photo of him popped up on my Facebook feed. In the comments section, I read that he was leaving Michigan to teach in Florida. I smiled. "Good for you," I said to the picture, with no one in my kitchen to hear me. "You're finally escaping the cold."

I lingered a moment longer on his face . . . . I felt *something*, but I couldn't identify what it was. It quickly disappeared, along with the thought of Chris, and I went back to cooking dinner for my family.

Chris had gotten every job he wanted, at prominent, well-recognized schools. He'd been a leader in the Michigan band world, president of the Michigan School Band and Orchestra Association. He had everything going for him. Why would he throw it all away?

I sat slumped in my office chair, studying the man in the mugshot. The black hair. The pitiful brown eyes, one eyebrow lifted slightly higher in what looked like a plea for sympathy. Suddenly, I wasn't just looking at his hair, a gathering of lifeless pixels on a two-dimensional screen. No. I was *touching* his hair. Not in real life, but something close to it. Somewhere between memory and reality, so vivid I could feel the soft strands between my fingertips, the fruity undertones of Aussie shampoo invading my nostrils. It was there for a brief moment. Then it was gone.

1999

In Honors English, I tried to keep myself from glancing up at the clock every thirty seconds. It would've been easier *not* to look at the clock if Mrs. Richards didn't stand directly under it. She was so tall that the top of her short permed hair made the clock's face look like it had a curly beard.

It wasn't Mrs. Richards' fault I was distracted that morning. I was rarely bored in her class. She was my favorite teacher at Armstrong Middle School. I loved her stop-sign-red lipstick, the halo of warmth that followed her wherever she went. She was also the after-school drama club director, which made her the coolest adult in the building. Best of all, she was the reason I wanted to be a teacher. I had thought about becoming a ballerina, an opera singer, a lawyer, a judge, a pediatric cardiologist (I liked the way I sounded when I said, "*Pediatric cardiologist*"). But one day I was in her class and another student asked me for help on the assignment we were doing. When I explained it in a way that made sense to her, her whole face lit up. I was hooked. I knew, right then and there, I wanted to spend the rest of my life making people feel that way.

Mrs. Richards finished her lecture on Anne Frank, then made her way to the front of the room. She began scratching out our homework assignment on the green chalkboard while everyone quietly slipped books and folders into their bags.

"*Meg*," a voice whispered to me from one seat over.

Out of the corner of my eye, I saw my best friend, Andi, slide an origami square across the table in my direction. I plucked it from her fingertips and unfolded the paper. In her familiar cursive was a message: *Good luck today!* She'd dotted the exclamation mark with a heart, the same one she always drew over the last letter of her name. I snuck Andi a smile, refolded the note, and stuffed it into the front pocket of my low-rise jeans.

The second the bell rang, I bolted from my chair into the hall, rushing to beat the crowd before I ended up a sardine packed between sweaty bodies that reeked of cheap cologne and chewing gum. As I sped toward the band room, the anticipation I'd been feeling all morning turned sour and began sloshing around in the pit of my stomach. I took several deep breaths, repeating the words my mom always told me: *Just be yourself, Megan. People will see what you are.*

Inside the band room, students were scattered across the tiered flooring that cascaded downward to a conductor's podium. Across the room, my boyfriend, Sean, was getting his saxophone ready, tossing the strap over his head and wetting a reed in his mouth. He threw me a happy-go-lucky grin, the one that could make me smile even after an argument.

Next to the podium, I saw my band director, Miss Prior, talking with a man I had never seen before. His raven hair was molded into a perfect Ivy League cut. He was wearing a gingham red button down and slacks that appeared too large for his frame, khaki polyester parachuting from his thighs down to his brown Oxfords. *That must be him*, I thought. I hurried to my instrument locker, grabbed my trumpet case, and made a beeline for my chair.

Once we were all seated, Miss Prior made the announcement. "I'd like to introduce you to the high school band director, Chris Blackmer." She gestured to the man whose steely-eyed gaze was now skimming across the sea of students in front of him. "If you plan to be in band next year, you must audition for Mr. Blackmer today. He'll be waiting for each of you in my office."

I thought the high school band director would be older. Mr. Blackmer looked to be somewhere in his twenties, though it was hard to pinpoint where. The sharp lines of his hair and arched eyebrows exaggerated the roundness of his cheeks and nose, giving him a slightly cartoonish appearance. He was a combination of boy and man, ambiguous in age but unmistakable in confidence.

Mr. Blackmer disappeared into the office with the first student while the rest of us rehearsed our end of the school year concert pieces with Miss Prior. When I wasn't playing, I held tightly to the trumpet that laid across my lap, trying not to let it topple over as my knobby knees bounced restlessly, knocking against the three-valve casing.

It was my fault for being so nervous. I knew incoming freshmen were typically assigned to the intermediate Concert Band their first year. But I didn't want to be like every other freshman. I had never been interested in being like everyone else. As a small child, adults were always telling me how smart I was, how talented I was, how mature I was. I knew exactly how to behave in the presence of adults, what made their eyes light up: speak intelligently, be polite, listen when spoken to, ask meaningful questions. To me, adults were extraordinary. They had the power to live exciting lives, fall in love, have meaningful careers, adventure to faraway places. When I became a teenager, I'd overhear adults laugh and say to my mom, "She's thirteen going on thirty, isn't she?" That felt like winning the lottery, to be told I wasn't like other kids. I was more like an adult. I was *extraordinary.*

I wondered how many students had made it into the advanced Symphonic Band their freshman year. I could be the first. After all, I was the best trumpet player in the middle school. I had sat first chair in my section all year. Plus, I was used to playing difficult music. I played weekly with my church's brass band, and we often performed college-level pieces. If anyone in the room had a shot at making it into Symphonic Band, it was me.

When I saw it was my turn to audition, I heaved a sigh and made my way toward the office door. I prayed to God, *Please let this go well.*

Mr. Blackmer was seated when I entered the office. He greeted me with a glance, then he looked at the list he was holding. "Megan . . . *Lucius.* Did I say that right?"

"You did!" I said, bobbing my head and smiling. I was impressed. Few people said my name correctly on the first try.

I plopped down onto the chair beside him and adjusted myself into an attentive position. In front of us was a music stand. On it, a piece of paper with several lines of notes and rests. Everything on the page was well within my playing ability, but that didn't guarantee I'd play it well. I often had difficulty playing solos for strangers or crowds. Sometimes, the fear would be so great, it'd melt me into a puddle of goop—hands shaking, body trembling, making the sounds escaping my instrument sputter and whine.

Mr. Blackmer gestured to the paper. "I just want you to relax and do your best." His voice was firm, but it carried an air of encouragement, as if he already believed in me even though we'd only just met.

The knot in my chest loosened. I put the trumpet to my mouth, drew in a deep breath, and blew a steady stream of warm air into the instrument, my lips vibrating inside the brass ring of the mouthpiece. A wave of relief washed over me when the first note came out sounding exactly as I hoped it would, then another, until I had made it through the entire exercise free of disaster.

Mr. Blackmer placed a second sheet of paper on the stand (*Hallelujah*. I had made it to round two). "Take your time," he said. "Play when you're ready."

I sat up a bit taller and tilted forward for a closer view. I followed the patterns of ascending and descending black dots, mountain ranges of music stretching across the white page. This exercise was a bit harder, but I was feeling more confident. I lifted the trumpet back to my lips and began.

It wasn't a perfect performance, but it was pretty close. I searched Mr. Blackmer's face to see if he was impressed.

His cheeks grew rounder. "You're good. How long have you been playing?"

"I was nine when I started, soooo . . . five years?'

"Do you play anywhere other than school?"

"I play at church two times a week. I go to the Salvation Army downtown."

His face lit up. "Salvation Army? So you play cornet too?"

"Yup," I said brightly. "I actually started on cornet."

Usually when I told people about the Salvation Army, they assumed I was talking about the thrift store. How awesome was it that Mr. Blackmer knew it was a church with a rich history of music? That instead of trumpets, Salvation Army brass bands used cornets?

Mr. Blackmer's eyes shifted to the page. He nodded, then looked back at me. "It's nice to meet you. I look forward to having you at the high school."

I smiled, stood from my chair, and made my way toward the door. But before I left, I turned back to him and said, "Thank you very much for listening to me."

Mr. Blackmer chuckled, as if my comment had caught him off guard. "You're welcome. See you later, Megan."

Days after the audition, Miss Prior posted two lists on the door. One was a tower of names assigning most of my eighth-grade classmates to the intermediate Concert Band. The second list, titled Symphonic Band, included only a few names—and there, in fresh black ink: *Megan Lucius.*

• • •

"My daughter, in the top high school band as a freshman," Mom gushed to herself while stirring a pan of scrambled eggs over our kitchen stove. It'd been several days since the audition results were posted, but she couldn't stop talking about it. She brought it up at home, at church, to her colleagues at work, shrugging and saying, "I'm not surprised . . . but I'm still proud of her."

That morning, my mom was wearing the weathered bathrobe she'd owned for a decade, and still, she wore it like an evening gown, her ballerina frame dancing from stove to sink, the loose ringlets of her hair cascading down her back like a waterfall. She was holding the only spatula to ever live in our kitchen utensil drawer. Worn or not, most of our kitchen items hadn't changed over the years. Plates, bowls, cups, silverware, spices—they were like old friends to me.

My three-year-old brother, Trevor, was sitting at the round glass table beside me, picking apart a piece of cheese.

"When's the last time you talked to your father?" Mom said.

I shook my head, avoiding eye contact. "I'll call him today."

With the slam of a door, my stepdad, Randy, charged into the kitchen, his hands speckled with dirt and oil. He'd been working in the garage all morning, and at the speed he was moving, I knew he wouldn't be in the house for long.

Randy yanked open the kitchen desk drawer, checked inside, then slammed it shut and scurried over to my mom. When he pinched her butt, she scolded him. "Hey! I'm cooking!" He threw his arms high in the air, as if the police had just caught him red-handed in a bank heist, then he moved quickly to the sink, flipped the faucet handle up, and started washing.

"Geez Louise, Randy, you're like a bull in a china shop," Mom said as she scraped the eggs from the pan onto a large plate.

Trevor dropped a piece of his cheese and shouted in his mouselike voice. Before I could reach down to get it, Mom had already beat me to it. She tossed the wasted food in the trash and went back to preparing breakfast.

Randy announced to the room, "Alright, I'm going back outside!"

"Good, go!" Mom said, pretending to be annoyed. Maybe she was actually annoyed, it was hard to tell the difference.

Mom set a plate down in front of me with eggs and cinnamon sugar toast while Randy kissed Trevor on the head, patted my shoulders with the roughness of a football coach, and dashed out of the kitchen. I called out to him, "Bye,

Dad!" But it was too late. He'd already slammed the door between our house and the front office.

Nibbling on a piece of toast, I asked Mom, "Are you gonna be home Monday?"

She sighed through a bite of eggs. "No, sorry, I work nine to nine."

I asked again why she didn't just quit the waterbed store and find a new job. Her answers were the same every time: *This job has health insurance, and we have to have health insurance . . . . I don't have a college degree, so I'm limited in what I can do . . . . They're understanding about family things.* I couldn't fathom how health insurance was worth twelve-hour days. All I saw was my mom downplaying her ability to achieve something greater. She was always telling me how smart and gifted I was. *Megan, you can be anything you want.* But I was her daughter. Why didn't she believe in herself the way she believed in me?

"Hey," Mom said, chewing and pointing the prongs of her fork at me. "Don't forget to call your father."

Visits with my father had evolved over the years. In elementary school, my parents had an agreed upon schedule where I would visit him every other weekend. When I started middle school, my father told me I didn't have to visit him unless I wanted to. "I don't want to interfere with your life," he said. "I want you to be able to do your own thing."

I was proud my dad thought I was old enough and smart enough to decide how I wanted to spend my time. I was so busy with school, after-school activities, and church . . . . With this new arrangement, I didn't have to feel guilty if we didn't see each other for weeks, or even a month. I knew he wasn't going to be upset about it. He knew how much I loved him. I was just living my life, and he was living his.

My father and his wife, Cheryl, had lived in Flint for almost a decade, but they had recently moved to a nearby city which was still less than twenty minutes from Mom and Randy's house. I didn't know why my father and Cheryl had moved, but I never asked too many questions. I had learned a long time ago to be careful at my father's house. Careful about what I said, about putting things back exactly the way they were, about keeping my long hair out of my food. Upsetting my father was something I wanted to avoid at all costs. When he was angry, it was like unscrewing the cap of a pop bottle that'd been violently shaken, liquid anger spewing everywhere until the bottle was empty. And when he was done, he would kneel in front of me, hold my hands in his and beg for forgiveness. He'd tell me how much he loved me. Sometimes he would cry and I would comfort him. *It's okay, Dad. Yes, Dad, I forgive you.* I never knew what I was supposed to be feeling in those moments. I didn't want my father to be sad, but mostly I just wanted the discomfort to be over.

Mom and Randy were cordial with my father and Cheryl, and vice versa, but their relationship didn't extend much beyond that. Each set of parents did their own thing. They were separate islands in the same ocean, and I was the boat that traveled between them, carrying the cargo of my experiences back and forth.

Randy pulled into the driveway of my father's house and asked if I'd need a ride back the next day.

"My dad's gonna bring me home," I said. I grabbed my duffel bag, filled with just enough to get me through one night, and hopped out of the truck.

Randy responded in his usual farewell drone. "Okay, Megan. Have fun."

When I stepped into the house, my father emerged from the kitchen, striding toward me with arms stretched wide. He hugged me, then he pecked me on the lips. "Hey, baby. How are things going?"

"Good," I said, lifting my shoulders.

Cheryl poked her head out from the kitchen. "Hi, honey!"

I waved. "Hi, Mom."

My father took a few steps backward, arms wide once again, the way a host might introduce the next act of a show. "Well, come on in. This is your house too."

The next morning, I asked my father if Sean could come over for a few hours. I knew better than to ask Mom and Randy if I could have a boy at our house. When I was in seventh grade, they refused to let me go to a co-ed birthday party, even though it was parent supervised. I sobbed uncontrollably, furious that every kid invited got to go except me, but no amount of tears could get them to change their minds.

My father would have let me go to the party. At his house, some rules were painfully rigid while other rules didn't exist at all.

Cheryl wasn't home that afternoon; she'd left earlier to go somewhere with my baby brother, Zach. Sean and I sat shoulder to shoulder on the family room couch watching TV while my father worked in his office. My eyes were on the television, but my focus was on Sean—the heat of his sweaty palm, the rough cotton of his khaki cargo shorts, his breath rising and falling with mine.

My father entered the nearby kitchen and grabbed his keys from the counter. "Okay, you two. I have to go to the store, but I'll be back in an hour. You're going to behave yourselves, right?"

The way my father said this gave me a prickly feeling. He was so clear about the length of time he'd be gone . . . . Either he wasn't really concerned about us behaving, or he was leaving so we had time to *not* behave. Sean and I had been alone together for small windows of time, mostly after school when we'd walk the empty halls and make out in places where no one could see us. But we had never been in a house alone with zero supervision.

My heart raced as I watched my father's car make its way to the end of the long neighborhood street, slow to a halt, then gradually pull out onto the main crossroad. When it had completely disappeared, I hurried back to the couch and dropped onto the soft cushion next to Sean. Our mouths collided, and my insides turned toasty, like hot chocolate running through my veins, melting the world around me into an obscure oblivion. I was fuzzy, floaty, achy, *happy*. Before long, I climbed on top of him, dragging the place between my legs back and forth against the zipper of his jeans, waves of pleasure rocking my body.

We didn't do anything beyond that. Nothing below the clothes. Nothing I would have felt guilty about.

When close to an hour had passed, Sean and I went into the bathroom and splashed cool water on our rosy-cheeked faces. Then, we went back to watching TV, careful to sit in the exact same position as when my father left. Not long after my pulse had returned to normal, I heard the sound of the garage door. My father was home. Right on time.

Later that afternoon, it was time for my father to drive me back to Mom and Randy's. I threw the dirty clothes from the day before into my duffel and waited by the door. I said my goodbyes to Cheryl as my father loaded Zach's car seat into the back of his sedan.

As we backed out of the driveway, my father tilted his head in my direction. "So. You and Sean. You seem to like each other a lot."

"Yeah," I said, gazing out at the cool, overcast sky, and losing myself in the murmur of the radio. The memory from earlier that afternoon played inside my head like a scene from a movie. The soft couch. The taste of Sean's mouth. The waves. If I was lucky, I'd spend the entire ride quietly lost at sea, floating on water as I stared up at a celestial blue sky.

Car rides used to be my favorite thing to do with my father. When I was little, he'd pick me up from my mom's for the weekend and the two of us would listen to "Enter Sandman" by Metallica and "Bad to the Bone" by George Thorogood & The Destroyers on repeat. He'd croon Stevie Wonder's "My Cherie Amour" and gaze lovingly at me from the driver's seat, the sun gleaming across the strands of his feathery blonde hair.

When we weren't listening to music, he was intent on cramming as much advice as any father could into the twenty-four-to-forty-eight-hour intervals we spent together. We played a quiz game every time we were in the car. He'd talk like the game show hosts on *Jeopardy!* or *The Price Is Right* and ask me to spell a word or solve a math problem.

"Spell . . . *apple*."

"A-P-P-L-E," I'd say, each letter hopping across my tongue.

He'd raise his pointer finger and hold his breath, keeping me in gleeful suspense. "That's right! What is . . . eight plus three?"

He'd barely finish the question and already I'd have the answer. "Eleven! It's eleven!"

I was five years old the day my father asked me to spell a word with an *R* in it. I don't remember the exact word, only that I couldn't pronounce my *R*s properly—they came out sounding something like *ah-oo*, the sides of my tongue resting limp inside my mouth. I may not have been able to pronounce all the letters, but I could spell the word. "Great job," he said, pride curling the corner of his lip.

I waited then, expecting another question. My father sat quietly, his eyes scanning the terrain in front of him. After what felt like an eternity of silence, he said, "I think it's time you know what sex is."

The word "sex" jumped out at me. I recognized it as being one of those words adults were careful to use around children, but that was all I understood.

I listened attentively as my father explained how a man and a woman engage in sexual intercourse. I didn't wonder why my father was sharing this information with me. Maybe a song came on the radio that mentioned sex and he thought I was curious. Maybe it was an impulse. Regardless, I didn't ask to know what sex was, and I didn't know I should be telling him to stop.

The reasons for sex were unclear to me. I don't remember hearing anything like, *Well, honey, when two people love each other*... only the names of body parts and the strange things people did with them.

When I got home, I couldn't wait to share the news with my mom. "I know what sex is!" I said. "My dad told me."

Her lips parted, but nothing came out. Finally—"What did he tell you?"

"A man sticks his penis inside a woman's vagina," I said. I was certain I held a magical key no other five-year-old knew existed.

As I grew older, car rides with my father grew quieter. We still talked, but I felt guarded by the possibility of what either of us might say. I missed the old days when we'd just put on a great song and get lost in it.

"I want to tell you something about me and Cheryl," my father said as he approached the intersection. The tempo of his voice slowed. "We might be getting a divorce."

My brain scrambled to make sense of what my father had just said. The word *divorce* sounded like a foreign word coming out of his mouth. I was so young when he and my mom separated, I couldn't remember a life that didn't include all four of my parents. I thought his relationship with Cheryl was practically perfect. I'd never seen them have so much as a small disagreement. Now they were breaking up?

Cheryl was a second mom to me. If my parents divorced, would I ever see her again? Where would my father go? Would I see him less than I already did?

I glanced over my shoulder and saw my brother, Zach, asleep in his carseat. He was still a baby, less than two years old. I was less than two when my father left my mom for Cheryl.

"I may need to be on my own," my father said. "We'll see what happens."

I prayed for God to turn my eyes to glass. *Don't cry. Don't cry*.... It was no use. I couldn't stop the tears from coming. Staring down at my lap, I managed to croak out a single plea. "I don't want you and Mom to break up."

My father reached over and placed his hand on the back of my head. "It's okay, baby," he said, smoothing down my hair with long, calming strokes. "This isn't anything you have to worry about. Let's just keep this between us, okay?"

When I got home, I did exactly as my father asked. I didn't say anything about what I knew.

For weeks I waited for something bad to happen. For the phone to ring. To hear my father's voice telling me what life was going to be like now that he and Cheryl were getting divorced. Or maybe the voice would be Cheryl's. Through her sobs, she'd say, *Even though your father and I are breaking up, I still love you. This doesn't change anything. I still love you.*

But every time I visited my father and Cheryl, they acted the way they always had. Loving. Happy. It was as if the conversation in the car had never happened.

So that's what it became to me, something that never happened. I learned to ignore what I didn't want to worry about. I took the thought of my parents divorcing, folded it up, stuck it in a drawer somewhere inside myself, and slammed that drawer shut.

2019

"Who are you trying to reach, ma'am?" The voice on the line was kind and inviting. She said she was with the Lansing Police Department.

I remained slumped in my office chair—face puffy, eyes sore and swollen. When I spoke, my voice was broken and hoarse. "I have information about a teacher that was arrested."

"What's the name of the teacher?"

My stomach tightened. "Christopher Blackmer." Speaking his name felt like sacrilege, like a violation of some unspoken promise. The words lingered in the air as I waited to be connected to one of the detectives in their precinct. When a stoic voice came on the line, I found myself missing the voice I had spoken to just moments before.

"What do you want to report about Mr. Blackmer?" the detective asked.

Once more, there was a gripping inside me, as if to lock up whatever might escape. I knew, once I spoke the words there was no going back . . . . Going back to *what*, though? Whoever I was before I saw that article, whatever life I had been living, it was over.

"I had a relationship with him when I was in high school," I said.

I was not prepared for what came next. The detective jumped into questions—*personal* questions—I didn't expect to be asked during an initial phone conversation. I thought I'd have time to consider what details I was comfortable sharing, but there was no time. So I played a game with myself—I pretended each question was nothing more than a simple math or spelling problem that I already knew the answer to. I didn't need to think about the answer, I just needed to say it out loud.

"This is turning into something," the detective said, sounding more like he was talking to himself. It seemed obvious from the detective's statement that I wasn't the first person to call about Chris.

Relief filled my lungs, followed by an exhale of sadness. What did it mean that I wasn't the only person to call? What was I supposed to be feeling? Glad that there were others out there who would make my story more credible? Or upset that Chris had lied to me?

Technically, Chris didn't lie to me. There were things we didn't talk about, and I preferred it that way.

"Would you be able to come in this afternoon?" the detective asked. Lansing was only an hour away. I could get there by one o'clock if I left in the next few minutes. But before I could leave work, the detective said he needed to check on a few things. He asked me to stay by my phone.

When he called back thirty minutes later, there was disappointment in his voice. "I'm sorry, ma'am, but this isn't the department that would handle your information."

My heart sank. "Who do I need to contact?"

He didn't know, but he could give me the number of an officer who might. I called that officer, who connected me to another officer, and neither of them could point me in the right direction. I was baffled. I had information the Michigan State Police had specifically asked for, and there was no one to give it to.

Finally, one of the police officers said he'd do some digging and (hopefully) have an answer for me, if not that day then the next. There was nothing more I could do to move things forward. I was at a standstill.

I returned to scouring the internet for every article I could find on Chris. Police had arrested him at his apartment Friday morning, they took him to the county jail where he was held on a $5,000 bond, and by early Saturday morning he had bonded out and was free to go home. News footage showed reporters swarming him the moment he stepped outside the jail, shoving cameras and microphones in his face, shouting belligerent questions and statements at him as he hurried to a nearby taxi.

I shook my head. *God, just let him by. Do you really think he's going to talk to you? Aren't things bad enough already?*

I watched the video again and again, studying his facial expressions and body language. I kept murmuring, "Who *are* you?" as if he could hear me. He looked practically the same as the last time I'd seen him. *God.* I hadn't thought about him in so long, it was almost as if his existence had been wiped clean from my memory. It wasn't something I did on purpose, it just happened. I thought I knew this man, and none of what I knew included what was in those articles. A *predator*? What did that even mean? He didn't prey on anyone, he couldn't have. Before moving to Florida, Chris had taught in Michigan for almost two decades, across five different school districts. Nothing had been made public about other allegations, only that school administrators in Grand Ledge, where Chris had worked his last five years in Michigan, stated there was nothing in his personnel file to indicate he had abused students while working there. If Chris had abused students, how could he have taught for over twenty years without getting caught? Without there being any evidence of it? Surely someone would have seen something and reported it.

This was more complicated than anyone would understand. Only I could know the truth, because I knew him in a way no one else did. I knew things about him no one else knew. He wasn't a monster. He was a human being.

In my desperate attempt to rationalize what was happening, I grabbed on to the first thought that offered a glimmer of hope. Maybe the Chris I knew was still in there, somewhere. Maybe he'd gotten sick over the years, and that sickness had led him to this. He didn't need judgment. He needed help.

I left work early and took a short walk across the street to the community auditorium where Ian's students were rehearsing for their spring musical. I found him in the back row, pencil and paper in hand, jotting notes as the students ran their scene on stage.

When he saw me, he smiled. "You came to visit me," he said, keeping his voice light and airy. "How are you?"

I rested my head on his shoulder. "I'm okay."

"Did that officer call you back yet?"

"Nope. Probably won't until tomorrow."

While Ian continued to take notes, I opened Facebook and started scrolling through my feed. I needed something mindless and numbing to distract me.

Within seconds, I felt a flash of fear surge through my legs. Chris's face was staring at me once again. Someone from my high school band had shared one of the arrest articles. In her post she wrote,

> I've been processing this all day, talking to friends from those years, and just basically in shock. I feel a little guilty for centering on my own experiences, because obviously the victims are the ones who need to be heard if and when they are ready . . . . To know that I was once so close to a predator is a feeling I'm still trying to work through.

Those words again. *Victim*. *Predator*. So simplistic and one-dimensional. I rejected them with every fiber of my being.

Below the shared article were dozens of comments from people I could tell had randomly come across the headline. My stomach ached reading the awful things strangers had written about Chris, many wishing death on him. *Death to all pedophiles,* someone said, next to a picture of a gun. How could people be so awful? They didn't even know him. There were people out there who cared about him. His parents. Colleagues. Students. Friends.

For the first time, I understood how painful it is to be a person whose family member or friend is paraded in the news for a terrible act. How hard it is to watch helplessly from the colosseum seats, listening to calloused cheers as your loved one gets mauled and bloodied on the sand below you.

I kept scrolling, but stopped abruptly when I saw that several comments were written by people I'd gone to high school with. *I remember the rumors*, one person said.

My breath caught in my throat. There were rumors about Chris while I was in high school? I remembered kids teasing me, but I didn't know there were actual rumors about us.

Wait, I thought. What if they weren't about me? Who else would they have been about?

This was my band director in high school, another classmate wrote. *There was a rumor he did this exact thing. Guess we can come to our own conclusion on that.*

I felt like I was in the Twilight Zone, like I had lived a completely different reality from my classmates. And with my current reality shattered, I wasn't sure what reality, past or present, to grab onto.

"I'll be right back," I told Ian. I left the auditorium and found a quiet corner of the atrium to call my mom.

She greeted me in her usual sing-song way.

"Mom . . ." I said, trying to keep my voice from shaking. "Chris Blackmer was arrested."

"Oh, Megan." She sighed. "I'm so sorry."

"Police found videos of him and a teenage boy."

Her voice shot up. "*What*? That's awful."

"I'm going to tell the police what I know," I said.

I could practically feel her reach through the phone and grab me. "Why would you get involved in this, Megan? You said he only kissed you when you were in high school."

I froze. *Hold on. No, that can't be true.* She had to know more than that. I scanned my memory for something, anything that would prove she knew more....

A memory emerged. I was in college—*sophomore year, maybe?*—and I needed observation hours for my education class. Mom and I were sitting across from each other at our kitchen table, and I was telling her I'd be going to observe the choir director at Chris's school in Walled Lake. I told her, to make the trip easier, I'd be driving down the night before and staying at Chris's apartment.

"I do remember that," she confirmed. "I mean, I figured you were sleeping with him, but I said to myself, *'She's a big girl. She can make her own choices.'*" My mom sounded like a near-perfect imitation of herself from years earlier.

"We're gonna have to talk about this later, when I can be alone," I said. Behind me, several students had exited the auditorium and were passing through the atrium.

"Megan, I don't know if getting involved in this is a good idea. I don't think it'll be good for you. It's a big deal to hold a man's life in your hands."

Did she think I hadn't considered this? Most of my concern was centered on Chris and what my coming forward would do to him. What if I added another five or ten years to his sentence in Florida?

Even so. I couldn't imagine a year from now, five years from now, looking back on this, knowing I could have done something and I didn't.

My mom's voice turned somber. "I thought something might have been wrong. I thought it, but I didn't want to believe it. I should have kept asking questions."

The sound of chatter rose up from behind me as more students began to pour out of the auditorium. "I'm sorry, Mom. I've got to go. I'll call you tonight and tell you everything."

I woke Tuesday morning with a nauseating headache. I had spent most of the previous evening on the phone with my mom, locked in my bedroom, pacing the floor and gesticulating as I word-vomited a full confession to her.

She was remarkably calm during our conversation, but when I tried calling her in the morning, there was no answer. It wasn't unusual for her to miss phone calls. She'd often forget to turn her ringer on, or she'd leave her phone stashed away in her purse on the other side of the house. I had a gut feeling, though, that her not answering that morning had something to do with Chris. I wondered if she was angry with me for keeping secrets from her.

No matter. There wasn't time to sit around and worry; I had to keep moving. I had to get the lunches packed, the boys to school, and me to work.

When I arrived at the church, it had been almost twenty-four hours since my first call to the Michigan State Police. So far, my experience with law enforcement wasn't at all what I had expected. I certainly didn't expect Chris to bond out of jail in less time than it would take for me to get ahold of the right police station.

In the early afternoon, I heard back from the officer who had promised to get me answers. "It's the county where the crime happened that needs to handle your case, ma'am. You'll need to contact Sergeant Perry at the Genesee County Sheriff's Department."

It took me a moment to realize, when he said "crime" he wasn't referring to the crime in Florida . . . . He was referring to me. *I* was the crime.

My aching head was now spinning. An entire day had passed since I'd learned about Chris's arrest, and I still believed I was contacting the police only to give them information they could use in the Florida investigation. It never occurred to me I was reporting an actual *crime* here in Michigan.

I had never viewed my relationship with Chris as being something that happened *to* me rather than something we did together. As a high schooler, I knew it was taboo for a teacher and student to be together, but back then I had never heard of a teacher being arrested for it. There were stories at my school about teachers and students having casual sex, but I didn't believe they were true. How could a teacher have sex with multiple students and still teach at our school? The only story I believed was the one my mom told me, about a teacher she knew who'd had a relationship with a student and eventually married her. I had said to myself, *He must have been in love with her. Why else would he have risked his job like that?* And him marrying her was the ultimate proof of his love. It was also proof to me that something like that was possible.

Of course, the early 2000s was a different climate—before the #MeToo movement, before society could no longer close its ears to powerful businessmen abusing their subordinates, or the oversexualization of teenage girls. It was the age of Britney Spears and Catholic schoolgirl outfits, of teenybopper films like *American Pie* and *Never Been Kissed*, where high school kids were played by twenty-something-year-old adults. I probably could have recited every line of *Cruel Intentions*, performed a faultless imitation of Sarah Michelle Gellar in a sultry pose, saying, "You can put it anywhere."

In hindsight, I understood how it was possible for me to go through my teenage years unaware of statutory sexual abuse laws. But why didn't I know about the laws when I became a teacher?

I thought back to my college education. Had we ever gone over teacher ethics? Had we ever discussed how to draw healthy boundaries with our students, to protect them and us? I couldn't remember that being a part of the curriculum. In the schools where I'd worked, had I ever attended a single professional development session that talked about student safety in regard to teacher-student relationships? I didn't think so.

As a teacher, I never needed a class to tell me I shouldn't have romantic relationships with my students. It was instinctively clear the power I held over students in a classroom. I knew I had the potential to raise them up or tear them down. I knew it was my job to be a role model, not an object of romantic affection. If a student even looked at me a certain way—as if they might have feelings for me that went beyond respect—I added caution to my behavior, because I remembered the feeling of being a teenager with a crush on her teacher, and I didn't want to do anything to encourage those feelings.

What I couldn't explain was how my body recalled the feeling of having a crush on a teacher without recalling actual memories of my teenage life. It was like Chris inhabited a different compartment of my brain, far away from the reasoning

I employed as an adult in charge of children. Maybe I didn't see myself the way I saw other students because I had never seen myself as a child. Now, when I thought back to memories of Chris, I couldn't picture myself appearing young. I tried to imagine us standing next to each other—Chris as my teacher and me as a high school student—but he was the only one I could picture clearly. I was more of an idea, a vague outline of a girl who wasn't quite in her thirties but also wasn't at all a child. What if I'd known years ago that Chris was breaking the law? Would I have let him? If it meant us being together, who knows what I would have done. I trusted him implicitly. I never questioned anything he said or did. Maybe if I'd had more information earlier, my life might have been different.

It was too late for that. Being told at age thirty-three that what'd happened to me was a crime did not offer some miraculous revelation. If anything, it made me cling tighter to the belief I'd held on to for decades: Chris wasn't a predator. I wasn't a victim. Whatever happened in Florida—that isn't what happened to me.

1999

The day I stepped into Kearsley High School as a freshman, I was certain of who I was and what I wanted to be. I viewed the next four years as a series of open doors—perfectly aligned, one in front of the other—and from where I stood I could see my whole life ahead of me. I'd earn leadership roles at school and church, graduate at the top of my class. I'd be the first in my immediate family to earn a university degree and become a successful English teacher. I'd marry the man God intended for me, and live happily ever after. These dreams were so deeply seeded in me, someone would've had to crack me open to remove them.

My two favorite classes were English & Grammar with Mrs. Domerese and Symphonic Band with Mr. Blackmer. The two teachers were polar opposites, but I adored them equally. Mrs. Domerese was a walking double shot of espresso with crimpy white-blonde hair, pink apples for cheeks, and a smile that took up half her face. When she laughed, she laughed with her whole body.

Conversely, Mr. Blackmer was stern and controlled. His laughter never rose above an enthusiastic chuckle. There were times, however, he'd display a youthful excitement over the music we were playing in class, lavishing praise on composers like Frank Ticheli and Percy Grainger. Sometimes, in the middle of rehearsal, he'd hurry to his office and retrieve his trombone so he could model how to play a particular passage. I could tell he was a talented musician by the beautiful tone emanating from the bell and the way he maneuvered difficult excerpts with ease. To hear him play was both stirring and soothing.

What connected Mrs. Domerese and Mr. Blackmer was their apparent love of teaching and their undeniable skill in the classroom. And while I continued to love English as a subject, my dreams of one day becoming an English teacher were beginning to morph. I still wanted to teach—more than ever—but instead of envisioning myself in front of a chalkboard covered in writing prompts, I envisioned myself on a podium, baton in hand. I could see the rows of students before me, hear the music I'd chosen for them, many of the same pieces Mr. Blackmer had introduced to me. Within months that vision sharpened, then it solidified. Before long I'd know with absolute certainty: someday, I was going to be a high school band director.

Symphonic Band was the last hour of the school day. The band room was located in an isolated corner of the building. To get there, I had to hurry across the school's hub, down a hallway in front of the auditorium's main entrance, and finally through a set of doors past which the only choices were to veer left for the choir room or veer right and follow a curved brick wall to the band room's heavy double doors.

Sometimes, Mr. Blackmer was already at the podium, looking deep in thought as he studied the score in front of him, a loose hand drawn to his chin. I would climb the tiered flooring to the corner storage room to get my instrument, and by the time I reached my seat, Mr. Blackmer would look anxious to begin.

"Quickly," he'd shout, his rich voice cutting through the cacophony of clanging lockers and instrument case latches. "Get to your seats and be ready to play." Within seconds, his hands were out in front of him. "Alright, let's go. Whole notes. Concert B flat scale. And . . . ."

I knew Mr. Blackmer was my favorite teacher, not because I paid meticulous attention to everything he said or did, but because of the way I felt around him. I knew that every time I saw him, something would light up inside me. I admired his teaching style, his intensity and desire for greatness. He conducted rehearsals like a NASCAR pit stop; with two claps and a gesticulation, he'd bring the band to a startling halt, tell us what we needed to fix, then start us up again. There was a strength to his conducting, the way he pushed and pulled with his hands, as if commanding buildings to move out of his way.

At the start of the year, I was ecstatic when Mr. Blackmer sat me second chair, directly beside the best trumpet player in the school—a senior named Lisa, who had long brown hair, big brown eyes, and sweet cherub cheeks. The first time we met, Lisa smiled at me and said, "Hey, freshman." It was like exchanging a secret handshake. I had passed her test. I was *in*.

One day, Mr. Blackmer announced he'd be holding challenges for anyone who wanted to move up in their section. He said he'd select an excerpt from one of our pieces, and whoever played the excerpt the best would win the challenge.

The wheels in my head kicked into motion. I wondered if a freshman had ever sat first chair in Symphonic Band. Not likely, I figured. If I won the challenge, I could be the first. Lisa was a skilled player, it'd be difficult to beat her. Moreover, I was concerned that challenging her might strain our new friendship. But the possibility of sitting first chair was too tempting, too shiny to pass up.

When Mr. Blackmer asked the class who was interested in challenging, I slowly lifted my hand toward the ceiling. The temperature inside the room rose ten degrees, and my face flushed in exhilaration. I avoided looking at anyone but Mr. Blackmer. I didn't want to face the possible reactions of the students around me.

Isn't that girl a freshman?

She's going to challenge a senior?

Who does she think she is?

I was sure Mr. Blackmer wasn't thinking any of those things. When he saw me with my hand up, I swore I could see the faintest hint of a smile as he went to write my name on the paper in front of him.

Maybe I imagined it. Maybe the thought of him being impressed with me was a way to block out the fear of what others might be thinking. From what I could tell, he was an ambitious man, always demanding the highest standard of excellence from us, and therefore, from himself. At the very least, Mr. Blackmer was intrigued by my boldness. At best, he wanted me to win.

The day of challenges came, and Lisa and I (along with several other students who wanted to challenge within their own sections) took turns playing for Mr. Blackmer. When the challenges were over and the class was packing up, Mr. Blackmer went to his office and sat at his desk. Not long after, he taped a piece of computer paper to the outside of his office door with several names written in a particular order.

From where I stood, I could see that I had won. Two upperclassmen approached the door to look at the sign. I watched as they exchanged looks, their faces stern with confusion. I imagined the question they were sharing in their heads: A *freshman beat a senior?*

The win didn't feel at all the way I thought it would. I thought I'd feel on top of the world, but instead I felt alone in it. I had three years ahead of me to sit first chair. Lisa only had one left, and I took it from her.

I waited for Lisa, who was avoiding eye contact with me, to leave the room before starting toward the door. As I passed by Mr. Blackmer, he said my name in his usual commanding tone. He was on the podium collecting papers off the stand. He carried them with him as he stepped down to greet me. "Great job today," he said, his voice turning from steel to silk.

My heart felt lighter. Did he notice I was acting awkward and wanted to cheer me up? He must have. I was grateful to have teachers in my life who cared about their students, who went out of their way to make sure they were alright. It was exactly the kind of teacher I was going to be someday.

In early November, I called Sean. "I wanna break up," I said.

I pictured him on the other end of the line, gripping the corded phone receiver in his kitchen, his boyish face twisted up in a scowl. "I can't believe you're doing this again . . . . We're gonna get back together. Can we just skip the breaking up part?"

I spoke firmly. "We're not going to get back together. We're not right for each other."

Sean sighed. "Yes, we are."

"How can you say that? We argue all the time."

"Well, stop finding reasons to argue with me. Can't we just have fun together? Why does everything have to be so serious?"

Okay. So maybe I was a bit serious for a fourteen-year-old. But so what? I didn't want to be like everyone else. Really, there were only two things I wanted to be in life. I wanted to be *good* and I wanted to be loved. That's why church had always appealed to me: it offered the promise of both. At church, I could learn what rules to follow in order to become the best, most *good* version of myself—don't swear, don't lie, don't use the Lord's name in vain, don't gossip, don't drink, don't have sex before marriage—and in exchange for being *good* was the promise that I would always be loved.

It wasn't that Sean was *bad*. He wanted to be a teenage boy. I wanted him to be fully formed and capable of meeting all my wants and needs. I hated when he swore, when he cracked jokes about marijuana or the male anatomy. My stomach would twist in knots every time he alluded to another girl being *hot*. Sometimes, he would say mean things out of the blue, like the time I got a painful cold sore on my lip and he embarrassed me by blurting out in front of his friends, "Ew, gross! You have herpes!" They all laughed, including Sean.

But on his best days, Sean was sweet and funny and a good listener. He wasn't afraid to hold my hand, or walk me to class, or kiss me in front of his friends. He wrote me love letters, told me I was beautiful, called me every day . . . so it hurt that much more when he would turn careless or rude. When I was hurt we would argue, and when we would argue we were like two fireworks, shooting sparks and smoke. Sometimes it felt like I was on a rollercoaster. One day up, another day down. It was hard to know which Sean I was going to get, so I was always on edge.

The other problem in our relationship had to do with sex. Not *real sex*—you know, the kind that could get you pregnant—but *other stuff.* I was devastatingly attracted to Sean, and by our freshman year we had gone from kissing to making out to touching above the clothes to touching below the clothes. As a *good* Christian girl, I was constantly going back and forth about whether or not it was okay to be doing these things, and this back and forth created even more tension in our relationship.

When it came to *real sex*, the church was very clear: you must abstain from it until marriage. I was told at church and church camps that God wanted me to save myself for the person God had made specifically for me, that to give away parts of myself before marriage was not only sinful but it would have a negative impact on my future marriage. Abstaining from sex in the face of desire was a way to prove your worth and dedication as a follower of Christ.

I had no doubt in my mind I would wait until my wedding night to have *real sex*. It was the *other stuff* I was confused about. The scriptures said that Jesus told people to avoid sexual immorality. I wanted to know what made something qualify as immoral. Was every sexual act outside of marriage immoral, or were only some things? Was there a list somewhere I could see that ranked things from "Acceptable" to "Absolutely Not"? Even simple gestures of affection, like hand-holding or kissing on the cheek, made other parts of my body light up with excitement, so I wondered if those, too, were off limits.

At times, I would feel very committed to my purity—that is, being pure sexually and, also, what the church liked to call "pure of heart." I'd play a game with myself to see if I could make it through a whole day only thinking pure and kind and happy thoughts. At some point, though, I would fall back into having impure thoughts about boys, or I might lose my temper with someone, or participate in gossip when I should have been strong enough to resist.

Overall, I was pretty good at the "pure of heart" thing. I didn't swear. I wasn't mean. I didn't want to hurt others. But when it came to boys, I could never really hold onto the guilt I was supposed to be feeling. I knew there were teenagers in the church that were making out or worse. I knew the adults telling us these things must have been teenagers who did the same thing, and it seemed like they were going to heaven. Something didn't add up.

To complicate the matter, approaches to sex and sex-related things varied depending on the parent I was talking to. With my father, it was guaranteed he would bring up the subject if we were watching a movie with a sex scene. Inevitably, he'd say, *Uh oh! Better cover your eyes. They're, uh, they're having SEX!* I would've preferred to sit in quiet torture until the scene was over.

My stepdad, Randy, said a person would have to be crazy to marry someone without first knowing if they were "good in bed." One day, he charged into the house with a movie rental in his hand. "Megan, have you seen this? American Pie? You have to watch it. You have to know how guys think, Megan. This is exactly how guys think." He popped the DVD in and stood by as I witnessed the opening sock masturbation scene. He laughed hysterically, then he said he had to go back to the garage to work. I was left alone to watch the rest of the movie and, I guess, to take notes.

My mom made an obvious effort to engage in meaningful conversations about sex. She told me, "Whoever you have sex with first will be your husband in God's eyes."

I wondered what that meant for her since she'd already been married to my father before marrying Randy. Was she still married to my father in God's eyes? Would she be demoted in heaven for having sex with Randy, or was there a forgiveness clause for second marriages?

She also warned me that having sex would tie me to someone in a way that would be hard to untie myself from, and it would make it harder to leave a bad relationship. That's why I needed to save as much of myself as possible for The One. "But once you're married, everything's fair game," she said. "And if you're able to give blow jobs, you can make your man happy and keep your man happy." This was advice I understood.

It seemed pretty obvious to me why my mom would talk about husbands and sex the way she did. She had mentioned a few times that she wasn't "adventurous" enough for my father, and that was probably one of the reasons he chose Cheryl. I could only assume she didn't want the same thing to happen to me.

So there it was, a hodgepodge of information I'd learned over the years about sex: what it was, what it wasn't, what God thought of it, what guys thought of it. I took it all and tried to arrange it into something that made sense to me.

When it came to Sean, what I did know was, between the arguing and the jealousy and the constant confusion surrounding sex, it sometimes felt like God was whispering that there was someone out there who was better for me, who was more like me. Someone who would always build me up instead of tearing me down.

"Megan," Sean said, tears building up in his voice. "I love you. Please don't do this."

"I'm sorry," I said, calm and in control. "I've already made up my mind."

Sean's voice turned icy cold. "Whatever." *Click*. He was gone.

In January, I auditioned after school for the spring musical *Seven Brides for Seven Brothers*. I really wanted the leading role of Milly Pontipee, but I knew it was a pipe dream. This was my first high school show, and it seemed highly unlikely the director would cast a freshman as the lead.

That night, my bedroom phone rang. It was the theater director, Mr. Carrizales. "I'm wondering if you'd be interested in playing Milly," he said.

"Are you kidding?!" I squealed. "I would love to!"

I ran up the stairs, into the kitchen, shouting, "I got the lead! Mom! I got the lead!"

She was doing dishes, and the plate she was scrubbing nearly came flying out of her soapy yellow rubber gloves. "You're kidding!"

"I'm not! Mr. Carrizales just called!"

"That's awesome, Megan!"

Together, we cheered—our hands flailing wildly in excitement, our voices ricocheting off the kitchen walls and tile flooring.

Mr. Carrizales asked if I could come down to the auditorium during lunch to rehearse a scene with Brendan, the junior playing the male lead. When I got there, Brendan greeted me in his character's backwoods Southern drawl. "Well, hey there, ah, Milly."

I blushed, charmed by his genuineness. "Well, hey there . . . *Adam*." I liked Brendan already. Rarely had I felt so welcomed by a stranger, especially a teenage boy.

In the scene we were practicing, Adam asks Milly to marry him. After she says yes, he hoots and hollers and lifts her high in the air. Before Brendan and I could run the scene, Mr. Carrizales said we needed to practice the lift. "Have you done this before?"

I shook my head.

"Here," he said, taking my hands and placing them on Brendan's shoulder's. Then he took Brendan's hands and placed them on either side of my waist.

A spark ignited in my chest. A boy I'd met only minutes ago was now touching me. Even though this was theater and we were pretending, the exhilaration I felt was real. As Brendan's eyes shined down at me, questions started to run through my mind. *What's he thinking right now? Does he think I'm attractive? What if we fall in love in real life?*

Mr. Carrizales instructed me to bend my knees as Brendan prepared for the lift, then to jump at the exact second he lifted me from the ground. Once we'd gotten fairly proficient at this, Mr. Carrizales told us it was time to move on to the kiss.

My blood ran hot. I knew there was a kiss in this scene, but I didn't think we'd practice it during lunchtime. I asked Mr. Carrizales, "How do we make it look like we're kissing?"

He grinned, eyes narrowed and brows drawn together in amusement. "You just *kiss*."

I stared, blinking at the boy in front of me, two years older and six inches taller than I was. *This cute junior is going to kiss me? For real?*

I wasn't going to let my nerves show. I was in high school theater now, a place where you were obviously treated like an adult and expected to behave like one. If Mr. Carrizales trusted me to be the lead as a freshman, I'd prove I was mature enough to handle stage kissing.

We started on the page where Brendan proposed. I said yes. He cheered, lifted me high in the air, spun me around—and when my feet touched the ground, he leaned in and put his lips to mine. It wasn't two seconds before I felt my lips being pushed apart by something wet. Pulling away in surprise, I yelped, "He stuck his tongue in my mouth!"

I expected Mr. Carrizales to be as surprised as I was. Instead, he barked a big belly laugh.

Brendan put his hands up. "Ahm sorry, ah was just playin' 'round, Milly," he said, continuing to stay in character. "Ah won't do it again."

His apology was silly, but there was sincerity in his eyes. "It's okay," I said, smiling to put him at ease.

We practiced our kiss a few more times, but Brendan kept his lips soft and closed. As the three of us were leaving the auditorium, Mr. Carrizales stopped me. "You need to look like a woman for this show," he said, placing his open palms flat against the left and right sides of his chest. "Is there any way you could fill this area out?"

I glanced down at the two tiny mounds protruding from my pink shirt. *He's right. How am I going to pass for a grown woman? I still have braces on my teeth.* Suddenly, I remembered seeing, on sale at JCPenny, rubber inserts for women to stick inside their bras. It seemed simple enough. I'd just ask my mom to take me to the store to buy some.

I nodded at Mr. Carrizales enthusiastically. "I can do that."

In the weeks leading up to the show, the musical's cast, crew, and pit orchestra were spending four to five hours in the auditorium every evening. One evening, I couldn't get the timing right in "Love Never Goes Away." Mr. Blackmer was down in the pit conducting, and I looked down at him in apology.

With patient eyes, he said, "You'll get it. Here, let me show you." He gestured a breath with an upward pull of his hands. Then, to demonstrate the correct timing, he began singing my part.

He had a nice voice. There was something alluring behind it. I wondered, *Does he know what it's like to be in love?*

Mr. Blackmer had always been a bit of a mystery to me. While other teachers told stories of their family members or spouses, I knew practically nothing about his personal life.

Don't be stupid, Megan. Of course he's been in love. He's twenty-eight. He's probably been in love more than once.

We tried the entrance again. As I gazed out into the dark auditorium, I saw, in my periphery, Mr. Blackmer's hands rise for the cue. I timed my breath to match his movement, and when it came together I looked him directly in the eye, a moment of *thank you* that he reciprocated with a warm smile.

We performed a two-weekend run of the show. Mr. Carrizales said the show was so well done that he might have us take it on tour. Whatever that meant, it sounded exciting. I was having so much fun, I didn't want it to end. However, after the final performance, once the set was taken down, I never heard mention of a tour again.

On the day of my fifteenth birthday, I was coming into the band room for an after-school jazz band rehearsal when a senior boy shouted to me from across the room, "Happy birthday, Megan!" Then he turned his attention to everyone else and shouted, "Hey, she's legal now!"

Laughter erupted from some of the students. Mr. Blackmer was exiting his office for the podium and didn't appear to notice.

Part of me felt like I should be embarrassed, but a larger part of me was warmed by the flattery. This boy had publicly declared me worthy of desire. What's more valuable to a teenage girl than to be desired? For me, very little. To be wanted was to be needed, and to be needed was to be loved. I knew how this worked, I had seen it time and time again in Disney films and TV shows. Of course, in a Disney movie, the prince would never use *"she's legal now"* as a pick-up line. But this was the real world, where boys didn't always know how to articulate their feelings. The important thing was that they *had* feelings . . . . A boy has to notice you before he can fall in love with you.

So while I would have much rather been called something more eloquent than *legal*, I chalked it up to teenage boy immaturity and took it for what it really was—a compliment.

• • •

The jazz band was invited to play at a community event in the cafeteria of my old middle school. For the performance, I chose my favorite knee-length dress—snow white with daisies embroidered on the soft cotton. Mom was at work and Randy had to be somewhere that evening, so he dropped me off before the band's call time.

When I peeked inside the cafeteria, Mr. Blackmer was alone, setting up chairs and music stands. His back was to me, but I recognized the outfit: camel-colored slacks and a sharp-looking navy blue blazer I'd seen him wear on only a handful of occasions. The clicking of my heels must have alerted him to my presence, because he stopped what he was doing and turned around.

When he saw me, his eyes softened. He sighed into an open smile. "That dress looks nice on you," he said. Then he turned back to finish his task.

I couldn't move. An ache surged in my gut, a pretzeling of my insides, knotted up and velcroed together. Men had complimented me on my appearance before, but Mr. Blackmer wasn't just *any* man. He was a man I admired above most men. And the way he looked at me, I could tell he admired me, too.

A revelation appeared, bringing giddy delight—like watching a magician pull a rabbit from his hat: *Mr. Blackmer thinks I'm pretty.*

2019

On the morning of Thursday, April 11th, I arrived at a police station twenty minutes outside of Midland to deliver my official statement to the Michigan State Police. With me, I brought the stack of yellow legal notepad paper where I'd handwritten everything I could remember about my time with Chris—dates, events, places, amateurish drawings of apartment layouts.

I was led into a large conference room with a long table surrounded by a dozen or so chairs. Sergeant Perry, a tall, broad-shouldered man around my age, with an oval-shaped face and an unassuming presence, sat two chairs down from me. I showed him my driver's license, gave him my name and birth date, then I began recounting the story of my relationship with Chris, starting from the day we met.

At one point, Sergeant Perry interjected, "I'm sorry to ask, but I need you to be specific about the physical interactions that took place. I need to determine the degree of each offense."

I walked him through each scene, doing my best to describe every detail. It felt like I was reading entries out of my high school diary, except I wasn't running my finger over the words in girlish delight the way I had years ago . . . I was marking sections in bold highlighter to be used as evidence of a crime.

"There are different types of penetration," Sergeant Perry said, listing them off one by one. "When you were sixteen, did some form of penetration occur?"

My response to the sergeant spawned a jolt of self-realization. As a teenager, I had created two distinct categories in my mind: *real sex* and *other stuff*. It was only now, while sitting inside a police station at the age of thirty-three, that I understood for the first time . . . what I had considered to be *other stuff* was actually *real sex* in a court of law, and *real sex* meant only one thing: rape.

Rape?

The word knocked the wind out of me. I turned it over again and again inside my head, examining it from every angle. There was no possible way I was a victim of rape. A person would know if they had been raped.

"Did he ever force himself on you?" Sergeant Perry asked.

Something about this question dug under my skin. Since finding out about Chris's arrest, I'd been asking myself, *How bad is it, really, what happened to me?* If I answered, *No, he didn't force himself on me,* it would imply what I had believed all along: I chose this. I wanted this. This was consensual.

"He never forced himself on me," I said.

Sergeant Perry glanced over his notes. "Well, the only reason this was illegal is because he was your teacher."

The word *only* jumped out at me. I gave him a look.

"*Hey*. I'm not saying it's right. I'm just telling you what the law is. Sixteen is the age of consent in Michigan. A sixteen-year-old can meet up with pretty much whoever and do whatever they want."

I couldn't believe what I was hearing. For three days, I'd been researching statutory laws and child sexual abuse. I'd read repeatedly that it's impossible for children—and even youth of certain ages and in certain situations—to give consent, because they can't fully comprehend the consequences of sexual interactions, especially when it involves a person in a position of authority or a trusted adult.

Sixteen-year-olds aren't legal adults. They aren't allowed to purchase cigarettes or lottery tickets, but legal adults with fully developed brains are allowed to have sex with them? Who does that benefit?

"You have two options here," Sergeant Perry said. "The first option is to pursue a civil lawsuit against Christopher."

"What does that mean?" I asked.

"You can take him to court and sue him for reparations. For the damage he's caused."

I heard my mom's voice in my head. *We don't believe in suing people*. She had said this many times over the years. Bad things were bound to happen in life, but you don't seek retribution for wrongdoing. You don't repay harm for harm.

What would I even ask of Chris? I didn't want what little money he probably had after losing his teaching job. What I really wanted was answers. I wanted my old life back. I wanted to feel like myself again, not two separate minds clashing inside one body.

"I don't want to sue him. It's not my intention to hurt him," I said.

"Did you believe you were in a relationship with him?" the sergeant asked, his eyebrows drawn together. He looked sorry for me.

"Yes. I did."

If I didn't want a civil lawsuit, the other option was for the police to launch a state criminal investigation that could lead to an arrest and maybe even a trial. This was the better option, because it wasn't me deciding his guilt or his punishment. I was simply allowing the police to do their job. Plus, it would help the prosecutors and the victims in Florida. They would know he had a history of criminal behavior, instead of believing he was a first-time offender.

With a stern look, the sergeant said, "If the state tries him and you end up on a witness stand, you'll be asked why you're doing this. What would you say?"

I pursed my lips and shrugged. "I just want to help. I want to do the right thing."

"We'll need to look and see if we can bring a case against him. You say the physical relationship started in 2001? That's a long time ago. But he did move out of state, and that can change things."

He said there was no telling how long it would take for the Genesee County prosecutors to decide whether or not the state could pursue an investigation. It could be a few days, maybe a week. Because I had reached the age of consent when the first incident of rape occurred, my allegations were subject to the statute of limitations, a window of time in which victims must report. If too much time had passed, there was nothing the police could do.

I picked up my purse, preparing to leave, when Sergeant Perry handed me a card with his name and a combination of letters and numbers handwritten on the back. "You're brave for coming forward. Not everyone would."

I didn't feel brave. In my mind, coming forward was the only option. I couldn't move on with my life without some kind of resolution. Trying to ignore this would only make it more painful—knowing I could have helped victims and didn't, that I threw away my one chance to know the truth about what really happened between me and Chris. But if I agreed to an investigation, it would mean sharing the most private details of my life. If people knew about my past, would it change their perception of me? What if I had to see Chris in a courtroom and testify against him? It felt like such a betrayal, I didn't know if I had the strength to do it.

All of these scenarios were *what ifs*. None of them might actually come to fruition. What I needed was to put one foot in front of the other and trust that, whatever was to come, I wouldn't be alone. There was no way around the storm, there was only *through* it.

Driving home from the police station, I felt a nagging inside to call my father. We talked on occasion, mostly through short text conversations. He knew I was delivering a statement to the police that morning, I was sure he'd be curious to know what came of it.

I thought he'd have questions. *What happened? What was that like for you? How did the detective react?* But no. He reminded me that people have it way worse than we do. "I try to thank God for the good things in my life, and I try not to worry about the rest," he said. "I hope you can find a way to let this go."

His words spurred me toward anger. I didn't need a lecture on gratefulness. I thanked God all the time, even in the midst of this nightmare. But I was allowed to be sad, and I wanted him to be sad with me. *Actually* sad. Couldn't he just pretend to feel a sliver of what I was feeling? One damn sliver was all I asked.

Why did I expect something different from what I'd always gotten? Maybe because I had never been involved in something like this. I thought, *This is it. This is the thing he's going to care about. It's too big for him not to care about it.* But I was wasting my time. My father knew nothing about Chris. He wouldn't recognize Chris if they were in the same room together. It seemed awfully ironic that the man who was supposed to care about me most knew so little about my life. What cut even deeper was the sudden realization that, between my father and Chris, I had more moments with Chris where I remembered being listened to. More memories of long, meaningful conversations.

I let my father finish his speech while I stayed quiet on the other end of the line. "I love you, honey." he said. I knew he meant it. He did love me. Love just looked different to the two of us.

After we hung up, I tried calling my mom for the fifth time in three days. No answer.

• • •

On Friday, I was scheduled to perform a noontime concert at my church with another singer in town. As I was leaving the house, I caught a startling glimpse of myself in the mirror. It had only been five days since Chris's arrest, but I could see a marked change in my appearance. I looked paler than normal, and gaunt, intensifying the naturally dark circles under my eyes. I tried to remember what I'd eaten that morning, or the night before, but time was a blur, and the sadness unceasing.

My mom had said she was coming to the concert, but that was before Chris was arrested. We hadn't spoken to each other since Monday night when I confessed everything I'd been keeping from her for almost twenty years.

When she didn't show, I refused to let myself care. I didn't have the energy, I was too focused on trying to get through each day without falling to pieces. Getting out of bed every day was a struggle. As soon as I opened my eyes, all my thoughts would pile up inside my brain, too heavy to lift. I would lie there, listening to the activity on the other side of the bedroom door—the opening of the fridge, the clanking of dishes, tiny voices and cartoon shows. It felt like I was trapped on one side of a glass wall, watching my family go about their lives on the other side. I could see them, but I couldn't get to them.

Every night I'd have vivid dreams, most of them about Chris. In one of the dreams, I was standing in a crowded sea of people. The sea parted, and Chris was standing six feet from me, too far to reach. He was in his twenties again, wearing stonewash jeans and a forest green polo. He looked at me with a peaceful gaze, eyes soft, a slight smile drawn across his face. I tried shouting his name but nothing came out. I lunged forward but my body was locked in place. Fiercely, I continued to struggle toward him, mouth wrenched wide open, shouting silence into the air, frantic tears streaming down my face.

As Ian shook me back to reality, I caught the tail end of my voice rising into the bedroom—one name warped inside a terrifying moan.

"Wake up, Megan. Wake up," Ian said, his voice fraught with concern. "You're having a bad dream."

In the darkness, warm tears trickled down the sides of my temple, running over my ears and soaking my hairline. Could Ian tell I was crying? Did he know whose name was struggling to escape my throat?

"Are you okay?" he said.

"I'm okay," I said, taking deep breaths to try and slow my breathing. "Thank you for waking me up."

Silence fell between us. I waited for Ian to move closer. I imagined him pulling me to him, the tension leaving my body in the safety of his arms. But Ian didn't move. The tension turned poker-hot and began burning a hole into the pit of my stomach. I'd forgotten how much I missed being held by him in bed. Our first nights together as a couple, Ian and I had spent every second holding onto one another, him on his back, me tucked into his side with my head resting on his broad shoulder. It wasn't a comfortable position to sleep in, but being close was more important to both of us than being comfortable. By our third or fourth night together we started sleeping in our own spaces, but Ian made sure we kissed goodnight. He was adamant about it, flirtatiously leaning over me with his lips puckered, demanding our nightly ritual. There were few things that made me feel so loved. So needed.

We kissed goodnight every single night for years. Then, one night, in the tired delirium brought upon by a long day of work and chores and children, we forgot to kiss. Without realizing it, one night turned into three weeks. Three weeks turned into three years. Then four. And five.

Now, as I laid in the dark, fevered by the dream of Chris and sick with longing for my husband's touch, more tears quietly slid down my cheek.

On Saturday, my mom finally called. Her voice was hoarse. "I'm sorry I missed your performance."

"It's alright, you can come to the next one. Are you okay?"

"I'm just tired . . . . I called into work for two days straight."

Something was wrong. My mom rarely missed work. She only called in on days she was too sick to stand.

"Does this have something to do with what we talked about the other night?" I asked.

"I'm just tired," she said. A beat of silence passed, then Mom sighed. "I've spent too much time on this already. But I'm done. I decided this morning I'm not going to give any more of my energy to that man."

Instantly, my mom was thousands of miles away. It must've been nice to be able to say, *'I'm done with that now,'* like a light switch you can just turn off whenever you want. I had tried that already, and it didn't work.

She began to plead with me. "Megan, you have so much to be thankful for. You are so smart and talented. You have a great husband and job and beautiful children. Stop giving your time to this man."

"I wish I could, but I can't. It's not that simple for me."

How could I explain to her something that I couldn't understand myself? Why Chris had meant nothing to me for over a decade, and now he was all I could think about. He was all I could dream about. I didn't ask for this. I would have loved nothing more than to snap my fingers and go back to the way things were before April 8th.

"I don't know what to tell you," she said, clearly irritated. "This is your burden to bear. You knew what you were doing."

Something inside me broke open, and anger spilled out into my chest. *I knew what I was doing? I knew I was being abused?*

"This is bullshit, Mom. I need to go." Before she could respond, I hung up.

That night, alone in my bedroom, I escaped into my journal. A memory had appeared to me earlier that day, of Chris finding me crying in a stairwell. I couldn't believe the memory still existed and was accessible to me, as if it had simply lived dormant somewhere in my brain until something else came along to wake it up.

As I wrote, new memories appeared. It was like walking through a mansion of endless doors and rooms. I'd open one door, step into a room that held a memory, and while I explored that room another door would appear. Some memories appeared fuzzy, but most of them were astonishingly intact.

Things that seemed insignificant at the time were now refusing to leave me alone. The whirring of a floor fan. The taste of coconut shrimp. The feel of an icy-cold Columbia jacket crinkling in the palms of my hands. I couldn't make sense of it, the way I could feel each memory, almost as if it was happening in real time. One smile from Chris and my chest would swell, one touch would set my fingers throbbing. I had never experienced anything like it. What scared me was the comfort I derived from it, the insatiable desire to sink deeper into each memory so I could loot the room and find the answers I desperately craved. *Did everything happen the way I imagined it? Who was Chris, really? Who was I to Chris? How am I going to get my old life back?*

2000

I was leaving the band room when Mr. Blackmer stopped me. "You're still going to sign up for drum major auditions, right?"

"That's the plan," I said.

He smiled. "Good. I'll see you tomorrow."

Before getting to high school, I never dreamed I'd audition for drum major at the end of my freshman year. Drum majors were typically juniors or seniors, but that year had proven I was capable of doing things other freshmen couldn't, like sitting first chair in the top high school band, or landing the biggest role in the spring musical. Who was to say I couldn't become drum major by my sophomore year?

When the day of auditions arrived, only two candidates were signed up: me, and a rising senior. We delivered speeches about why we were the best choice for drum major. We took turns conducting the band. Then the two of us waited outside the band room as Mr. Blackmer invited comments from students.

I paced back and forth in front of the heavy double doors, attempting to ignore the faint dialogue leaking into the hall. I could hear only the lilting of Mr. Blackmer's voice as he prompted the students to engage in dialogue. The sudden roar of talking and shuffling meant the voting was over. Within seconds, Mr. Blackmer stepped into the hall. He secured a piece of paper to the smooth, shiny surface of the door. In hastily written handwriting, it read, *Drum Major 2000—2001: Megan Lucius.*

In August, just weeks before the start of my sophomore year, I arrived at marching band camp. That year, the camp was held at a different location than it had been previously. There was one main building that housed the dorm rooms, a gym that doubled as a cafeteria, and a room where students and staff could watch movies and play games when we weren't rehearsing.

I preferred the mornings. The air, though warm, was still breathable. By mid-afternoon, the blinding sun beat down on the open field, laying a blanket of glistening sweat across our foreheads and arms. The junior drum major, Stephanie, and I would stand spaced out in front of the band, waving our arms in a mirrored four pattern—down, in, out, up, down, in out, up—while the band ran drill. Inevitably, Mr. Blackmer's voice would ring through the megaphone. *STOP. You're not keeping your lines. Do it again*. The band would exhale a subdued groan and trudge back to their original spots, then they'd stand at attention while Mr. Blackmer ambled across the uneven grass, checking formations. He didn't walk, he *strode*—shoulder-heavy, arms swinging like pendulums, his tight lips and dark sunglasses making him look like an out-of-shape drill sergeant.

One hot afternoon, Mr. Blackmer approached me while I was conducting. I could tell he wanted to say something to me, but the band was so loud I knew I'd have to lean in close to be able to hear him. He put his mouth to the opening of my ear. "They're getting tired, aren't they?" His voice vibrated inside my head, sending tingles down my neck.

I liked that he wanted validation from me before making the decision, as if out on the field I was more of an equal than a regular student. I gave him the answer I assumed he already knew. He nodded, then lifted the megaphone to his mouth. "I want everyone to go to their rooms and take a mandatory thirty-minute rest. You don't have to sleep, but you must stay in your bed."

Everyone looked relieved as they trudged across the field toward the dormitory.

One evening, the students and staff gathered in the gym for a game. I was excited when Mr. Blackmer put me in charge of explaining the rules, but as I was addressing the group I noticed the sour look on Sean's face.

We had broken up on and off throughout freshman year, and like the previous summer, we had spent this vacation apart. Our relationship followed the same predictable cycle. I'd break up with him, vowing to be done with the relationship, and when I would see him again months later, all the old feelings would come rushing back. No one had the power to make me feel like I was either having the best day or the worst day more than Sean did.

Sean looked at the people down the row and shook his head. "This is so dumb."

My cheeks burned with embarrassment. I felt the sting of tears damming up behind my eyes, but I held them back long enough for the game to start. Then I hurried out of the gym to a nearby stairwell to be alone. I fell to the cold concrete steps that led up to the dormitories and slouched into myself, head in my hands, tears streaming down my face.

Moments later, I heard the groaning of a door. I lifted my head and was surprised to see Mr. Blackmer peering into the stairwell. He stepped inside, guiding the heavy door as it slowly fell shut behind him. Softly, he asked, "Are you okay?"

"I'm fine," I said, using the back of my hand to wipe tears from my wet cheeks.

Mr. Blackmer stood with his hands in his pockets, timidly rocking back and forth on his feet. His head was bowed in sympathy, the brown pools of his eyes lifted to meet my face. "Boys are stupid," he said. "If you want, I'd be happy to give him some advice. It might help."

I imagined Mr. Blackmer pulling Sean aside to lecture him on how to treat girls while Sean glared at him, red-faced and ready to explode with anger. "Thank you," I said, "but that's okay. I'll be back soon."

Mr. Blackmer nodded, offered a caring smile, then left the stairwell.

The warm autumn brought the first home football game of the season, and the marching band was preparing to play our first official halftime show, with music from *West Side Story*—Mr. Blackmer's favorite musical. There was a solo in the show's ballad number, *Maria*, and instead of giving it to the second chair trumpet player, he asked me to play it while Stephanie conducted.

As the band made its way around the track to get into place, I went to Mr. Blackmer for encouragement. He smiled at me like I was being ridiculous for worrying. "You're going to be fine," he said, placing a calming hand on my shoulder. Mr. Blackmer had a way of making me see myself the way he saw me, as capable and confident. I loved that whenever he saw me, he seemed to light up the same way I lit up when seeing him. When he looked at me, he *really* looked at me, as if he understood what I was thinking or feeling, whether I was happy or sad or nervous.

Following the halftime show, I raced up the stadium steps to find my best friend, Andi, decked out in our school's colors, complete with sparkling blue and gold face paint. "You look awesome!" I shouted, hugging her.

"Thanks! Great job on your solo!" she shouted back.

We huddled together, observing the organized chaos around us. After a while, she leaned in close and said, "I don't want this to sound weird, but I think Mr. Blackmer likes you."

"What?" I said. I'd heard her the first time, but I wanted her to say it again. I liked the way it made my stomach flit and flutter.

"Mr. Blackmer!" Andi said. She pointed down at the track where he was standing, arms folded, watching the game. "I think he *likes* you!"

Suddenly, it was impossible to keep a stupid grin off my face. "What makes you say that?"

"It's the way he looks at you. And the way he touches you. It's like he's flirting with you."

I remembered the way I felt the night of the jazz band event, when Mr. Blackmer said to me, *That dress looks nice on you.* I had the same feeling now, as if Andi's words had reached into my stomach and squeezed my insides, making them beg for release.

I stood still for a moment, imagining what it was like to be Andi up in the stands, watching me and Mr. Blackmer together, noticing the obvious closeness between us. I wondered if other people noticed it, too. I knew we shared a special connection, but I had never considered that he might have romantic feelings for me.

The rest of the night, if Mr. Blackmer spoke to me, touched me, if he even looked in my direction, I observed it through a different lens. Was it really possible for him to like me? I had to imagine that anything was possible. How many times had I seen older men with younger women, both in movies and in real life? There were rumors that teachers at my high school had been involved with students. I'd even heard that one of the school staff had married a student. He wouldn't have married her unless he was in love with her. So, I guessed it was possible. But was it possible for Mr. Blackmer to feel something for me? And if he did, what did I feel for him?

My mind paged through memories of me and Mr. Blackmer, tiny moments that might add up to something. But it seemed foolish to think too much about it. He was my teacher, that was clear to me, and even if we had feelings for each other, we couldn't be together—at least, not until I graduated.

I decided I would try to forget about what Andi said. I would try to forget whatever warmth was stirring inside me that night in the autumn air.

In October, the band took a field trip to see the show *Blast!* at the Masonic Temple Theater in Detroit. After the show, I followed my group of friends—which happened to include Sean—to the back of the bus. But before I sat down, Sean made a rude, tasteless joke. The type that always felt like a screw was being twisted into my gut. It was all the reason I needed to leave the back and go searching for another place to sit.

Gripping the top of each cold green leathery seat, I pulled myself forward, pushing through the crowded aisle of protruding arms and legs. When I noticed an open seat directly behind the driver, excitement washed over me. Mr. Blackmer was probably going to sit somewhere near the front of the bus. If I sat in the front, I might get to talk to him. At the very least I would be near him, which was enough to make me forget about how irritated I was with Sean. I plopped down and scooted myself toward the window.

Minutes later, Mr. Blackmer climbed the bus steps. He stopped when he reached the landing next to the driver and began surveying the herd of antsy teenagers in their post-concert squirreliness. I watched him scan the back of the bus, then the middle, until he made his way to the rows directly in front of him. When his gaze landed on the front row, his eyes darted between me and the vacant spot next to me. What was it I saw in his eyes? Nervousness? Apprehension?

My excitement melted into anxiety. *I put him in a bad position by sitting here. What am I gonna do now? Get up and move? It looks so obvious I want him to sit with me. Oh my gosh, Megan. What were you thinking? Stupid. Stupid. Stupid.*

Mr. Blackmer gave the okay for the bus driver to take us home. As the engine roared into motion, I stared out the window, holding my breath, waiting for his next move. When I felt him sit down beside me, my heart leapt into my throat. I kept myself statue-still, arms crossed over my stomach, my knees lifted to rest against the seat that divided us and the driver. I was aware of every inch of my body—the rise and fall of my breath, the lines of my thighs extending out from my dress, my long hair falling across my shoulders in his direction.

Mr. Blackmer crossed his arms and leaned in slightly. "Did you like the show?"

"I loved it," I said, allowing myself to look directly at him. When our eyes met, my body breathed out a sigh. He looked less intimidating on a cramped bench seat than when he was a giant perched atop a conductor's podium. We fell into easy conversation, and before long it was like we were the only two people on the bus. We had spoken before, obviously, but never for this long and never in such close proximity to one another. He asked about my family. I told him that my parents had been divorced since I was a toddler, but they had both remarried. That I had two brothers—one from each set of parents—ten and twelve years younger than me. I talked to him about my church, my grandparents, my friends. In exchange, he told me where he had grown up and gone to high school, how he'd attended Central Michigan University for his teaching degree and had even been the drum major of the marching band.

We also talked about church and compared notes on our different religious backgrounds. "Let me get this straight," I said, wrinkling my nose in judgment. "If I'm not Catholic, I can't take communion at your church?"

"Nope. Not allowed," he teased through a toothy grin.

It was so easy to talk to him. So easy to get lost in the sound of our voices mingling with the roar of the road, the sight of his boyish face shining in flashes of light that passed through the windows as we traveled down the highway. Each time I made him laugh, he'd playfully bump his shoulder into mine as the back of his hand swung out to tap my leg, and as he withdrew his hand I could feel his index finger glide across the nylon of my sheer black tights. Sometimes, while I was talking, his gaze would fall to my mouth and jump back up. I'd hold my gaze at him, pretending not to notice as my heart danced around inside my chest. Was he flirting with me? It felt like flirting, but I couldn't be 100 percent positive. Maybe he was just really comfortable around me. I mean, I had never seen him interact with anyone the way he interacted with me, student or adult. I had never seen him look at anyone the way he looked at me. The way he was looking at me now.

I reminded myself that he was my teacher. Not that I *needed* reminding or anything. I knew nothing could realistically happen between us. But it was fun to live in the world of make-believe, to float on air high above everything and everyone else, to dream that I was beautiful and smart enough that a man like Mr. Blackmer would choose to give his undivided attention to me.

As we neared the high school, an ache blossomed in my stomach. I knew our time together would be ending soon, and already I was longing to rewind time and do the ride all over again. For that one hour, we were in our own world. There was nothing but us. Nothing but good feelings.

That night, I laid in bed, warm and weightless, thinking about Mr. Blackmer and the bus ride. Every look, every touch, the sound of his voice—it played in a continuous loop inside my head until, finally, I drifted off to sleep.

As the school year progressed, Mr. Blackmer invaded more and more of my mind. It used to be that I only thought about him when I was in his classroom. Then I started to think about him during other classes. By winter, he was with me everywhere I went—at school, at church, at home.

One weeknight, I was pacing the length of my basement bedroom floor, stifling tears as I listened to the barrage of shouts seeping through the ceiling above me. Mom and Randy were in a full-blown argument, which I had rarely seen in the past five years. Most of their fighting had taken place when I was younger and still sleeping on the main floor in the bedroom next to theirs. I would lie awake, listening to the sound of Randy's pleading voice, and my mom's irritation escalating to anger. A few times, my mom was so angry with Randy, she marched into my bedroom and told me we were leaving. She didn't give me time to grab clothes, we just hurried outside into the dark of night. I would lie down in the backseat of her burgundy sedan and stare up at the window, watching the white lights of the lamp posts fly by as she drove through the city to a friend's house. At some point, she would turn around and drive us back home, and the next morning everything would seem to go back to normal.

It was only later that I realized the fights were always about sex—Randy wanting too much of it, my mom not wanting enough of it. I vowed to myself that when I got married, my husband and I would never have a reason to fight about sex. The sexual interactions I had experienced up to that point proved to me that sex—*real sex*—was going to be so phenomenal, there would never be a time when I would want to refuse it.

The fight they were having now was worse than any of their previous fights. I wasn't afraid that they would physically hurt each other, but I hated the yelling and I was desperate to talk to someone.

The moment Mr. Blackmer popped into my head, there was nothing I wanted more than to hear his voice. He had given us his home number at the beginning of the school year in case we ever had questions. I picked up the black cordless phone from my nightstand and slowly began pressing buttons on the numbered keypad.

Before pressing the final number, I stopped. What would he think if I called him at home crying? Would he be annoyed? Would he be freaked out? Would it ruin our relationship? I knew it was a bold move to call a teacher about a personal problem, but Mr. Blackmer had shown an obvious interest in my life outside of school. He seemed to care about me as a person, not just as a student.

When the phone started to ring, I imagined being a fly on the wall of his home, listening to the phone ring on his end. I pictured him walking out from another room, across the living room and—

"Hello?" the voice said.

My stomach tightened. It was too late to back out now. "Hi. Um . . . This is Megan Lucius."

"Hey, Megan. Are you okay?" He sounded both genuinely concerned and genuinely happy to hear my voice.

"I'm sorry to bother you. It's just—my parents are having a bad argument and—" As the words were escaping my lips, I regretted my decision to call. *This is stupid. He's going to think you're weird and emotional and ridiculous.* "I'm so sorry to bother you," I said.

"You're not bothering me. You can always call if you need me."

He stayed on the phone with me until the shouting subsided. There was something so comforting about listening to his voice as I sat on the edge of my bed, staring at my wallpaper border, a repeating pattern of white and purple flowers. It was almost like he was in my bedroom, sitting right beside me.

"Are you going to be okay?" he asked.

"Yes. Thank you so much for talking to me."

"Of course. I'll see you tomorrow. Goodnight, Megan."

Before going to bed, I wrote Mr. Blackmer an email thanking him for the conversation. By morning, he had already responded. He told me again that he would be there for me if I needed him, and I could feel free to call him whenever.

When I walked through the band room doors later that day, Sean was waiting for me. "Please don't be mad, but I saw the emails between you and Mr. Blackmer."

An unfamiliar terror gripped my chest. "You *what*?"

Sean once showed me how he could gain access to information on other people's computers. *It's called hacking*, he said. But I didn't think he would do that to me. We weren't even together. I would have been angrier with him if I wasn't preoccupied with the fear that something important was about to be taken from me.

"I shouldn't have done it," Sean said, "but you really shouldn't be talking to a teacher like that. I should tell somebody—"

My hand shot up, as if to block a physical attack. "Don't do that. Nothing's going on, he was just being nice to me. It's nothing." My mouth was dry and my pulse was pounding in my ears. Before Sean could say anything else, I walked away from him and into the storage room to get my trumpet.

After school, I told my mom that Sean was threatening to go to the principal about a harmless email I'd sent to Mr. Blackmer. She was immediately agitated. "Why would he do that to you? He's going to stir up trouble for no reason, and it's going to hurt your reputation." She took a breath, as if having to calm herself down. "If he makes a big deal out of this, I'm going to tell the police he's hacking into my daughter's emails."

I told Sean what my mom had said, hoping it would put an end to the whole thing. But I still spent the rest of the week on edge, waiting for a knock at one of my classroom doors, to hear the principal's voice saying, *I need to speak with Megan Lucius*.

I waited, but no one came.

2019

Six weeks we'd been living in the new house, and there was still very little furniture in the spacious living room: two hand-me-down recliners, one end table, and a small flat-screen television perched on one end of the fireplace hearth. I was hopeful that in the next month or so we could save enough money to buy a sofa and some new chairs. The shag carpet was growing on me, but it would also need replacing, especially if we were going to host our family for Thanksgiving later that year.

Ian sat in one recliner, feet propped up, scrolling through his phone. Through the picture window we had a clear view of Evan and Eli. They were in the backyard starting to argue over whose turn it was on the tree swing.

I got up from my recliner, walked to the window, and started to knock hard on the glass with my fist. The boys' heads spun toward me, their faces wide with surprise. "Be nice to each other!" I shouted, overenunciating each syllable, hoping they'd hear me through the thick glass. Even if they couldn't, my body language was enough to warn them to stop. Evan surrendered the swing to Eli, then he ventured off, no doubt to find a giant stick to use as a sword.

"They're fine," Ian groaned, his eyes still scrolling the phone screen.

I picked up my empty wine glass from the end table and went into the kitchen. I poured another glass and called to the living room, "I don't like it when they argue."

Ian called back. "They're brothers. They're going to argue."

Of the two of us, Ian had always been the more easygoing parent. The last one to lose his temper. Sometimes, if I spoke harshly to the boys, Ian would step in. *That's enough*, he'd say in a calm, restrained tone, which would infuriate me. I didn't understand why it made me so angry. Was it that my own spouse had to correct me like I was a child? Or was I angry because Ian was always acting like things were fine when they clearly weren't? It was only when things became nearly unmanageable that he'd take action, like how he'd wait until the trash can was overflowing to change the bag. Every day I would walk by, watching the trash line rise and, with it, my irritation. I wasn't the best housekeeper, but I did what I could to pick up after the four of us, every day bending down to gather toys and stuffed animals, socks that Ian had removed after a day at work. If I made dinner, the dishes would sit staring at me until I picked them up. Several times I had tried to talk to Ian about my discontent. I told him it was unfair that we both worked the same job but I had to also be the housekeeper and the one to get the boys ready in the morning even though it took me twice as long as him to get dressed.

It didn't make sense to me how Ian could be the best man in almost every way, but then there were glaring holes that refused to be filled. He would do anything for me, except make the daily chores an equal responsibility. He wasn't lazy, far from it. He could spend an entire day on a difficult project, but when it came to laundry or dishes, it's like they weren't even on his radar. It was only when he ran out of underwear or the sink was piled sky high with dishes that he'd intervene, and then he'd complain to me about how we needed to rinse the dishes before they crusted over and became impossible to scrub. Since it felt like a losing battle, I tried my best to stay quiet and ignore the urge to lash out. I told myself I should be grateful. This was the way it looked for a lot of women. Why couldn't I just swallow my anger and move on?

"Has the sergeant checked in with you?" Ian asked, looking up at me as I returned from the kitchen. It had been five days since I'd given my statement. Now it was up to the prosecutors to decide whether or not Chris could face charges.

I sat the newly filled glass down on the table, curled up into the recliner, and pulled my open journal onto my lap. "No," I said.

"He taught here in Michigan for almost twenty years. There's no possible way you're the only one he did this to. You won't be alone."

"I hope you're right," I said, my eyes fixed on the page in front of me. I didn't want there to be more victims out there, but I also didn't want to be the only person stepping forward. If I knew there were others like me, it would be undeniable proof that I wasn't special, that I was a victim, and I wouldn't have to feel like I had betrayed Chris by going to the police.

Ian's attention drifted back to his phone as the world around me dulled to nothingness. I finished writing out a memory. Then I carried my empty glass back to the kitchen.

Exactly one week after giving my statement, I was at church busily preparing for a Holy Week service. Members of the choir were trickling into the worship hall for rehearsal when my phone lit up. When I saw Sergeant Perry's name, I quickly removed myself from the room and hurried down to the nearby parlor to be alone.

"The prosecutors say we can move forward with the investigation," he said. "The statute of limitations is fifteen years. Because Christopher left the state in 2013, the counting stopped at twelve years, which meets the requirement. But we need your permission. Since you're the main witness, we have to know you're going to cooperate."

I paced back and forth, rolling heel to toe into the plush carpet. "What would you do?"

"I can't tell you how to feel, but this guy is definitely a predator. He's using his position to get with kids."

I knew what I was supposed to be feeling in that moment: anger, disgust, a readiness to pull the trigger and send the police after Chris. But instead, my skepticism was aimed at the sergeant. How did he know what Chris was? And what did he mean when he said Chris was *using his position* to get with kids? The boy in the video wasn't even his student. According to the articles, they had met through an online dating app. What did that have to do with being a predator?

Regardless of my feelings, the facts were the facts. Chris had broken the law. There was at least one known victim, and in no possible scenario could I see myself abandoning them.

A large part of me wanted the police to do the investigation. I wanted to bring everything into the light. After all, it was secrecy that made this mess possible in the first place. But another part of me feared Chris's reaction. If I went through with this and he found out I had gone to the police, would he be angry with me? Would he be hurt? If I could forgive him on my own, would I even need to involve the police?

"Can I think about it before I make a decision?" I said.

"Yes, absolutely. Take a day or two."

I remembered what Ian had said to me: *You won't be the only one.* I thought back to the first detective I spoke with the day I found out about Chris's arrest, the one who said, *This is turning into something*, like I was one of several calls about Chris that day.

"What about the other victims?" I said.

"We reached out to other police departments in the counties where he worked, to see what allegations had been made."

"Okay?"

"So far, you're the only person who's come forward. If we arrest him and bring him back to Michigan to be tried, it will be for you."

The next morning, I went to one of my church pastors for advice. Pastor William was one of the most beloved and respected men in the community, spiritually grounded and trustworthy. I knew that whatever I asked him, his response would come from a place of love.

I was too exhausted to recount all the details of what had happened and what was happening now. Thankfully, I didn't need to. It took only a snapshot of the story for him to sympathize with my brokenness. I sat across the desk from him, my body collapsing onto itself, and cried, "How do I show love to someone who's hurt me?"

Pastor William leaned forward at his desk, one hand on top of the other, the lines on his face shifting as he pondered my question. With all the tenderness of a surrogate grandfather, he answered. "Megan . . . you hold them accountable."

If we bring him back, it will be for you.

It felt like such a burden to bear, to know that because of me, Chris could be tried not once but twice. It seemed impossible he'd win the Florida trial, not with the police in possession of the video—and if he was tried here in Michigan, what chance would he have at winning here? Would he ever get out of prison?

If we bring him back . . . it will be for you . . .

. . . bring him back . . .

There was something strangely appealing about the possibility of Chris coming back to Michigan, even if it was in handcuffs. If I was the only one in Michigan to come forward, that meant I was the only one he'd have to answer questions about.

If they put him on a witness stand, what would he say? Would he deny everything? Would he try to convince a jury that what we had was real? Would he avoid eye contact with me, or would he look at me the way he used to?

. . . it will be for you . . .

What if, once the police brought him to Michigan, he asked to see me? Would they let us be in a room together? Could I sit at a table across from him and ask all the questions that were burning a hole in my chest?

I had to admit, it was a bit delusional to think the police would actually let me be in his presence, unless it was in a courtroom. But a voice inside was telling me I could make the impossible *possible*. I had to believe in something, because there was no happy ending to this story. At least there could be some kind of closure. I needed to believe that every question would eventually be answered, that every loose end would be tied up when this was all over. But in order for that to happen, Chris would have to reenter the story.

On April 17th, I sent Sergeant Perry an email: *I have made the decision to proceed with the investigation.*

2001

I returned from winter break carrying the brand new Bach Stratavarius trumpet Mom and Randy had given me for Christmas. When I got to Symphonic Band, the room was fairly empty. I couldn't wait to show Mr. Blackmer my gift, but when I noticed he was standing at the podium talking to two girls, a spark of jealousy flickered inside my chest. My body stiffened as I made my way to my seat, my mind continually drifting to the conversation happening at the front of the room. I set my pristine case on the ground and flipped open the latches.

I was in the middle of removing my trumpet from its case when Mr. Blackmer glanced in my direction, putting me on edge. He made a joke to the two girls that was loud enough for me to hear, and in my doe-eyed laughter the trumpet slipped from my hands, hitting the hard floor with a loud *clang*. I bent down to get it, trying hard to swallow my stupidity, when I saw a glaring dent in one of my shiny new valves.

Fifteen hundred dollars. That's how much the instrument had cost my parents. They must have saved up for months to get it, and on the first day back to school I damaged it.

Lost in stomach-churning guilt, I lifted my head. But when I looked up, the guilt was overcome by an acute awareness of Mr. Blackmer's gaze. He was staring straight at me, his lips locked in a knowing smirk.

The blood drained from my face. I could tell he wasn't concerned about the trumpet I had just dropped. His stare, which was now burning a hole through me, told me he knew *why* I had dropped it.

• • •

There's no way to pinpoint the exact moment I knew I was in love with Mr. Blackmer. Somewhere along the line, respect blurred into admiration, admiration into affection, affection into infatuation, and all of it fueled by a thousand microscopic moments that made him familiar to me and me vulnerable to him.

I had tried so hard to act normal around him before we left for winter break. I didn't want him to suspect that anything had changed between us, but every day was like trying to escape a forest fire. When a strange or funny thing happened, he'd make eye contact with me from across the room as if we were sharing an inside joke. As the first chair trumpet player, I was directly in his line of sight. When the band reached the end of a piece and he gave the final cutoff, his eyes frequently locked on mine. Time would stand still, and at his command the band remained frozen until he lowered his hands, granting us all permission to move and me to breathe again. It was like I didn't fully belong to myself anymore. Part of me now belonged to him.

Fantasies took shape in my mind of what it would be like to go on a date with him, to kiss him, to have him fall in love with me. I searched for clues that this was possible, from him and the world around me, in songs and stories that seemed to mirror my experiences and desires. I took note of any couple where the man was significantly older than the woman, like my hairdresser who told me she was married to a man twenty years older than her. *Twenty years*. That made the thirteen year age gap between Mr. Blackmer and me seem like nothing.

I played a game with myself, negotiating what ages we'd have to be for our relationship to be socially acceptable. I was fifteen and he was twenty-eight, so . . . sixteen, twenty-nine . . . eighteen, thirty-one . . . I decided twenty and thirty-three were the perfect numbers because I wouldn't carry the label of *teenager* anymore. I'd be a few years into college, practically a grown woman by that time. And thirty-three wasn't old, especially because Mr. Blackmer looked at least five years younger than his actual age. We could be out in public together and no one would think anything about it.

It wasn't unusual for students to be in Mr. Blackmer's office before or after school, mostly to ask questions. I stopped in one day, and before I could leave he asked if I'd heard the Muppets song "Mahna Mahna."

"I have no idea what that is," I said, shaking my head and trying not to smile too wide.

He leaned back in his chair and feigned a gasp. "*Megan*," he said, as if scolding me, "you have to listen to it." He searched the computer until he found a song file in one of the folders. He gestured for me to switch places with him so I could sit in his chair while he stood nearby. It could have been that I was tired that day, or maybe there was something genuinely hilarious about that song, but I got to laughing and I couldn't stop, and because *I* was laughing he started laughing. By the end of the song, we had laughed so hard for so long that we were both wiping tears from our eyes.

It wasn't only Andi who thought the relationship between me and Mr. Blackmer was unusual. Students in band were starting to tease, saying it was obvious Mr. Blackmer had a crush on me. I pretended to brush off these comments, or label them as absurd. Secretly, I wanted them to be true.

In January, I auditioned for the musical *Guys and Dolls*.

I didn't get a lead. Mr. Carrizales gave me the minor role of a hotbox dancer, which wasn't so bad because Andi had also tried out for the musical that year, and Mr. Carrizales made her a hotbox dancer as well.

The cast was gathered on stage one day when Mr. Carrizales said he wanted to teach proper stage kissing. He pointed to Andi. "Andrea, come here," he said, beckoning her with a sweep of his hand. Andi approached Mr. Carrizales and stood square to him. He asked her to tilt her head to the side—which she did, exposing the soft edges of her neck and jawline to everyone watching. Mr. Carrizales tilted his head in the opposite direction, his mouth aimed at her cheek. He explained to us that he would barely touch the corner of her mouth, and he leaned his face in, putting his lips to her skin. While Andi remained frozen, a shiver crawled up the back of my neck. I tried to ignore it, reminding myself that this must be what serious theater is like.

After that day, however, I started to pay closer attention to events involving Mr. Carrizales, like the time he stared at my chest and said, "You're really starting to fill out," or the night I was leaving rehearsal and he stopped in his truck to say hello.

"We're going to see a movie," he said. "Wanna come?"

I didn't understand what he meant by *we're* going to see a movie, until I took a closer look. Under the white glow of the parking lot lamps, I saw two students crammed into the tiny cab with him, the interior's deep shadows draped over their faces.

I thought it odd he'd be going to a movie with two students late at night, but I also assumed their parents knew where they were. Plus, why would Mr. Carrizales stop to talk to me if he had something to hide? Wouldn't he have just driven by, hoping no one would see him?

"No thanks, I'm tired. But you guys have fun," I said, waving goodbye.

One evening, musical rehearsal was being held in the cafeteria. The room looked a bit like a zoo when I arrived, with students scattered everywhere, dancing and shouting. I overheard a group of students talking about the dinner they'd just had with Mr. Carrizales at a Chinese restaurant. They were laughing—but about what, I didn't know.

Mr. Carrizales approached me and said, "Megan, come here!" He led me to a corner of the cafeteria, hovering over me, his hot breath on my cheek. I stared down at the floor so I could block out the noise and focus on what he wanted to tell me.

"Do you want to see my cock?" Mr. Carrizales asked.

The hard *k* in the word *cock* lashed at my eardrum, stunning me. Before I had time to react, he shoved an object into my line of sight: a Chinese restaurant menu covered in animals.

"See?" he said, pointing to the rooster. "Here's my cock."

"Oh!" I said, forcing a laugh. I was still trying to process what had happened when he walked away, leaving me in the corner.

A day later, the cast of *Guys and Dolls* was called into a meeting with the principal. We were informed that Mr. Carrizales was no longer allowed on school grounds, and we were to tell someone immediately if we saw him near the building. Apparently, Mr. Carrizales had been asking several kids the same question he'd asked me at rehearsal. The rumor amongst students was that one of the girls in the cast had reported Mr. Carrizales' behavior to her father—who happened to be a pastor—and he had contacted the school immediately.

It was never discussed in detail the reasons why Mr. Carrizales was fired. He wasn't arrested, only let go from his job, and no one interviewed me or anyone else that I knew to see if he had done other inappropriate things. We were told another teacher would be stepping in to direct the show, and I left the auditorium that day thinking one dirty word was the reason he was no longer our theater director.

When I saw Mr. Blackmer later that day, I could tell we were both thinking the same thing.

"What an idiot," Mr. Blackmer said, shaking his head.

"Right? Pretty stupid." I let out an awkward laugh, thinking again how crazy it was for a teacher to have said the word *cock* to me and to other students.

"Stupid" was the word that came to mind when I thought of Mr. Carrizales. Not "dangerous." Not "abusive" or "criminal." I had an idea in my head of what criminals looked like and how they behaved. As far as I was concerned, the people in my world were flawed but they weren't *bad* people. I hoped Mr. Carrizales would use his firing as a lesson to not be such an idiot in the future.

In February, our band took a field trip to a nearby school that was hosting an annual band festival. We performed our rehearsed pieces in the school's auditorium. When that was done, we moved to the sight reading room where we'd be given five minutes to look at a piece of music we'd never seen before, then perform it for the sight reading judge.

The judge was on a short break, so we stood around the room chatting and waiting to take our seats. I started to panic when the second chair trumpet player had an emergency and needed to leave the room. Without him, I'd have to play the most difficult trumpet part by myself. It must have been obvious how anxious I was, because Mr. Blackmer locked eyes with me and motioned for me to come to him. He took my arm and walked me through a side door, out of the library, and into a half-lit empty hallway. Everything happened so fast, I didn't have time to wonder why he'd taken me there or if anyone would notice we were gone. The only thing that mattered to me was what would happen next.

Mr. Blackmer stepped toward me, forcing my back against the scratchy gray brick that lined the hallway. With one foot in front of the other, he leaned forward, looming over me with his hand pressed flatly against the wall above my shoulder. "I need you to relax," he breathed, his brown eyes boring into me with an intensity I'd never seen in him. He spoke in a controlled, unhurried manner, the way I'd seen people do in movies when casting a spell.

"I'm trying," I said, swallowing hard, disoriented as time seemed to be moving too fast and in slow motion simultaneously.

He leaned in closer, his face now inches from mine. "Take a deep breath. I know you can do this."

My heart was pounding in my ears, my blood racing through my shaking hands and into my throbbing fingertips. *He's going to kiss me. Oh my God, he's going to kiss me.* I pressed my back to the wall harder, held my breath, and waited for him to close the space between our mouths.

There was a long pause, as if time had stopped completely. Then, as if a switch had been flipped, he broke my gaze and removed his hand from the wall, pulling away from me.

He tugged at his tuxedo jacket. "Okay," he said, stern and teacher-like, "let's go." He opened the door, outstretched his hand with an air of gentleman-like formality, and ushered me back into the room where the rest of the students had been waiting, seemingly unaware of our brief and unexplained absence. My hands were still shaking when I sat down to play.

That night, I wrote in my journal every detail I could about that afternoon. *I'm not making this up in my head. Mr. Blackmer almost kissed me. Something is definitely going on between us.*

Early spring was a blur. Day in and day out, I waited for another moment like the one Mr. Blackmer and I had shared at the band festival. There were hints here and there—a small touch, a warm glance, but nothing like what happened in that hallway.

In April, following a band event at school, I approached Mr. Blackmer in his office. "I need a ride home. Do you know anyone who could take me?"

He answered without hesitation, "I can take you."

I felt particularly lonely that night and I just wanted to spend time with him. It wouldn't be a big deal for him to drive me to my house, which was less than fifteen minutes away. I had already been in his car for long periods of time, when he'd taken me and a small group of students on a trip to Central Michigan University and to one of the big music stores in the state.

I tried not to look awkward as I lingered in the band room, sparks flying through me as I waited for everyone to leave so he could lock up and we could go.

"I have to make one quick stop on the way. Is that okay with you?" he said.

"Yup," I said, excited that this stop would extend our time together.

On the way to my house, Mr. Blackmer pulled into the 7-Eleven convenience store just down the road from the high school. He went inside to use the ATM while I stayed in the car. It surprised me he would stop at such a public place. As far as I knew, we weren't breaking any rules, but if someone were to see me alone in his car, they might wonder if something strange was going on. Through the giant storefront window, I watched him meander to the ATM and back. He didn't seem nervous. And if Mr. Blackmer wasn't nervous about what others might suspect, why should I be?

We were getting close to my street when I pointed to the business sign in front of my house. "That's it," I said, then added with a shrug, "*Yeah*. I live on a car lot."

He lifted one eyebrow and offered an impish smile. "You *do* live on a car lot."

He drove his blue Saturn up the angled driveway into the open space in front of my house. When he reached down to shift into park, my muscles tensed. His hand had been close to me before, but not in this setting. Alone in a dark car—*his* car—with warm air breathing through the vents, cloaking us in artificial heat. A few more inches and his hand would be touching my skin.

I turned toward him and smiled softly. "Thanks for the ride."

"Anytime," he said.

I didn't want to leave, but I also didn't want to make him uncomfortable by trying to prolong our time together. I opened the door and stepped out onto the cracked pavement. "Goodnight," I said, leaning down to steal one last moment with him.

He lifted his hand in one elegant motion, as if conducting a farewell. "Goodnight, Megan."

On the Friday leading up to my sixteenth birthday, I had planned to go on a field trip with Mr. Blackmer and a few students to see *Phantom of the Opera* at the Masonic Temple in Detroit. This wasn't like the field trips where Mr. Blackmer requested a school bus and openly welcomed all band students to attend. This was a special trip, where he had invited only a handful of students.

On the day of the show, I asked him who else was going. Casually, he said, "It looks like you're the only one."

My stomach dropped ten floors.

On the surface, it seemed like an absolute dream—spending the entire evening alone together, just the two of us bantering to and from Detroit in his car, shoulder to shoulder in a dark theater for almost three hours. But instinctively I knew it wasn't a good idea. It looked too much like a date, and students were already suspicious of our relationship. I worried this would throw open the door for vicious rumors. And even though Mr. Blackmer didn't seem worried, I wondered if he could get in trouble for taking only one student to a show an hour away.

It didn't matter what I wanted, I couldn't put either of us in that situation. I realized, however, if I could convince another student to come along, we could still go to the show. I'm not sure why, of all the people I could have invited, it was Sean I called that afternoon.

Over the course of three years, Sean and I had developed a predictable cycle. We'd get together, hoping that things would be different from how they were the previous time—but the arguments would start and they'd escalate to the point of me breaking up with him. After a few months apart, we'd become friends again, and the friendship would be going so well that I'd regret breaking up. I'd long for him, remembering only the good times we shared, because when things were good between us, they were great. We genuinely enjoyed each other's company. We laughed together a lot. His taste in music was superb—The Hollies and Mazzy Star—and we often liked to watch the same shows and movies.

Sean and I were in the friendship part of our cycle and getting along fairly well, so I took a leap of faith and asked him to go. I knew that with him there it was less likely for people to make up rumors about something happening between me and Mr. Blackmer. As tumultuous as our relationship was at times, I believed there was always some kind of love between us. In Sean's best moments, I could rely on him for shelter and support.

Sean must have felt *something* when I told him I was the only person going on the trip, and it probably wasn't a warm, fuzzy feeling. He was acutely aware of Mr. Blackmer's behavior toward me, and it was an occasional point of contention in our relationship, whether Sean and I were dating or just friends.

But that night, none of that seemed to matter. On the way to Detroit, Mr. Blackmer and I sat in the front. Sean sat in the back center, leaning forward so that his head hovered just above the center console. The radio was kept to a dull hum as we all talked and laughed and told stories. It was surprising how easy it was for the three of us to be together. If Sean was uncomfortable, he wasn't showing it.

When we got to the theater, Mr. Blackmer went ahead of us to get refreshments in one of the ballrooms. Sean and I explored the theater and eventually met up with him. Then the three of us went up to our balcony seats, located on the right side of the house. Mr. Blackmer sat on my left and Sean on my right.

I had never seen *Phantom of the Opera*, but I was familiar with it because my mom kept a music book in our house with songs and pictures from the show. Sometimes, she would sit down at our piano and play excerpts from three or four of the songs. I didn't know the names, but I knew the melodies well. I loved that my middle name—aside from the spelling—was the same name as the main character's in the musical. Megan *Kristine* Lucius.

When my mom was pregnant, she read somewhere that the names Megan and Kristine, when put together, meant "strong, faithful Christian." From the moment she first held me in the hospital bed, that's exactly what she thought I'd become—strong and faithful, courageous and compassionate, honest and forgiving. And because she believed those things about me, I believed them, too.

The second reason for my name I'd always found more entertaining than anything. Along with reading baby books, my pregnant mother endured all eight hours of the television miniseries *The Thorn Birds*, a dramatic saga akin to *Gone with the Wind*, only twice as long. She was drawn to the character of Meggie, stubborn and strong-willed, with red-gold hair. I had never seen it, but I knew it involved two people of a considerable age gap and a lot of crying. To sum it up, young girl meets older priest, girl and priest fall in love but can't be together, and everything sucks. It's the kind of show you watch when feeling miserable somehow feels good.

Occasionally, I'd tease my mom for naming me after such a tragic love story. "Don't you know you've cursed me in love?" I'd say, throwing my hands to the sky for theatrical effect.

She'd always respond with a look of genuine surprise. "What? I just liked the name!" Then she'd look away, perform a cute little half-shrug, adding, "And I liked how confident she was."

The beginning of the show was eerily quiet. I didn't know what to expect, so when the chandelier lit up and loud music burst from the pit, I visibly jumped.

I looked back at Mr. Blackmer, so startled I was almost laughing. He looked back at me, eyes soft, smiling in amusement. There were moments throughout the show when I would whisper to him about different things, whether it was to ask a question about the plot or just to say, *That was amazing*, but for most of the show I was immersed in the story, the costumes, the lighting, and most of all, the music. I was enamored with the romance between Christine and Raoul, childhood friends turned lovers, how Raul had never forgotten about Christine all the years they were apart. When they sang "All I Ask of You," I nearly melted onto my velvet seat.

The Phantom had some great songs, but he was fairly simplistic—the quintessential villain, interfering with the picture-perfect romance between Christine and Raoul, terrorizing the theater with ominous voices and letters and, of course, *murder*. What I didn't understand, really, was the relationship between Christine and the Phantom, the strange power he had over her. She seemed to both fear him *and* love him. In the end, I was relieved to see Christine and Raoul escape the Phantom's lair to go off and live happily ever after, and for the Phantom to disappear.

The ride back to Flint was similar to the ride there. Easy-going. Fun. And when we arrived at the high school, we said our goodnights and Sean drove me home. In a way, it felt like a perfect night. I'd gotten to spend the evening with Mr. Blackmer, but in a way that wouldn't stir up trouble, and Sean and I didn't have a single argument. It was a simple, carefree night. Nothing more.

On May 2nd, I turned sixteen years old. Mom and Randy surprised me with my first car, a white two-door Monte Carlo. Having the freedom to drive ushered me into a new world. Now I could take myself to school and church. If I wanted to visit my father or a friend's house, I didn't have to bother anyone for a ride. I could just *go*.

I was headed to Andi's house one late afternoon when I stopped at a traffic light. "Tearin' Up My Heart" came on the radio, so I cranked it up to full volume and began singing loudly as if I were in a stadium at a packed NSYNC concert. The light turned green, and as I pulled forward I caught a glimpse of a navy blue hood to my left. When I looked over, Mr. Blackmer was driving beside me, our vehicles neck and neck. His eyes were hidden behind dark sunglasses, but I could almost hear the laughter in his wide grin. I continued to sing and dance, throwing him looks between our cars and gesturing to him in an effort to keep him smiling.

I had fantasized about a moment precisely like this one. Every time I saw a blue Saturn on the road, my heart would leap into my throat and refuse to drop back into my chest until I was certain the car wasn't his. And now, there we were, locked in this snapshot of cinematic euphoria. It was like I had manifested it simply by wanting it.

Eventually, he slowed. I watched his car in my sideview mirror turn onto a road, moving further and further into the distance. He was gone, but the movie inside my head played on. It was enough to get me through until the next time I could see him.

A day later, I was heading out of the band room with a friend when Mr. Blackmer called out to me. "Hey, Megan. Do you need a ride home?"

I turned to look at him, butterflies swarming my stomach. He knew I had my license and a car, he had just seen me on the road the day before. Why was he offering me a ride?

Then it dawned on me.... This wasn't him offering help. This was something else.... He was *flirting* with me, out in the open.

"Nope," I said, tossing him a coquettish smile. "I drive now, remember?"

He threw me a playful look of rejection. "I guess you don't need me anymore then, do you?"

2019

May—Three weeks into the investigation

Aside from the receptionist behind the thick glass window, I was the only person in sight. The waiting area was smaller than I'd expected—a dimly lit cove lined with a handful of chairs, pamphlets fanned out on corner tables. As I waited for my name to be called, I wondered what to do if another patient were to walk in. Do I make eye contact? Do I smile and say hello?

A woman my age, with a pixie haircut and childlike features, appeared in the only hallway visible to patients. Her hands were buried in the pockets of her roomy oatmeal sweater. She looked at me and smiled. "Megan?"

I stood from my chair and offered a slight smile in return. "That's me," I said.

With a tilt of her head, she gestured for me to follow. "I'm Becca. Come on back."

Until I stepped foot into the Evergreen Counseling and Wellness Center, it had never occurred to me how little I knew about being a therapy patient. What questions does a therapist ask during an intake session? How do I know if my therapist is any good? What if I don't like my therapist? What if they don't like *me*? How do I stop seeing them and find another therapist? It felt like I was going on the most intimate first date ever. *Hi. It's nice to meet you. Now let me unveil to you my deepest, darkest secrets.*

As a teenager and young adult, seeing a therapist would have never crossed my mind. If I was sad, my mom told me to eat better, drink more water, exercise, sleep, pray. Therapy, as I understood it, was for people who had suffered massive, life-altering tragedies like car accidents or cancer or divorce. Therapists were so mystical and out-of-reach, I thought you had to be referred to one by your family doctor.

Becca led me down the short hall to one of only four rooms. "Sit where you're most comfortable," she said. The room was lit by a tall floor lamp tucked in the corner behind the door. A few decorative pillows added a hint of color to an otherwise bland collection of gray furniture. On one of the end tables was a Kleenex box and a fully stocked candy dish.

"Is this your first time in a therapy session?" Becca asked as she sat down at a bulky wooden desk with a hutch displaying an array of crowded books.

"It is."

"Can you share with me the reason you're here?"

By the end of the hour-long session, Becca's yellow legal pad was covered in notes she'd taken while listening, all the while doing her best to keep her eyes on me. I thought we would only talk about my past with Chris, but she prompted me to talk about my present life too—my recent difficulty with concentrating or making decisions, my rapidly changing moods, excessive guilt, anger, irritability, loss of energy. I told her that Chris's arrest wasn't the only big thing to have happened in the past year—that in my final months of teaching in the public schools, a student had attempted suicide in one of the music practice rooms. I recalled leaving my classroom in the days following the incident, unable to remember where I had parked my car earlier that morning. I stood cemented to the parking lot, unable to move left or right until I could call Ian and explain where I was and what was happening. That was the first time I could point to something and say, *That's trauma.*

"So. That's *a lot*," Becca said, her eyes crinkled in empathy. There was a weightlessness to her voice that made everything seem more bearable, if only for a brief moment. "We're going to start unpacking this next week. As an exercise, I'd like you to write a letter to Chris expressing everything you'd like to say to him. You won't actually send it, but make sure to bring it when I see you again."

I left Becca's office feeling lighter than I had in weeks. It felt safe inside that 10x10 cube, with its simple walls and simple furniture. With Becca, my thoughts could fly freely around the room, always with a soft place to land. The next session couldn't come fast enough.

• • •

"What do you want to do for your birthday?" Ian asked.

An old anxiousness bubbled up behind my lips. I wanted to say, *Ian, what I want is for you to plan something special.* But I didn't, because it seemed a lot to ask considering the circumstances. "Dinner sounds good," I said. It was something that wouldn't take a lot of effort.

I remembered, though, we used to get a hotel room not far from where we lived, just because. Ian used to surprise me with flowers and notes. He would leave long voicemails on my phone proclaiming his undying love for me. Maybe it was ridiculous to want those things ten years into a marriage. I loved our life together, but I still craved adventure and excitement, and the demands of life made it difficult to make space for those things. Even with the church job, I felt like we were in a deficit, and I didn't know how to pull us out.

Like any marriage, we had experienced hard times. Pregnancy, pregnancy loss, and caring for infants were the most difficult seasons of our marriage. My morning sickness lasted all nine months, complete with vomiting. Evan slept through the night at five weeks, but Eli didn't sleep through the night until he was eight months old. And even when I returned to work, I was still the one getting up in the middle of the night. There were times I felt less than human, that I wanted to scream and rip the hair from my head, to break everything in sight. In my worst moments, when my babies would not stop crying, I wanted to take those precious bundles of joy that I loved so dearly and launch them at the wall. It turned out, I just needed a full night of sleep.

For the first eight years of our marriage, Ian and I lived near the border of Michigan and Indiana, over three hours away from our parents. We learned to rely on each other, on the help of students or parents of students for babysitting our young children. Ian's job was in Indiana, where teacher pay scales were removed and merit pay was introduced, a measly $1,000 annual bonus for proving you were effective in the classroom. Years into his position, Ian was still making a first-year teacher salary while the cost of health insurance continued to rise. That's why, in 2016, when two choir positions opened in Midland, we decided we had to try for them, to be close to family and afford to pay our bills.

Ian joked that he DJed so he could "afford to teach." Every year on Saturdays stretching from May to October he'd be gone, not returning until the middle of the night or the next day, depending on how far away the event was. It was hard to watch him leave the house, free of diaper bags, only himself to care for. I imagined him inside his peaceful truck cab, listening to the radio, watching the quiet road and grass pass by. My resentment of his freedom started with our oldest but worsened after our second child when I suffered from what I later recognized as postpartum depression.

Ian had been patient with me through the years when I'd go through unpredictable periods of melancholy that seemed to have no cause and no cure. He would patiently wait for me to regain my spirit and join the ranks of everyday living. Ian sensed something was wrong much earlier than I did. A few years into our marriage, he asked me, "Have you ever talked to a doctor about depression?"

His insinuation was disconcerting. How could *I* have depression? I've always been happy and energetic, ambitious and high-achieving.

"I know you got good grades in school and everything," Ian said, "but you also slept half of freshman year away in your dorm room. That's not normal."

I'd always thought I had everything together, from the moment I realized having everything together was what made you worth something. I was near the top of my graduating class. I'd known I wanted to be a teacher since eighth grade. I got into the college I wanted, married the man of my dreams. I had two beautiful children. And yet, for as long as I could remember, something hadn't felt quite right in my body, like a drawer that's off kilter inside its desk, refusing to slide smoothly in and out, catching as it opens and closes. When I wasn't receiving constant affection from my husband, or surrounded by people who adored me, or busy planning rehearsals, concerts, or events . . . when I had to be alone with myself, that's when I could feel it. The discomfort. The boredom. The gnawing that used to lead me to a parking lot with an old flame but now led me to the kitchen at night to grab a glass of bourbon and a calorie-loaded plate of snacks.

The last time I felt like Ian and I were able to relax and connect on a deep level was our tenth wedding anniversary trip in August of 2018. We spent three days at our honeymoon spot, a guest house in Suttons Bay, Michigan, where we did nothing but sleep and eat and make love. We strolled the streets of Suttons Bay, sat on the quiet balcony of our quaint bed and breakfast, and drove to the nearby cities to shop and try new places to eat.

"Hey, *you* like to write," Ian spoke excitedly to me while we waited for our food at a Traverse City restaurant, sipping on spicy alcoholic cider. "I have a great idea for a romance novel."

Ian had always been a great storyteller, but with teaching and DJing and "dadding," he rarely had the energy to be creative for reasons other than work. But in that restaurant he spun for me a Nicholas Sparks-esque tale that was so simple yet enthralling, that had all the quintessential romantic tropes that make Hallmark movies worth watching, and I couldn't wait to get back to the guest house to start writing it.

When we returned home from our trip, there was a sudden shift in Ian's behavior. Back in the real world, he was already absorbed by thoughts of the school year starting. The dreaming and the playfulness of our trip was gone in a terrifying instant, and I felt a new kind of loneliness, one that touched a place deep beneath the surface, raw and bruised.

I was so sure that getting the church job and moving into town would fix our problems. But I was coming to the realization that all of these things were mere bandages over an unhealed wound. Until I figured out the source of the problem, the wound would remain and the loneliness would continue to follow me.

I returned to therapy with my letter to Chris, the last of many iterations I had feverishly scratched out over the course of a week.

As I read aloud, I envisioned myself inside a large courtroom like the ones I'd seen on TV, everything from the walls to the desks a honey-maple color. I'm seated in a tiny box of a witness stand while Chris stares up at me from a desk below. He's in his late twenties again, boyish and innocent looking, the only way I can remember him.

> *Chris,*
>
> *I don't fully understand how I feel about everything that has transpired since you were arrested. I have spent countless hours trying to make sense of your actions, to figure out where things went so incredibly wrong and how I fit into that picture. Up until the arrest, I thought our relationship—though unconventional—was born out of genuine care and concern, but I see now that true care and concern would have prevented you from starting a romantic relationship with me, since I was a child and you were an adult who knew better. At some point, I*

grew enough to realize we could never actually be together in a healthy relationship. It would have been too complicated to remain friends with our history, but I have always cared for you and wished good things for your life. I thought you would continue to be the same talented, caring, influential teacher you were for me and for so many others. I imagined you would find someone to love, get married, and live a happy, fulfilling life. To see you throw everything away is devastating. To think that you would use your position of authority to manipulate and abuse me is something I cannot comprehend even now. You had a chance to make things right. I was never going to report you because, to me, you weren't a predator. I saw you as someone I cared about, trusted, even loved. I'm sorry to those who have been hurt because your behavior was allowed to continue. I desperately wish you would have seeked help. I wish you would have faced your demons. I wonder how my adolescence was affected by our relationship, how it affected my relationship with others and myself. Still, I feel no anger toward you, and I pray you will find understanding, forgiveness, and peace within yourself.

If you really cared about me and wanted what was best for me, you would have waited. You wouldn't have let me lie to my parents and my friends. I never should have been responsible for such a secret. Because of your arrest, I am taking the memories of the time we shared that I thought were meaningful and consensual and I'm reliving those memories through the eyes of a sexual abuse victim. I think about how your choice to pursue me in adolescence affected my relationship with my parents, friends, boyfriends, and I can't take those things back. I can't rectify my wrongdoings. But I can do something now. You made me love you, but I loved you first as a teacher and a mentor. I looked up to you. I wanted to become a band teacher because of you. I went to CMU because you went there. I wouldn't be me without your influence in my life. The problem is, you took the love I had for you and used it for your own gain. You knew I wouldn't be able to resist you. For me, it was never a choice. I lied to other people because of you. I had others lie for me to protect you. I went against my values because I trusted you to have my best interest at heart, that you would never do anything to hurt me because it was your job as a teacher to take care of me and protect me.

You will always be a big part of my life. I can't just remove that fact. It will take a long time for me to separate the love I felt for you which was healthy and brought good things into my life, and the love that has now brought pain and confusion.

When I looked up at Becca, she was gazing at me thoughtfully. She lifted the pen from her notepad and let her wrist drop in my direction. "In the letter, you mentioned something about being devastated. Would you mind reading that again?"

I thumbed backward to the second page and found the line Becca was referring to. I took a deep breath. "Chris . . . to see you throw everything away is devastating."

Of all the sentences, I wasn't sure why she had chosen this one.

Becca spoke calmly. "Do you know why you said that? Why you used those words, specifically?"

As soon as the question left her lips, the answer appeared on mine. "Because I love him."

My eyes went wild with shock. I didn't say, I *loved* him, past tense. I said, *I love him*. As in *today*. As in *right now*. I wanted to shove the words back into my mouth and swallow them, but instead I repeated the phrase with increasing volume until I was shouting. "I love him . . . I love him . . . I *love* him?!"

Becca's expression was collected, unshifting. "When your relationship with Chris ended abruptly, it's possible you had a lot of unresolved feelings—not just about Chris, but the situation you'd been in. The secrecy and intensity surrounding the relationship. It's possible you never dealt with any of those things."

Any of those *things*. . . . What did that include? If I had never dealt with *this*, what else had I not dealt with?

Overwhelmed, I started to cry. "What's happening to me?"

Becca hesitated, as if contemplating a move on a chess board. "Do you know what Stockholm syndrome is?"

I grabbed a tissue and pressed it against the corner of my eye. "No."

"It's when a victim bonds with their abuser. Victims can feel affection, trust, loyalty. They can even feel love. I'd like you to spend some time researching it this week and let me know what you find."

I opened my journal and wrote *Stockholm syndrome*, adding to the list of words I'd been Googling constantly: *abuse, grooming, molestation, sexual assault*—words I'd been privileged not to have in my world because they had never applied to me previously. I'd never see any of those words the same way again.

• • •

"I need to tell you something," I said. Ian and I were in the kitchen discussing dinner plans before heading out to Evan's baseball game. "At therapy today, I told Becca that I love Chris."

Becca had specifically advised me not to tell Ian what I had said to her. She said I needed to take time to process the statement, and to think of ways to express those emotions without using words that could be hurtful to my husband.

But I was impatient. Ian was my sounding board, the person I told everything to. How could I keep something this big from him?

Ian winced. "What does that mean, you *love* Chris?"

It was clear I had inflicted damage. I scrambled for an explanation to diminish the hurt, then spoke as casually as possible. "I think it means I haven't acknowledged what an important part of my life he was for so long."

Ian's eyes dropped to the floor. "I'm sorry, but I don't know how to respond to this."

"You don't have to respond," I said, keeping my voice light. I began to fidget with a stack of envelopes, unpaid bills that had been left on the kitchen counter. "I'm just working through some things."

At the game, we watched as the tenth kid stepped up to bat with no hits to speak of. Ian and I were sitting close to each other in our folding lawn chairs, but he felt miles away from me—withdrawn and slightly irritable, talking only in monotone phrases and short sentences.

I regretted having said anything in the kitchen about Chris. How could I make this right? How could I make *any* of this right?

I wanted to be honest. I didn't want to withhold information. I worried what it would do to me if I kept my feelings hidden. Something was wrong, and I didn't know how to explain it in a way anyone would understand. It was as if there was an invisible thread between me and Chris, connecting us, and it didn't matter that he was over a thousand miles away in Florida. He was with me everywhere I went, invading my mind and body, stealing the life I could have had.

I could only picture Chris in one of two scenarios: with me in a courtroom or with me in the world we used to share. There was no reality where we weren't tethered together in some way. Risky as it was to tell Ian the truth, I had a sinking feeling that it was far more dangerous to hide it from him.

• • •

That night, I did as Becca instructed. I Googled *Stockholm syndrome.*

An article caught my eye, "STOCKHOLM SYNDROME: THE TRUE STORY OF HOSTAGES LOYAL TO THEIR CAPTOR." It was published on April 9th, 2019, only one day after Ian came to my office to tell me about Chris's arrest.

The article told the story of what happened on August 23rd, 1973, when escaped convict Jan-Erik Olsson stormed at an upscale bank in Stockholm, Sweden, with a loaded submachine gun. He took several women and one male hostage, demanded money, a getaway car, and the release and delivery of another convict, Clark Olofsson.

Within hours, Olsson was given everything he asked for, including Clark Olofsson arriving at the bank, but then Olsson wanted to leave with the hostages. The police would not allow it. So the two convicts and the hostages remained holed up together in the bank while the police figured out what to do next.

The situation was highly visible to the public. People showed up to the police station offering suggestions on how to end the standoff; one wanted to send in a swarm of bees to sting the convicts into submission, another was offering a concert of religious music played by a Salvation Army band.

It would take over 130 hours for the situation to end. But before it did, police noticed a strange bond had formed between the hostages and their captors. They were on a first name basis. The hostages had become increasingly warmer toward their captors and hostile toward the police. When police launched tear gas into the bank vault, the hostages were concerned about the safety of the convicts. They wanted to protect them from potential harm. "Don't hurt them!" two of the female hostages yelled. One hostage, Ms. Enmark, while being wheeled away on a stretcher, shouted to Olofsson, "Clark, I will see you again."

The hostages displayed irrational attachment to their captors that was confusing to them and to outside observers. The hostages said the captors had shown kindnesses to them, like soothing someone after a bad dream, giving them a bullet as a keepsake. Hostage Elisabeth Oldgren, who was claustrophobic, was allowed to walk outside the vault attached to a 30-foot rope. Oldgren later asked a psychiatrist, "Is there something wrong with me? Why don't I hate them?"

A chill ran down my spine. I had said similar things to Becca at my therapy appointment. *What's happening to me? Why can't I be angry or disgusted with Chris? Why am I saying that I love him?*

Multiple articles defined Stockholm syndrome as being a type of *trauma bond* (another term I had never heard before), where the victim finds the relationship virtually inescapable. The victim relies on the relationship as a source of survival, and they wait out the abuser's bad behaviors for "crumbs" of good behaviors.

I noticed the words *captor* and *abuser* were often used interchangeably. I performed an experiment: I replaced those words with *Chris* to see if any symptoms applied to me.

> Positive feelings toward *Chris*;
> a strong connection to or bonding with *Chris*;
> being in an emotionally charged situation with *Chris*;
> feelings of love and empathy for *Chris*;
> seeing *Chris* as a victim;
> a desire to protect *Chris*, which includes hostility toward others;
> a relationship with *Chris* that includes an imbalance of power.

Physical symptoms of Stockholm syndrome include cognitive delusion and flashbacks, confusion, anxiety, irritability, estrangement, lack of feeling, and something called Splitting, where victims inadvertently detach bad qualities from good so they can create a fantasy-based view of their abuser. Even though Stockholm syndrome is a well-known condition, it's not recognized as an official mental disorder in the 5th edition of the Diagnostic and Statistical Manual of Mental Disorders, more commonly referred to as the DSM-5.

If it was true I had Stockholm syndrome, how would I get support for it? Who was going to believe that I had it when it's not even considered a legitimate disorder? We have AA meetings, but what about SS meetings? (I could just see it . . . . *Hi, everyone. My name is Megan and I have Stockholm syndrome).*

I wanted to talk to my mom about this, but she wouldn't understand. I wanted to talk to Ian about it, but it would only make him feel terrible. What if I never got over this? Ian wouldn't want to be married to someone who loved him *and* someone else, even if it wasn't my fault. Or was it my fault? I had no idea what to feel, what was normal, if I was overreacting or underreacting. Mostly, I just felt tired and sad and lonely all of the time. And there was the shame. The white-hot shame for the secret I was hiding: I missed Chris. I missed Chris so much it hurt, and the more I tried to deny my feelings the stronger those feelings became.

I closed my computer and left the basement in search of Ian. I found him in the garage, leaning with his back against the workbench, eyes aimed at the floor. His arms were crossed, eyes wet, cheeks red.

"Are you okay?" I said.

He shook his head. "I can't stop thinking about it."

"Can't stop thinking about what?"

"That I didn't turn him in. I let those kids get hurt. But you were so convinced he wasn't a predator. You would've hated me if I did anything to him, and I would have lost you."

I stared at Ian, blankly.

Pity filled his eyes—not for himself, but for me. "You really don't remember, do you?"

2001

Mr. Blackmer was in his office after school, chatting with a few students, when I overheard him say something about leaving for a new job. Without thinking, I darted across the room and interrupted the conversation with a voice so abrupt, so shrill and pinched, it visibly startled anyone within earshot. "Wait, you're *leaving*?!"

The students froze, wide-eyed with confusion. Mr. Blackmer said nothing—only exhaled a long, apologetic sigh.

Panic shot up from my gut in one uncontrollable shout. "*No!*" I ran out the back door, toward the parking lot, tears streaming down my face. I didn't care that I'd made a fool of myself. My world was crashing down. The person I cared about most at the school wasn't going to be there anymore.

He had never mentioned looking for another job. He seemed happy at our school. Why was he leaving? Why would he say he was going to be there for me just to take that away?

I climbed into my car and slammed the door. I let the sound of my sobs fill the interior. A minute or so later, a curiosity crept into the periphery of my mind. *Does Mr. Blackmer care that I'm upset?* Would he come find me to see if I was okay? If he did, it would mean he cared about me. It would prove there was something more between us, and I'd know I wasn't losing him for good. This wasn't the end. This couldn't be the end.

Slowly, I pulled up the service drive near the exterior band room door and waited. *One sign*. That was all I needed from him.

My tongue swelled when the door opened and Mr. Blackmer stepped out onto the sidewalk. He was alone. He approached the passenger side of my car. I brought the window down, allowing him a better view inside. My shirt was blotted from the tears that rolled off my cheeks, my face hot as he bent down and stared at me sheepishly, clearly aware that he was the cause of my pain.

"Are you going to be okay?" he said.

I sniffled, sucking the snot back into my head. "I'm sure I will be."

That wasn't what I really wanted to say. Words were piling up in my mouth. *Please don't go . . . I love you . . . I know I shouldn't feel this way . . . I'm so sorry . . . I didn't mean for this to happen*. All I had to do was open my lips and free them.

Maybe he wants me to tell him . . . Maybe he's waiting for me to be the first one to say it . . .

My mind was waging war against itself, a battle between telling the truth because it was hurting me not to, and withholding the truth because I didn't want to hurt him. As much as I wanted to pour my heart out to him, I knew it would be reckless and selfish. What was I expecting him to say in return? Even if he felt the way I did, he could never say it.

"I need to go," I said, trying not to look at him.

"I'm sorry, Megan. I *will* see you tomorrow."

I pulled away from the building. In my sideview mirror, I saw him waiting on the sidewalk in the spot where I'd left him, watching me drive away. Once he was almost out of sight, I saw him slowly turn and head toward the back door.

By the time I rounded the corner for home and pulled into the driveway, I had stopped crying. It was strange. When I was at the school, I felt like I was never going to be happy without Mr. Blackmer there. But now that he wasn't in front of me and I'd had several minutes to think, I found a way to look for the positive changes that were coming. Underneath my sadness was a growing sense of relief. I would miss Mr. Blackmer, but with him gone, school would be less complicated. I wouldn't have to feel every day like I was wearing a sign around my neck that said *I'm in love with my band director*. I wouldn't miss being teased by kids in band.

They thought this was a game, but this was my life. Being in love with a teacher was not something I planned on. It just happened. I was tired of being under a microscope every second, wondering if Mr. Blackmer could see through me. At last I could relax and be myself again. And, like all things in life, if it was God's plan for us to be together someday, it would happen. Against all odds, it would happen.

• • •

"Hey Mom. Tomorrow, a group of band kids are going to Mr. Blackmer's apartment for lunch before we have to rehearse for graduation. It's this cool 'farewell to seniors' thing."

Mom finished loading Randy's work jeans into the washer. "That sounds like fun." She scooped out a cupful of powder detergent from the Tide box and closed the lid. "It won't be just a group of seniors and you, right?"

I exhaled a laugh. "Oh no. Of course not."

It was bright and sunny when I left the house around eleven that Saturday morning. I followed the directions Mr. Blackmer had jotted down on a scrap sheet of paper. "Look for the train tracks," I muttered to myself. The entrance to his apartment complex was just beyond them.

He lived in Davison, less than fifteen minutes from my house, and as I passed the places that were familiar to me—friends' houses, video rental stores, restaurants—they all seemed to take on a new meaning. They were a part of my old life, a chapter that had passed. Now, I was entering an exciting new one.

It was mostly true what I had told my mom. I *was* going to Mr. Blackmer's, and I *was* leaving there for the auditorium. Two days earlier, Mr. Blackmer had asked if I wanted to have lunch at his apartment before the band had to rehearse for graduation. "What's your favorite food?" he said.

I knew what he was doing. The question was about food, but it was really about me. He didn't ask what foods I *like*. He asked what food was my *favorite*. He wanted to please me.

"Strawberries," I said.

He smiled. "I'll make sure to have some at my place."

Being invited to his apartment seemed too good to be true. I wondered if maybe he'd invited other students and just didn't mention it to me. But I paid close attention to the conversations around the band room and no one was talking about lunch at Mr. Blackmer's on Saturday.

It felt like we were sharing a secret. Except, he didn't say it was a secret, and he didn't ask me not to tell anyone. Of course, I wasn't going to tell anyone about it. There was no way I was going to ruin my last opportunity to spend time with him before the school year ended and he moved away. This was a once-in-a lifetime chance. I needed to make sure he had enough memories of us that he wouldn't forget about me.

A short staircase led me down to the lower level of one of the apartment buildings. His door was on the right, but there were others nearby. He had neighbors. I wondered if they ever talked. If they knew each other's names. *What would they think if they saw me standing here?*

My skin was tingling when I knocked on his door. I pulled taut the fitted black dress I'd borrowed from my mom's closet that morning, remembering how Randy would always say to my mom, *Don't let her wear that dress. She's curvier than you, she's going to stretch it out*. My mom would always ignore Randy's pleas. *The dress will be fine. She's fine. And anyway, I wish I had a backside like hers.*

Footsteps appeared, faintly at first, then louder until they were just out of reach. A turn of the lock and the door opened, revealing a grinning Mr. Blackmer. He was wearing stonewash blue jeans and a forest green polo. "Hey, Megan," he said, dragging out the *heyyy.* (If he'd dragged it out any longer, I would've fallen into it and been swallowed whole.)

When I stepped inside, a fresh new aroma drifted into my head. It was as if every object inside had been doused in the same detergent. The apartment was exceptionally tidy—at least, what I could see of it from the entrance mat. In front of me was a small dining space, beyond that a galleyway kitchen, and to my left a living room.

He gave me a tour of the apartment, leading me through the main living area, down a narrow hallway. When we got to his bedroom, I pretended to be only mildly interested. I acted like he was showing me something boring, like a broom closet *(nobody's heart races looking at a broom closet)*. His bed was neatly made with a plain-looking comforter and matching pillowcases. Two dark colored dressers lined the walls. A digital clock in one corner. A lamp on a bedside nightstand.

"Just a bedroom," he said.

With all the nonchalance I could muster, I nodded and spoke the first word that popped into my head. "*Nice.*"

We went back to the kitchen, and Mr. Blackmer pulled open the refrigerator door. He bent over and placed his hand on a carton of bright red strawberries. "I got these for you."

"Thanks," I said, outstretching an open hand. "I'll wash them."

I leaned against the sink and ran cold water over the open carton as Mr. Blackmer looked on, hands in pockets, leaning his shoulder against the opening of the kitchen. My insides were buzzing. I could feel his eyes on me. Watching me. Adoring me. One by one, I sliced the strawberries into heart-shaped halves and sat them neatly aside on a round Corelle plate. I wanted to show I was comfortable in his home. That I was helpful. That I belonged there with him.

We ate sandwiches on the couch, holding the plates of food in our laps. There wasn't anything particularly special about the conversation, just that we were having it alone in the place where he slept and showered. I noticed he hadn't touched me once while I'd been there, not even casually to brush by me as we moved around the small apartment.

He's being safe. As long as nothing actually happened between us, there would be nothing to hide. Besides, it didn't matter if he touched me or not. Just being near him was enough to make me happy. We were sharing something I never would have dreamed of until I met him. A student having a crush on a teacher? That was common. But a student and teacher sharing a genuine connection and mutual attraction? That was fate. Him inviting me to his apartment was, in my mind, an unspoken message: *I have feelings for you, even if I can't act on them*. Me showing up to his apartment was my way of saying, *Me too*.

"Have you thought about where you're going to go to college?" he said.

I nodded, chewing up a bite and dabbing the napkin to the corner of my mouth. "I'm gonna look at the major universities here. Michigan State, U of M . . . the one in Ann Arbor, not Flint."

He chuckled, his brown eyes drawing together. "What? You don't want to stay here in Flint?"

I smirked and rolled my eyes. "I don't want to go too far away. I'd like to be able to drive home on the weekends. But *no*—it'd be nice to live somewhere other than here."

"Have you thought about CMU?" he said. Since it was his alma mater, and he had stayed connected to the school's faculty and events, he had taken a group of us to Central Michigan University to see a performance earlier that year.

I had to admit, I loved the aesthetic appeal of the music building. It was fairly new and brightly lit, with full-length windows in many of the practice rooms. "I'm definitely thinking about it," I said.

"You should. It's a great school. I think you'd do really well there."

It occurred to me, another benefit of going to Central was that Mr. Blackmer would probably visit for different events. I wondered if a small part of him was thinking the same thing I was—that maybe, someday, when he visited, we could go out on a real date.

After lunch, it was time to leave for Whiting Auditorium. I slipped my feet into the black heels I'd set neatly on the entrance mat.

Mr. Blackmer opened the door for me. "See you soon," he said.

Staring down from the highest balcony, I watched the band students meander to their chairs. In about an hour, family members and friends would pour in to take their seats for the graduation ceremony. The band had just enough time to rehearse our featured piece, "American Elegy" by Frank Ticheli, before we needed to be off stage. Mr. Blackmer wanted the trumpet solo for the Ticheli piece to sound distant, so he asked me to play from the uppermost balcony while he conducted the band on stage.

"American Elegy" was my favorite band piece of all time. It was written in memory of those whose lives were lost in tragic events, but the music was so moving and inspirational, it could transport you to a million beautiful places. I played recordings of it at home on repeat, envisioning different scenes in my head. The scene I envisioned most was me in a wedding gown walking down the aisle of a breathtaking cathedral as Mr. Blackmer stood at the front waiting for me. It was a fantasy, but in my lovesick heart and mind, it was a fantasy within reach. For months I had wondered if I was making it all up in my head that Mr. Blackmer had feelings for me. But after spending time with him at his apartment that day, I was almost certain he liked me.

This had to be more than *like*, though. What we were doing was taboo, there was risk involved. He wouldn't take that risk for someone he simply liked. But he would for someone he *loved*. Mr. Blackmer wasn't a boy playing stupid games. He was a man who knew what he wanted. He wouldn't have let himself fall for me unless I was really worth it. And if other teachers and students had fallen in love and gotten married, why not us?

I was lost in thought when I heard rustling behind me. I turned to see Mr. Blackmer in the doorway to the balcony. "Checking in on you," he said. "Are you ready?"

I smiled at him. "I think so."

• • •

On the first morning of summer break, I was up early, showering, blow-drying my hair, putting makeup on. I smeared French vanilla body lotion from Bath & Body Works all over my arms, legs, and neck, and pulled on a dark denim jean skirt and a pink rose-colored top. I slid my feet into a pair of Old Navy flip-flops, hustled to my car, and started the drive toward the high school.

Mr. Blackmer had asked me to come in that day to browse marching band shows on the computer while he still had access to the band room. He said if I picked the music it would help ease the transition for the new band director. Since he didn't ask the other drum major to come, I suspected that picking music, though useful, was a good excuse to spend a few last hours together before he would be packed up and gone for good.

I sat at his office computer perusing different shows, but my mind wasn't on the music coming from the tiny desktop speakers. It was laser-focused on the sound of Mr. Blackmer's movements in the band room behind me. I listened to his steps as they moved from one area of the room to another, opening and closing lockers and cabinets, shuffling items and stacking them into boxes.

My heart was pounding like a drum trapped inside my chest. I wondered what he would do before we said our goodbyes. Would he trust me enough to finally confess what I longed to hear? The *truth*—that it didn't matter our age difference or that he was my teacher. We were just two people who had fallen for each other. When he looked at me, he didn't see an ordinary teenage girl. He saw a young woman who was special and smart and worthy of his affection. And when I looked at him, I saw all of my dreams becoming a reality, a dream I didn't know I wanted until I met him.

I didn't care that I had to wait another two years. I'd wait ten if it meant that, someday, I would be with the man who was not only everything I desired, but everything I desired to be. It finally made sense why I had never been like everyone else. It was because I was meant for this. For *him*. We were meant to be together.

The room behind me grew alarmingly quiet. The footsteps had stopped. I heard a faint *click* from outside the office, and there was only one conclusion in my mind. *He just locked the band room door.*

I filled the silence with the click-clack of typing, my fingers nervously tapping the grooves of the hard plastic keys. His footsteps appeared again, starting at the entry to the office and making their way slowly forward, becoming more purposeful as they approached the chair from behind me. With a caressing touch, Mr. Blackmer's hands corralled the wandering strands of my hair to the center of my back. The tips of his fingers began pressing into my neck and shoulders.

Oh my God.

This is happening.

This is actually happening.

My mind slipped into oblivion as he spoke to me in hypnotic tones and short, lulling phrases. I tried to focus on what he was saying, but I was too intoxicated by the touch of his hands. The only words I understood were molded into a single question: ". . . even a man that will buy you strawberries?"

I moaned approval, my head dropping to one side as his fingers circled my ears, neck, and collarbone. I sank further into myself, heat swallowing my body whole as if someone had poured lighter fluid over my head and lit a match. In an abrupt move, he spun my chair around and dove forward, pressing his lips to mine. I was in such a state of disbelief, I opened my eyes to make sure I wasn't dreaming. His eyes stayed closed as he remained waist bent, expertly guiding my mouth open and shut.

After what seemed like a full minute, he pulled away from me, allowing our mouths to separate. The second my body was freed from his, I surged into an embarrassing display of trembling, eyes drawn wide, mouth agape in a state of shock. I stared down at my quivering hands and let out a series of sounds that resembled words, but I couldn't string them together in a way that made sense.

Mr. Blackmer calmly grabbed a second chair and sat down in front of me, pulling himself close enough that our knees became intertwined. He hunched reverently, taking my hands in his and stroking my knuckles with the flat, smooth surface of his thumbs. He stared up at me with glassy-eyed affection, a loving gaze I could only have pictured in my wildest fantasies. It was a look that said, *Yes. This is real.*

The next thing I knew, I was driving to Andi's house. Whitney Houston blared on the radio as I sang at the top of my lungs, tossing my head around and pounding my tingling palms on the steering wheel to the beat of the music.

Andi's front door was unlocked, as usual. I rushed inside and called her name from the bottom of the living room steps. She called back from the second floor. "I'm in the bathroom. Come on up!"

Andi was finishing her hair in front of the mirror when I charged up the stairs and whisper-shouted, breathlessly, "He kissed me! He kissed me!"

"*Who* kissed you?" she said.

"Mr. Blackmer."

Her eyes flung wide open. "Shut up! No way."

"He did!" My heart was still racing, every fiber of my being pulsing with electricity. "It was so . . . " I didn't have the words to describe it, so I put my hand to my heart and shook my head, lost in the memory of him touching me, kissing me, risking everything to be with me.

I wasn't dreaming. *He loves me. He loves me. He loves me.*

Andi had been my best friend since sixth grade. She was honest, which I admired about her. But as worry drifted into her ocean-blue eyes, I found myself wishing she knew how to lie.

"I'm happy for you Meg, but . . . are you sure this is okay? I mean, he's your teacher."

I straightened my spine and took a deep breath. Before her words could pierce my tender chest, I willed them into vapor, unable to touch me. "Officially speaking, he's not my teacher anymore."

The next day, I told my parents I was going to Andi's house, when really I was headed back to the high school. As I crossed the parking lot toward the performing arts wing, nausea unfolded in my stomach. He'd had twenty-four hours to think about what happened. What if he regretted kissing me? What if he told me it was all a huge mistake? I could feel my heart breaking just thinking about the possibility of it.

Before I reached the band room door, it opened, and he stepped out holding a box of miscellaneous items.

"Hi," I said, trying not to sound anxious.

"Hey, Megan." He was calm. Not a hint of regret in his demeanor. He set the box down. "Come here, I want to show you something."

He led me through the band room to his office and motioned for me to sit down. Then, with a look of pride, he presented me with a rectangular object covered in floral wrapping paper. "This is for you," he said.

My chest swelled. *A gift. He hand-wrapped a gift for me.*

I pictured him in his apartment, bent over his coffee table, thinking of me as his fingers worked to carefully fold and tape each edge. I pulled back the paper flowers as delicately as possible. I didn't want it to tear—the wrapping seemed as meaningful as the gift itself.

It was a *book.* Something inspiring about becoming a music teacher. I ran my hand over the cover and clutched it to my chest. "I love it. Thank you so much."

We left the office and walked back into the curved brick hallway that separated the band room from the auditorium. We were walking side by side when he came to a sudden halt. Not realizing this, I kept walking, until I felt his hand grab mine, causing me to stop and look back at him. We locked eyes—and in one fluid motion he drew me to him, wrapping his arms around me as his lips parted into a smile, then closed to meet mine.

I'd been kissed before, and by boys who knew how. But this wasn't a boy.... *This* was unlike anything I had ever experienced. I didn't know it was possible to feel so much in my body at one time. Never had I been held so tightly or kissed so passionately. There was zero hesitation in his movement, no question how much he desired me. It was like being in a movie. I wanted to freeze that moment and live in it forever.

In the midst of our embrace, I felt his hands slide from my head and upper back down to my waist, then my butt. When he pulled my pelvis into his, my body lit up, firing on all cylinders, my head a tilt-a-whirl. Through the intoxicating haze, I imagined a door opening, a voice gasping in alarm at the sight of us. But the vision was distant and blurred. The only thing that felt real was what was right in front of me: his mouth pressed against mine, his fingers in my hair, the smell of his clothing.

Eventually, our bodies slowed. His arms returned to fully embrace me, squeezing and caressing as he continued to steal my breath with each kiss. He allowed our mouths to part long enough to murmur, low and wistfully, "I want to see you."

"You *are* seeing me," I teased.

He groaned. "When can you come back to my apartment?"

Feverishly, I calculated how much time would have to pass before I could leave the house again without suspicion. "Tomorrow night," I said.

I woke the next morning with guilt needling my insides. I laid in bed, staring up at the ceiling, thinking about what my life would be like now that Mr. Blackmer and I were together. How much would I have to lie? And for how long? I knew that lying was wrong. But if God brought us together, then God knew we'd have to lie. Wouldn't I be forgiven for that?

I trudged upstairs and found my mom in the bathroom getting ready for work. She was poised in front of the mirror, bent forward, head tilted up, applying her makeup.

Watching her, I felt sick. I wanted so badly to go to Chris's apartment. I wanted to be with him. But a small voice was begging me to empty my pockets of the secrets I was hiding. I had never kept anything from my mom, but I'd also never told her anything like this. Would she be furious at him? Would she go straight to the school and tell someone what had happened?

Maybe, I thought, *if I tell her the truth before things get worse, whatever happens next won't be so bad.*

"Mom," I said, in a voice barely above a whisper.

She let out a garbled "*Wha?*" her mouth hanging open as she held the eyelash curler against her slender face and concentrated on squeezing it.

"Mr. Blackmer kissed me. At school."

The hand that was holding the eyelash curler fell to the counter as she jerked her head toward me, her mouth still open. "He *did*?"

I panicked. There was no taking back what I had just said. But perhaps there was another way out . . . . I painted a vague picture of a spontaneous, awkward kiss, omitting details that might have demolished my chances of seeing him again.

She filled in the missing pieces, composing a story of relative innocence: *Mr. Blackmer got carried away in the moment, and he made a mistake.*

"So. He accidentally kissed you? Out of nowhere? Like, a one-time thing."

I nodded. "Mm hmm." The lie tasted like metal in my mouth.

"And he's not teaching here anymore." She said this as a statement to herself more than a question to me.

My mom stood still, eyes to the floor, searching left and right as if she'd lost something and was trying to remember where she'd last seen it. Then, she looked at me and said, "Well, I'm not going to ruin a man's entire life over one kiss. Besides, I'm not shocked. You've always gotten along with adults. And I don't want to ruin your junior and senior year by making a big deal of this."

Mom was right. I had always gotten along with adults. Why should she be surprised that one would kiss me? Especially a man I had a close relationship with who shared the same interests as me. And of course it would be a huge deal if she went to the school and told them what happened. It would get around to everyone, and it's all anyone would think about when they saw me. Everything I am would disappear in the shadow of my new title: The Girl Who Kissed Her Band Director. There'd already been enough discomfort with students teasing me about our relationship. For them to know we kissed . . . that would be the worst thing that could happen.

"You're okay, though. Right?" she said.

I thought honestly about her question. My mom wasn't mad. She understood why my teacher had kissed me. And if she understood that, then I wasn't crazy to believe what he and I shared was real.

To my relief, when I answered her, I didn't have to add to my lies. "Oh yeah. I'm good."

It was past nine when I arrived at his apartment, my head buzzing as I stepped out into the night air. The breath of early summer filled my lungs—the fresh cut grass, the warm nighttime breeze. When he opened the door to greet me, the lights in his apartment were off. The television in the corner of the living room cast a chromatic glow over the couch where he invited me to sit.

We huddled together, holding hands, kissing from time to time. I paid barely any attention to what was on TV; I was too busy glancing over at him, thinking about the soft skin of his forearm, the folds of his ear, how the couch gave way to our bodies.

So far, he hadn't asked me to lie to anyone about anything, and he hadn't questioned me about what I had told other people. But I felt an urge to tell him about the conversation with my mom. I loved him. I trusted him. There wasn't anything I was going to keep from him.

"I told my mom you kissed me," I said.

His eyebrow went up. "What'd she say?"

"She said she understood why you would kiss me. She thinks it was just one kiss, though, and only one time."

He looked back at the TV, saying nothing.

Suddenly, I felt a need for reassurance. "So . . . what's happening here?" I said, pointing to him and back at me. I wanted him to say it out loud—that we were in a relationship, even if it was a secret relationship for now.

He searched my face for a brief moment, then he took my hand and brought it to his mouth, pressing his lips to my skin. "Do you want to come with me to a band concert tomorrow?" he said.

Wait. He wants to take me somewhere in public . . . like a real date?

"I would love that," I said. "Do you want me to meet you there?"

"No. Just come over around one. We'll take my car."

As planned, I met him at his apartment the next afternoon. He drove us to Chesaning's Showboat Park Amphitheater, about thirty miles northwest of Flint. We exited his car in full view of others who were parking, gathering their belongings, and walking toward the entrance to the amphitheater. No one seemed to bat an eye at the two of us. But why would they? Why would anyone be on the lookout for something suspicious at an otherwise ordinary event?

To my amazement, he chose a spot for us near the center of the open stadium. Before the concert, a woman I didn't know approached to say hello to him, but she didn't inquire about the girl seated at his left.

On the way back to his apartment, we took a detour to a drive-through ATM. Respectfully, I kept my gaze forward as he typed in his password, withdrew the money and tucked it into his wallet. Then he drove us to a VG's grocery store near his apartment. We went in together, and he allowed me to wander the aisles looking for what to make for dinner. Again, I was curious as to why he wasn't concerned about being in public with me, but I guess he knew better. We left without as much as a sideways look from the cashier. Then, we went home, ate dinner, and watched a movie.

"I'm staying the night with Chris," I told Andi over the phone. It was the first time I had used his first name out loud to anyone. The name Mr. Blackmer didn't fit anymore. I didn't know anyone who addressed their boyfriend that way, except for Carrie Bradshaw in *Sex and the City*. "I'm going to tell my parents that I'm staying at your house tonight," I said. "Will you cover for me in case anyone calls?"

There was a pause on the other line. "I'll do it this time, but please don't ask me to lie for you again. Don't use me as your excuse."

Andi and I used to have fun talking about Chris, indulging in *what if* fantasies of romance and adventure. But now that those fantasies had become reality, things between us had changed. It was in her eyes, the way they flinched at the sound of his name, as if every comment about him was a brick I laid down between us. I told myself she just needed time to adjust. And maybe I could work on telling her less. It was a sacrifice I was willing to make to keep the peace between us.

Sneaking around was easier than I thought it'd be. Between my friends' houses and my father's house, I always had an alibi. My father and Cheryl had moved back to Flint, only five miles from Mom and Randy. The freedom to travel freely and alone between households offered a surprising benefit—a wide window of time that was both assumed and unaccounted for by my parents. No one ever called the other parent's house asking for me. And who would've imagined their hard-working, honest, reliable daughter—a straight-A student heavily involved in band, theater, student council, and church—sneaking around to be with her teacher?

For the sleepover, I chose a pair of soft running shorts and a spaghetti strap tank top, an outfit that was sexy without screaming, *I'm trying really hard to be sexy*. I wasn't sure what type of clothing was best. I had never stayed the night with a boy, let alone a man. Lingerie was out. Not only would I be uncomfortable buying it at a store, but I ran the risk of Mom finding it in the house. Then she'd think I was having sex. Women didn't wear lingerie unless they were *sexually active*, as most people put it. But I wasn't going to have sex until marriage. Well, not *real sex*, anyway.

Chris had to have known I was a virgin—I had just turned sixteen one month earlier. Was *he* a virgin? I wasn't sure, but I had to assume he was not. He was twenty-nine. Besides, he was popular enough in college to get voted in as the university's drum major. Of course that would make him popular enough to get dates. Maybe he just hadn't been in any serious relationships since he started teaching. No one was good enough. Not until me.

What did it matter whether he was a virgin or how many people he had dated? We were together now, and no one in his past could possibly compare to me.... A man *that* in control of himself—for him to break the rules meant I was different. I was special.

In the apartment living room, the light of dusk saturated the closed curtains in a misty yellow. Chris thumbed through his collection of movies and asked if I'd ever seen *An Affair to Remember*. I hadn't, though my mom had mentioned Cary Grant's name a time or two, always with a bit of a sigh. A boy my age would have never chosen a classic romance film—it seemed like teenage boys only wanted to watch raunchy films about hot girls with big boobs.

I sidled up next to Chris on the couch, and he held my hand throughout the movie. In the final scene, when Cary Grant realizes why his love couldn't get to the top of the Empire State Building to meet him, and the music swells in giant waves of longing, I thought my heart was going to burst.

Chris looked over at me and smiled, seemingly amused by how moved I was by the whole thing. "You okay over there?" he said, gripping my hand tighter.

I rolled my watery eyes at him. "You're a jerk. You knew this was going to happen."

It was dark outside when the ending credits scrolled across the screen. My knees turned to jello when Chris shut off the living room lights, and together we moved to the lamp-lit bedroom. I couldn't believe this was real life. This was *my* life. I was a balloon trying not to burst open and shoot rainbow-colored confetti all over the walls.

Chris grabbed a T-shirt from one of the dressers and took it across the hall to the bathroom. As I waited for him to return, an idea popped into my head. I reopened his dresser drawer where his T-shirts were neatly folded and stacked. I pulled one out, careful not to disturb the others, and leaving only my bra and underwear on, removed my clothes and set them in a pile on top of the dresser. I pulled Chris's shirt over my head, finding my way through the tunnels of cotton. He wasn't a giant man by any means, but his mass far exceeded mine. His shirt hung like a blue tent on my 110-pound frame. The fresh aroma that filled the apartment was embedded in the shirt I was now wearing. I grabbed the collar, put it to my nose, and inhaled.

I climbed onto the bed and faced the doorway in a kneeling position, my hands placed flatly on my thighs in a prayer-like reverence. Chris entered the room, dressed down to a T-shirt and loose boxers. When he saw me, his mouth widened into a sly grin. He stepped toward me, took my head in his hands, and stared me straight in the eyes. "We're being bad," he said. As soon as the words left his lips, he was kissing me open-mouthed.

I couldn't imagine an earthly pleasure that exceeded what I was feeling at that very moment . . . until he began kissing my ear . . . then my neck. My cheeks burned as my body grew heavy and limp. I'd been kissed on my neck before, but it had never felt like this. Boys rush and paw at you. His kisses were somehow impassioned and controlled, artfully placed and precisely executed. I was sure he'd leave no visible marks.

As my bones turned to liquid, he leaned in, pushing against my body until the weight of him forced me down onto the bed. The air thickened as he climbed on top of me, coaxing my legs apart and bearing down in a rocking motion. The thin cotton of our underwear provided the only barrier between what was happening and the probability of *real sex*. I became so lightheaded from euphoria that the room began to tilt on its axis. It was a feeling of absolute surrender and also immense power. *Look at what I can do to this man.* He had always been so guarded and in control of himself, and now he was feral. Unrestrained. The epitome of passion.

After an hour of relentless intensity, the bedroom had become a furnace. My body was growing tired, and so were my inhibitions. As much as I enjoyed being kissed and touched by him, in my experience the only thing better than receiving pleasure was giving it.

"I want you to sit up," I said.

Chris cocked his head, his eyes narrowed.

I pushed on him, half-laughing. "Just do it."

"Yes, ma'am," he said, looking pleased by my forwardness.

He sat on the edge of the bed, his feet planted firmly on the carpet. I stood up and made my way to him, edging myself between his legs as he buried his face in my neck, setting my head spinning once again. When I reached down to touch his boxers and he let out a moan, a surge of energy shot up through my body, enough to power a football stadium. As if gravity put its hands on my shoulders, I began to slide to the floor.

"*Wait—*" he said, staring down at me with sudden concern. "Are you sure?"

There was zero doubt in my mind. I was desperately in love with this man. I wanted nothing more than for him to hold me up above any woman that came before me. Since *real sex* was off the table, I wanted the next best thing. I was going to make him feel things no one else could make him feel. I was going to make sure he would never forget this night. He would never forget *me*.

I woke the next morning to the sound of drums beating in the distance, starting small then growing in volume as if they, too, were waking up.

For a split second, I forgot where I was. But the scent of the bedding brought me back. It was then I realized the drums were coming from Chris's alarm clock, which was sitting on the dresser just past the foot of the bed. I got up and hit the snooze button as Billy Joel's "River of Dreams" came abruptly to an end, then I laid back down and stared up at the shadowed ceiling that only hours before had been soaked in the dandelion light of a bedside table lamp.

As I lay there in silence, I half expected to hear frantic knocking at the apartment door, the sound of Mom and Randy shouting for me from down the narrow hallway. *Megan! We know you're in there! You need to come with us right now!* But there was no knocking. No shouting. It was quiet and peaceful inside the apartment.

Relief filled my lungs. *I'm not in trouble. No one is looking for me.*

Chris was on his side, his back to me, his soft black hair matted and disheveled. I watched as he slowly rolled in my direction, eyes still closed, and released a steady hum. He opened one tired eye, peering at me while the other remained shut. "Good morning," he said groggily, the corner of his mouth raised in a sleepy smile.

"Morning," I said.

He swept the tangled hair from my face and kissed my forehead. I reached under his shirt and ran my hand over his skin, catching the light patches of hair across his chest and shoulders. Only one day earlier, the thought of chest hair was nearly repulsive to me, and now it was a source of comfort, a symbol of warmth and safety.

I moved closer to him, nuzzling my head under his chin, inhaling the sweet aroma of his T-shirt, same as the one I was wearing. Maybe I should have felt guilty for lying to my parents about where I was. But lying there in Chris's arms, feeling the beat of his heart against me, the only thing I could think was how lucky I was, how grateful that God had given me everything I had asked for. I couldn't be happier.

The sun had been up for less than two hours when I left the apartment and arrived at Andi's. Her house was silent. I crept up the stairs and into her bedroom where I found her asleep under the covers. I crawled onto the bed and laid still, looking up, tracing the lines of her ceiling in peaceful silence.

Andi's muffled voice appeared from under her blanket. "How was it?"

"It was amazing," I said, my cheeks sore from smiling.

"I'm glad," she said.

I wanted to tell her everything about my night with Chris, but she sounded legitimately happy for me. If I went into too much detail, I'd make her uncomfortable and ruin the moment.

Andi yawned. "I'm just glad you aren't dating Sean."

We both let out a quiet laugh, careful not to wake anyone else in the house.

"Thanks for covering for me," I said.

"No problem. Love you, Meg."

I put my hand on the blanket Andi was tucked safely beneath. "Love you, too."

During the remaining days of June, I spent as much time with Chris as I could. On the days we couldn't be together, we talked on the phone or AOL Instant Messenger.

Before the month was up, Chris left for a week to chaperone a trip, the longest we'd been apart since our relationship began. The day he left, I felt an unfillable void. I knew what it was like to miss a boyfriend. I had physically ached for Sean many times, but this was almost paralyzing. I knew I should be doing things to keep myself busy, but I had little interest in doing anything except waiting for the day Chris would return and I'd feel whole again.

Because our home received calls from Randy's customers in addition to our friends and family, my parents decided to give me my own phone line and answering machine. All my calls went directly to my bedroom, and since it was tucked away in the basement I had little fear of anyone picking up the phone if Chris called.

One evening after dinner, I went down to my bedroom. When I saw the answering machine's green light flashing, dull pain shot through my stomach. I took a breath and pressed the play button. "*You. Have. ONE. New. Message,*" the robotic voice mocked.

"Hey, Megan. It's Chris. I'm sorry I didn't catch you. It's beautiful here, but I miss you. I'll call you when I get home."

I replayed the message at least five times, his voice filling the gaping hole in my chest.

The day before Chris's return, I was already preparing the story I was going to tell my parents about why I'd be gone the next night. I knew I couldn't use Andi, so I told them I was going to my father's.

I left for Chris's apartment the next day, driving well over the speed limit and listening at full volume to Train's "Meet Virginia."

When he opened the door, I saw that his skin had tanned to a warm olive tone. I wanted to jump into his chest like a little kid, but instead I played it cool, and casually stepped through the entryway, inhaling the now familiar scent of his apartment.

I set my duffel bag down on his dining room table and immediately felt his body against my back. He wrapped his arms around my waist and nuzzled his nose and mouth into the crook of my neck, kissing the fleshy spot behind my earlobe. My hand wandered up to his rabbit-soft hair. I tugged at the ends. "You know I can't resist that," I said, closing my eyes and melting in his embrace.

His subdued laughter vibrated against my skin. "Why do you think I do it?"

That night, as we laid in bed, it occurred to me it would probably be our last night together for a while. In a few days, we'd both be leaving for drum major camp, where I'd be a student camper and he'd be on the staff. Drum major camp was an annual six-day event at Chris's alma mater, Central Michigan University. High school drum majors from all over the state would be spending the week there learning about marching technique, leadership, and conducting.

Chris didn't mention the camp to me before I left his apartment the next morning. He didn't ask how I'd feel going to a place where he'd be my teacher again, and we didn't discuss a plan for how we'd interact when we were there. I took his silence to mean he wasn't worried about it, so I said nothing. It was easier to live in the present, to avoid thinking about a future where he'd soon be moving away to work in another city. The more invested I became, the more I feared losing him, and the less I was willing to risk disturbing our perfect world.

2019

June—Six weeks into the investigation

I awoke from a morning nap in a sweat. I crawled out of bed and went searching for Ian, who was sitting in the living room on our sofa—a new addition to the home, along with two mid-century swivel chairs in cobalt blue and a wide drum chandelier Ian and I had chosen for the dining room because it looked like something straight out of *The Incredibles*.

The basement television was on, and I could hear music coming from whatever show the boys were watching. I kept my voice low so they wouldn't hear me. "I remember more about the nights I spent at his apartment in Davison."

"Do you wanna tell me what happened?" Ian said.

Of course I wanted to tell him. This was my husband, the person I shared everything with. Well, not *everything*. We knew about each other's past relationships, but we had never shared a play-by-play of what had happened in bedrooms with other people.

This was different though, right? This wasn't just some past relationship. This was supposed to be abuse.

It was almost formulaic what happened in that bedroom. It would always start the same way—with Chris kissing me, clutching me, digging his fingers into my hair. The tension inside me would grow, until I was ready to do just about anything for him. I was like a toy. A play thing. All he had to do was wind me up and let go.

Just as every night began the same way, it always reached the same conclusion. "There are different types of penetration," Sergeant Perry had said during my statement. "When you were sixteen, did some form of penetration occur?"

Why did I have to wait until I was sitting in a police station to know I'd been a victim of rape? Why was it that when I was growing up, sex was either something to be idolized or something to be feared? If the church claimed to be the reigning authority on sex, why were there so many gaps in my education? Why were people more concerned about my purity than my safety?

Ian already knew some of what had happened in the apartment. At the very least, he knew why the police were pursuing rape charges instead of a lesser offense. But there was something else I was afraid to tell him. Something I remembered only because I had dreamt about it that morning.

I was back in the Davison bedroom, lying on the bed, only my light beige skin and purple bra visible above the covers. I held onto Chris's hair as his mouth roamed the edge of my bra, teasing at the seam with his fingers, worming the padded cup downward. When my full breast was within reach of his lips and tongue, a searing sensation tore through my gut. I yanked his hair as my body contorted. "OKAY! OKAY! STOP!"

His mouth had returned to the crook of my neck, his laughter vibrating against my goosebumped skin as he rolled off to my side.

"Just give me a sec," I said, a mixture of panting and laughing and wiping my brow as if there was any real sweat to wipe off.

"Okay," he said, and kissed the soft spot behind my earlobe. "*One . . .* "

I raised my shoulder to block him. "You think you're pretty funny."

"I know I'm funny," he said, gazing into my eyes.

Then the whole thing would start again.

"Wait—" Ian put his hand up. "—that's why you recoil every time I try to do that, isn't it?"

I had never thought about it before. Every time Ian even came close to me in that way, nausea would bloom inside me, and I could feel my body retreating. It had never occurred to me that it might be connected to what happened in the Davison apartment, because I had stopped thinking about it long before we got married.

All this made me wonder . . . I had attempted—and failed at—nursing both of my children. I watched other mothers breastfeed, and they seemed to enjoy it and have this deep bonding experience. But all I felt was deep shame, because every time I tried to breastfeed I had to go somewhere else in my mind to escape the sick, twisted feeling in my gut. At both of the boys' initial doctor's appointments, they had been losing weight due to the fact I was barely lactating, so I switched to formula. As soon as I stopped thinking about breastfeeding, that's when my milk finally let down. But I wasn't willing to go back, and I felt shame for that too.

If adults bitten by dogs as children still reacted to dogs with fear, was it crazy to think that such an intense event from my teenage years could live in my body and continue to be triggered by a similar situation? I didn't know for sure, but it felt true in a way that only a person who's experienced something would know. My body had held onto the memory of Chris long after my mind had supposedly forgotten all about him.

On a Sunday, after getting home from church, I felt a small burst of energy. I carried a few boxes from the breezeway into the dining room. I also brought in pictures to hang on the walls—a collage of family members, of our first dog together who'd passed away five years before. In the office, I hung the painting Ian had given to me for my twenty-second birthday, protected by a wooden frame he had built for it that Christmas.

As I was unpacking the boxes on the table, I noticed one of them was filled with my high school yearbooks. I took out the one from 2000–2001 and thumbed through the pages until I reached a two-page section on the marching band. Among the smattering of text blocks and pictures was an image that made my blood turn cold. It was of me in my drum major uniform, standing profile to the camera. I would have been fifteen at the time. Tucked behind me and partially hidden from view was Chris, his hand wrapped around my right arm, just below my shoulder. He looked like he was speaking in my ear. The caption read: *Mr. Blackmer gives Drum Major, Megan Lucius, advice before the marching band takes the field.*

I put the yearbook down and went looking for Ian. "I need you to take me to the storage unit," I said. Sergeant Perry had asked if I had any physical evidence of the crime. I told him no, but after looking through the yearbook a memory came to light, and it occurred to me—I was wrong. I did have evidence: the tape recorder.

In sixth grade, I asked my parents to buy me a small handheld recorder. I wanted to tape conversations with my friends or audio from movies when I went to the theater. Later, I used it to record a message that was left on my basement bedroom answering machine. I could remember many days where I had gotten home from school and walked into my bedroom with the hope that Chris had left me a message.

In the winter of my junior year, I returned home to a blinking light. My heart leapt wishfully.

"Hey Megan. It's Chris." The sound of city streets and wind was whipping through his voice. "I'm at the Midwest Music Conference in Chicago right now. I'm walking down the street, and guess what I just saw? A real live Salvation Army band. Of course it made me think of you . . . . Anyway, hope to talk to you soon. Take care. Bye."

I wanted to keep the message, but I knew it couldn't stay on my answering machine so I captured it onto my little recorder. I was certain the recorder was in a plastic bin. So Ian drove me down to the storage unit. I found the bin, along with several others containing memorabilia from elementary, middle, and high school. Ian and I loaded everything into the back of his truck and brought it back to the house.

It didn't take me long to find the recorder and the tapes that were tucked away with it. I went from beginning to end on every tape—*play, forward, play, forward*—waiting to hear the familiar tones of Chris's voice. I discovered forgotten moments from movies, including audio of one of the *Scream* films. There were silly conversations with my friends, sleepovers with my cousin, and even some embarrassing singing of my own. But no Chris.

Did I tape over it accidentally? Or was it on purpose?

I knew I had always loved the idea of fresh starts and new beginnings. If there was something I needed to rid myself of, I usually found some grand gesture to make sure it was *forever* out of my life. That's why, my freshman year of college, I destroyed my journals from high school where I'd documented all of my romantic escapades—everything with Chris, Sean, boys I'd dated for a shorter periods of time. Stories of parking lots, bedrooms, camp cabins, all traces of where I'd been and what had happened.

Maybe I had wanted a fresh start. Maybe I was worried someone would read the journals. Or maybe this was the period where I became obsessed with *The Passion of the Christ* and vowed to change everything about me that wasn't perfect and Holy. Whatever the case, I went through every journal, reading each page one last time, ripping it from the spine, and placing it on a pile that I then tore into tiny, indistinct scraps. It was a cleansing ritual, an effort to rid myself of things I no longer wanted in my life. Now I realized I could never really remove any of these things. They stayed with me, whether I wanted them to or not.

I didn't have the recording of Chris's voice, but something told me to stay the course and keep searching. I opened two more bins and read through old birthday cards, concert programs, awards and certificates, short stories I'd written in elementary school. I was nearly to the bottom of the second bin when I spotted a purple Caboodle, the one I used as a child to store rings, necklaces, wallet-sized school photos of friends, and random personal belongings that were perfectly suited for its tiny compartments. As my fingers picked and prodded through the nostalgic treasure trove, the top compartment wiggled, reminding me it could be removed. I lifted it up and out of the box, revealing a white object underneath.

Sitting at the bottom of the Caboodle was a poorly constructed origami square, made from what I could tell were several sheets of computer paper. I unfolded the square and inspected the paper, starting with the top sheet. It was a printed picture of me standing next to my high school best friend, Andi, on a campaign poster that read, *Megan Lucius for Junior Class President*. Examining the page, I noticed faint lines of text visible on the other side.

When I turned the paper over, I could barely believe what was in front of me. It was an AIM conversation between me and Chris from the summer of 2001—the summer our physical relationship began. I had printed a portion of our conversation history on the only computer paper I had nearby and hid it away where I thought no one would find it. Now, almost twenty years later, I was holding the one piece of physical evidence that proved, without a doubt, the legitimacy of my story.

I rushed to Ian, who was sitting in the living room, and shouted, "I've got it!" I shoved the pieces of paper under his nose, pointing wildly. "Look at this! I've got him!"

Ian took the papers from my hand and started reading. "Oh my God," he said, shaking his head. The conversation definitely proved a secret relationship. In it, Chris invited me to his apartment, we had flirtatious banter, he even mentioned names of school board members and the man who would be his replacement at the high school. It was all there, in black and white. I emailed a copy to Sergeant Perry and went to bed feeling better than I had in months.

• • •

I thought finding the AIM conversation would be a war-winning victory. It would prove to me who Chris truly was and what little I had meant to him, and I could finally move on. But the next morning, I brought the printed conversation with me to work and locked myself in my office. I read through it twenty or so times, dragging my finger over top of Chris's screen name, aching to transport myself back to that moment in time. I wasn't looking for proof that he didn't love me. I was looking for proof that he did.

2001

Driving to Central Michigan University, the only thing I could think about was how excited I was to spend every day with Chris for the next six days. So what if we had to pretend not to be together? For a short time, he'd be Mr. Blackmer again—the same caring, attentive teacher he had always been, and I would be the enthusiastic, hardworking student I had always been. And when the camp was over, we'd plan an overnight at his apartment, where we'd talk about our week and how much we'd missed each other.

I parked in the lot next to Robinson dorm and lugged my overstuffed duffel bag down the sidewalk. It was gorgeous outside, rays of sunshine covering the well-groomed landscapes of the university lawns and flowerbeds. A group of drum majors were being checked in at a lobby desk when I entered the building. The only two people I knew at the camp were Chris and our other drum major, Stephanie, who was going to be a senior that year. This was mine and Stephanie's second year as drum majors, so we'd had some time to get to know each other. We weren't the closest of friends, but we'd always gotten along really well.

Everyone was instructed to drop their belongings in their rooms and assemble in the lobby for an evening meeting. When I got to the lobby, Stephanie was already there. I joined her at the back of a gathering crowd. Chris was on the other side of the room mingling with a few campers and staff members. He was grinning, arms crossed at his chest, head tilted to the side.

I stood there, admiring him from a distance. He appeared relaxed and at home, which put me equally at ease. I was secretly enjoying the pride I felt in being his . . . *girlfriend* wasn't the right word. It was too conventional, and our relationship wasn't conventional—at least it wouldn't be for a while. The label didn't matter, though. What mattered to me was that, in the world we shared, I was his and he was mine.

During the meeting, I waited for him to notice me. When he finally turned his head in my direction, a dull pain shot through my stomach. He looked right through me, as if I wasn't even standing there.

I took a breath and assured myself that everything was fine. It was possible he just didn't see me. But when he looked again and didn't meet my eyes, not for one second, a terrible sinking feeling told me this wasn't by accident.

Was he really ignoring me, or was I imagining it? And if he was ignoring me, *why?* Didn't he trust me to be smart about this?

I told myself to stay calm. It was only the first night, and I knew neither of us had been in this kind of situation before. It would obviously take time to find our rhythm in this environment.

At the end of the meeting, the staff director sent us off to our rooms for the night. Many of the drum majors stayed in the lobby a while longer to hang out. Saying hello to Chris at this point wouldn't have drawn any unwanted attention, but I wanted to respect his boundaries and prove I could give him the space he was clearly asking for. A grown woman wouldn't seem needy. She'd do her own thing and let him be.

I asked Stephanie if she wanted to go up to the room. When we left the lobby, I ignored the impulse to look behind me to see if Chris was watching.

The next morning, in the dining hall, I saw Chris at a long cafeteria table eating breakfast with a group of staff members and drum majors. A spark of confidence ignited in me. I took a seat at the same table. I wanted him to see me interacting with people, being myself. After all, being *me* was what made him fall for me in the first place.

When I attempted to make eye contact with him, he refused, but in a way no one else would notice. The anxiety I'd been perpetually swallowing was now rising like hot bile in my throat. *He's doing this on purpose. He's avoiding me.*

Throughout the week, I held onto some hope that Chris's behavior would change, but every day was the same—it was like I didn't exist. He maintained distance from me during activities. He passed me in the lobby like I was invisible, and so that's what I became. The confident, bubbly girl I used to be disappeared, and in her place was a quiet, skittish ghost of a girl. It hurt to smile, and it hurt to talk, and it hurt to feel anything. I soon learned that it was easier for Chris to stay as far away from me as possible, because his nearness pulled my body in one direction, his rejection pushed me the opposite, and I felt it splitting me in two.

One evening at dinner, I sat with Stephanie and two other campers whom I'd spoken to only a few times. In a surprising turn of events, Chris sat down at a nearby table, his chair a mere six feet from mine.

I kept my eyes on my tray, attempting to swallow food down without throwing it back up. Enrique Iglesias started playing over the cafeteria speakers. "I hate this song," I said to myself, loud enough for him to hear.

"You have something against love songs?" Chris said.

There they were. The first words he'd spoken to me since the morning he kissed me goodbye at his apartment a week before, the morning that followed a night of passionate kissing and touching and holding and every little thing he'd done that made me believe he actually cared about me.

Burning, I stared at him and said, "I have something against this love song." I turned away and went back to eating. My tablemates went on with their conversation.

The next day, I was on the football field practicing the marching show with the other drum majors, the daily activity I feared most. All the drum majors were staged on the field performing a drill to Jamiroquai's "Canned Heat" while the staff members lined the top of the stadium bleachers, peering down at us. Chris was always standing with his arms crossed like a drill sergeant, wearing dark sunglasses that concealed the direction of his gaze. I was a caged animal, put on exhibition to entertain, and it was a living hell on earth. In the most pathetic display of beggary, I watched him from below, my twisted-up face desperate to send a message to him: *Please stop this. You're hurting me.*

There was a section of the show where we had to break out into a free-style dance. This was the absolute worst moment of every single day. First, I wasn't a dancer—this situation would have been social suicide under normal circumstances. Second, I was painfully embarrassed by every movement of my body, which, less than a week prior, had been on full display in Chris's bed. While kids around me did cartwheels and paired up with friends to perform cool dance moves, I was alone looking like a penguin dancing a drunken jig. I kept my eyes forward and prayed to God Chris wasn't watching from behind his stupid drill sergeant glasses.

In the midst of this nightmare was the one reprieve I got every day: the conducting clinic. The drum majors had all brought their instruments from home so we could form one large band. For a couple hours, the campers took turns conducting on the podium in front of the band.

I'd always been somewhat confident of my conducting, mostly because I'd attended summer music camps for years that allowed me to practice the skill. Even better, I was one of the best trumpet players in the room, so playing in the band gave me some of my confidence back, some of *me* back.

For every student who conducted, either the director of the camp or Chris acted as the clinician. They'd come up to the front, take comments from the campers about the conductor's performance, then provide their own feedback. I'd been certain all along that Chris would avoid being my clinician, just like he'd avoided me at every turn since we'd arrived. But that day, he was the one who called on me to conduct.

As I approached the podium, the ball of fire in my gut expanded. Conducting was the only thing I had left to look forward to at the camp, and he was going to ruin that too. Not only that—I knew this would be videotaped, and I'd forever have a memento of that moment, of him and I together but not *really* together, and of how God-awful miserable I was.

I stepped onto the podium and gripped the large clear stand in front of me for balance. I reminded myself to breathe. *Inhale. Exhale. Inhale. Exhale.* Chris stood behind the band, arms crossed and shifting his weight from side to side until he was planted in one spot. *Inhale. Exhale. Ignore him, Megan. You can do this.*

By some small miracle, I found the strength to narrow my focus to the campers in front of me and no one else. I extended my arms, readied myself to conduct, and while staring out into the eyes of supportive peers who wanted only for me to do well, I remembered who I was.

Standing alone on the podium, I dug deep for the best of what was inside me. I didn't break. I didn't falter. When the piece was over, I lowered my hands and let out a huge breath of relief. The students applauded, their praise melting away some of the misery that'd been clinging to my bones. For the first time all week, I was being seen.

Chris stepped up to the front of the room and began taking comments from the campers.

"You looked all professional or something!"

"I wanted to play for you better than I'd ever played."

"When you brought us in, it wasn't a startling rush. It was relaxed. You looked peaceful."

I smiled. If she believed I was peaceful, maybe I could believe it, too.

"I wish you guys could be more positive," Chris said, turning on the charm.

I wanted to believe he was Mr. Blackmer again, returning to his former self—a supportive, nurturing adult in my life. But this was a deception. After the way he'd made me feel that week, I knew things could never go back to the way they had been before.

When the clinic was over, I sat back down in my chair. The next student got up to conduct, and I went back to being invisible.

On the last day of camp, as I made my way down the stairwell to the lobby, a part of me still believed Chris would find me before I reached my car. He'd pull me aside and say, *I'm so sorry about this week, Megan. I had to ignore you or people would know about us. Will you forgive me?* Then, before anyone saw, he'd kiss me and I'd know this had been one big misunderstanding.

I searched the lobby for him, but he was nowhere to be found. I had never felt more alone in my entire life.

As I walked out of the dorm and stepped onto the sidewalk, I allowed myself to feel everything I'd been bottling up all week. I broke wide open. The pain, the anger, the loneliness . . . it all came rushing out of me in one sweeping tsunami of grief—eyes flooded, tears streaming down my face. I held my palm to my stomach as if someone had stabbed me, my body bent in half, releasing cackling cries that I tried to stifle as I hurried toward my car.

I got to the driver's side door and frantically dug for my keys, but my vision was blurred from the tears. I prayed no one would see me, this absolute wreck of a girl. When I finally got into my car, I rummaged through the pile of CDs in the center console—Janet Jackson's *Rhythm Nation*, No Doubt's *Tragic Kingdom,* my assortment of Mariah Carey albums, until I found the one that called to me. Something as miserable as I was—the Dashboard Confessional album *The Places You Have*

Come to Fear the Most. The trip home was more than enough time to blare the entire album, twice, beginning with the third track: "The Best Deceptions."

I returned home in the afternoon light, face red, eyes puffy and swollen. Unnoticed, I crept into the house, down the basement stairs, and shut myself in my room. My mom had made my bed while I was gone, and for some reason it made me even more sad. It was an empty bed, cold and lonely. I buried myself under the covers, wanting to fall asleep, not caring if I woke up again.

Mom stood at the kitchen stove cooking pork chops, each one sizzling as it made contact with the scalding skillet. The aroma of soy sauce floated through the room, and the microwave glowed and hummed as it heated a porcelain dish of buttered corn.

She looked over at me. "It's good to have you home."

"It's good to be home," I said, slumped over the kitchen table, elbows pressed into the clear glass that made my legs visible below. I studied the imperfections of each leg, the way the fat of my right thigh spread wider than my left, the knobbiness of my left knee compared to my right. I combed my fingers through my hair. If I allowed my mind to drift away, I could pretend they were someone else's fingers.

"You haven't said anything about camp yet," she noted.

I made a short droning sound. I wanted to smile but I didn't have the energy. The nap I took when I got home that afternoon only made me more tired, and the only reason I got out of bed for dinner was to prevent my parents from worrying that there was something more to my sleeping than just exhaustion.

Mom started prying. "Well? Was it fun?"

A familiar pricking needled at my body. I wanted to tell her the truth—about the camp, about sneaking around with Chris the past month, about my shattered heart.

I could do it, I thought. I could open my mouth right now and say, *Mom, I messed up. Mom, I'm sorry. Mom, I love him.* Then she could hug me and tell me everything was going to be okay.

But what if I tell her the truth and Chris changes his mind and wants to be with me again? What if he really was keeping his distance to protect us? What if I can't see him again and it's my fault? I couldn't risk it.

"Camp was pretty good," I said, raising my head up slightly.

"Pretty good? That's it?"

"Yeah. It was fun."

"I'm surprised," she said. "I thought you'd have more to say about it."

"I'm just tired. I'll feel better after a full night of sleep."

By this time, Trevor was begging for his food, and the doors to the house were slamming, which meant Randy would be there any second.

A few days passed, and still no communication from Chris. No phone calls, no texts, nothing on AIM. Every once in a while, I saw his screen name pop up on my friends list. It would stare at me for a few minutes and then disappear. The hourglass was almost empty; if Chris hadn't found a new place to live yet, he would soon. Then he'd be gone forever.

Before the week was up, I got the courage to send him a message: *Hey Chris.* (The words looked tiny and insignificant on the computer screen.)

He wrote back, *Hey there. How are you?*

There were so many things I wanted to say, but I was too afraid. As much as I wanted to ask him what happened at drum major camp, I didn't want to start an argument that might ruin any chance of me seeing him again.

I typed back, *I'm good. What are you up to?*

Busy. Getting ready to move. I found a place to live.

Our sickeningly sterile conversation ended without as much of a hint that he wanted to see me. A few days later, I sent him another message on AIM. It was a similar conversation. Emotionless. Stagnant.

One night, when I knew for certain he had moved away, I drove to the parking lot of his old apartment complex, listened to the radio show *Love Songs with Delilah*, and wept.

For days I hid in the basement, crying, wondering what I had done, what I could have done differently. I poured over our AIM conversations. I watched the conducting clinic video at least a dozen times, searching his body language for clues, aching every time he looked directly at the camera. Was he trying to send me a message? What message? Why was he doing this to me?

Had I been delusional for thinking we could be together? He *made* me believe we could be together. If I meant nothing to him, why did he kiss me? Why did he invite me to his apartment and let me spend the night with him, just to toss me aside like some piece of garbage?

There was only one explanation I could stomach: Going to drum major camp, being in an environment where I was once again his student, made him feel guilty about our relationship. He was regretful, so he distanced himself. He did the only thing he *could* do.

The thought didn't make me less sad, but it made me less angry. It was something I could understand. Something I could forgive.

I pulled up an AIM conversation from earlier that summer and printed it on the back of the only computer paper I could find, a leftover campaign poster I'd made when I ran for class president the last month of school. I folded it up and tucked it away in a place I knew no one would look—the hidden compartment of my purple Caboodle jewelry box.

The next day, as I cleaned my room, I found the information for my upcoming bible camp. I had attended this camp the past two summers with friends from church, and I'd be going back again in a few weeks. It was a silver lining to that awful summer. The camp took place out of state, and I couldn't wait to get out of Michigan. I didn't want to be in the same state as Chris. I needed new scenery, new beginnings, a new *me*.

In the camp paperwork, I saw the option to sign up as a group bible leader. A weight lifted from my chest. This was the first time since before drum major camp that I felt genuinely excited about anything. Being a group leader meant spending more time with my bible and my journal, planning devotionals for discussion. It would be a good distraction and a way to heal.

I was going to be *good* again. I was going to get my life back on track.

Since Andi and I had been drifting apart that summer, I stopped going to her when I needed a friend to cry to about Chris. Instead, I sought solace in a friend from church. Heather would invite me to her house, and we'd sit cross-legged on her bedroom floor as I recounted stories of that summer, before the drum major camp. Talking to her about Chris helped remove some of the sting of missing him, and Heather was the perfect listener—wide-eyed with excitement, swooning and sighing at all the best moments. It helped pass the time before we left for the bible and leadership camp.

When August came and we arrived at camp, all the group bible leaders met to reflect on how we could best lead the group of campers assigned to us. We gathered in a large carpeted room and sat in one large circle, a sheen of natural light entering through the open blinds.

"I want you all to share about a time when you were holy," said the adult leader.

If the question had been *How are you struggling as a Christian?* I would've had plenty to say. That was a question I was qualified to answer. But *holy*? What did it mean to be holy? If God was holy, that seemed unattainable, especially for someone like me. I thought about that summer, the lying and the secret-keeping. It was easy to see all the ways I'd been failing as a Christian.

I chose to take a breath and look for the good in who I was at that moment. I thought back to the times I felt closest to God, when I was living the best version of myself, when I didn't have to hide anything. I thought about my family and friends, about the kindness and love I'd shared with others. I could recall many spiritual moments in my life, but to say that I was *holy* because of them? I wasn't sure of that. I did know one thing: to say, with any degree of certainty, that I'd ever been holy would feel like a lie, and I had lied enough already.

We went around the circle, each person sharing a story. Most people described a specific moment in time, an act of generosity or self-control. One boy said he'd been holy for an entire afternoon. Before they got to me, our time ended, and I walked away relieved.

Later that day, while eating lunch with some friends in the dining hall, a counselor came to my table and asked me to step outside. She led me away from everyone to a semi-secluded area near the building. "It's been brought to our attention that you're making certain choices in your life," she said.

The blood drained from my face.

As she continued to talk, I felt like I was sinking into the ground, growing dizzier by the second. It was clear she knew I was having a relationship with a teacher, that I'd been lying to my parents and my friends and my church.

I tried to keep the panic from showing on my face. I tried to keep from shaking. What were they going to do to Chris? Was he going to get fired from his new job?

"We can't let you be a group bible leader," she said. "You'll be assigned to a new group that already has a leader."

At first I was relieved. She didn't mention contacting anyone about Chris. Removing me as a group leader seemed a small price to pay. So even though I was embarrassed and wished I still could be a group leader, I nodded and said that I understood.

The counselor left, and I stared down at a patch of grass, pondering the implications of the conversation that had just taken place. Not a conversation, really, but the doling out of a consequence. I had done something really bad. I didn't deserve to lead others in their spiritual journeys.

When I got back to the table, I saw Heather staring down at her plate. She looked like she was going to cry. "I'm so sorry," she said. "I thought someone needed to know."

I put my hand on hers. "It's okay. It's not your fault." I knew Heather was a good person. She did what she thought was right, even if it meant losing our friendship.

That night, while I laid in bed unable to sleep, I thought about the other group leaders. Had they ever sinned? Ever done anything sexual with their boyfriends or girlfriends? Was I so different from everyone else? So much worse? And if what I'd done was so terrible, why hadn't anyone called my parents?

2001

June—Ten weeks into the investigation

The Genesee County prosecutors made plans to send Sergeant Perry and another police officer down to Florida to interview Chris regarding allegations of my abuse. When I heard this, I was overwhelmed by conflicting emotions. If the prosecutors were willing to fly the officers down to Florida, that meant they were taking my story seriously, which gave me hope. But the thought of them seeing Chris was almost too much to bear. It was something I couldn't wrap my head around. Chris wasn't just a memory. He was real. He was living in the present, and these detectives were going to talk to him about me.

"He's not obligated to talk to us," Sergeant Perry told me over the phone. "We might get down there and come back with nothing, but the prosecutors believe it's worth trying."

I couldn't imagine why Chris would choose to talk to the Michigan police. His lawyer would probably warn against talking to any authorities. But there was always a chance. I sent the sergeant a text: *I'm praying for whatever happens in Florida.*

The day Sergeant Perry and his partner flew out of Michigan, I checked my phone obsessively for an update. In the early afternoon, I received a text message.

> SGT. PERRY: When did you attend Kearsley?
> MEGAN: 1999—2003.
> SGT. PERRY: Going good. Keep praying.

That was the last text I received from him that day. By evening, I was desperate to reach out, but I didn't want to seem needy so I decided to wait until morning to do anything.

It was a particularly hot summer night, so Ian decided to sleep in the cool basement. I laid in bed, searching for new information on the investigation in Florida. As far as I knew, Chris was still out on bond awaiting trial, and now he had something else to worry about—the Michigan State Police were also investigating him.

An article popped up, one that had just been posted that day. It read:

- Blackmer now faces 14 felony charges:
- One count of transmitting child pornography by electronic device, third-degree felony
- Five counts of unlawful possession of materials depicting sexual performance by a child, third-degree felony
- Five counts of using a child in a sexual performance, second-
- degree felony
- Three counts of sexual activity with a 16 or 17-year-old by a school authority figure, first-degree felony

I had never seen so many charges attached to one person. It seemed unreal that it was a person I not only knew but had been close to for years. I read through each set of charges, trying to determine the specific crime. All but one charge—*transmitting child pornography by electronic device*—seemed to be related to the video that police discovered on his phone. If he was a serial predator, wouldn't his phone or computer have been filled with pornography? If crime shows portrayed even a fraction of truth, one piece of evidence would lead to more. It had been over two months since the arrest, and still, I knew of only two people Chris had actually laid a hand on: the boy in the video and me. If Chris was a monster, where was the overwhelming evidence?

The boy in the video had met Chris through an online dating platform, which meant he was looking to hook up with someone. He must have known Chris's age, and yet he made the choice to see him. Just like I had made the choice to be with him.

My eyes scrolled the article, until I saw a sentence that I could not comprehend. *According to court documents, Blackmer faces anywhere from 30 years to life in prison if convicted.*

It was like hearing the news of his arrest all over again—a blade slicing me clean down the middle. Grief poured out of me in violent gasps of air, my stomach twisting itself into knots. I leapt from the bed and headed for the basement door. I made my way down the stairs in a panicked rush and stood awkwardly on the bottom stair peering into the darkness. "Ian?" I said, trying to keep myself from shaking.

The sound of my voice jolted him out of his slumber. "Are you okay?"

"No."

"What's wrong? Come here."

I stumbled toward him and collapsed on the couch, sobbing loud, piercing wails, like a wounded animal. "He's going to go to prison for life!"

Ian held me tight, stroking the top of my head. "Aren't you glad he isn't going to be able to hurt anyone again?"

I tried to stifle my yells so I didn't wake the boys two floors above. "I'm not glad about anything. I was part of this. This is my fault, too."

Chris might have committed the crime, but I helped him. I fueled his unhealthy desires, allowed him to believe what we were doing was okay. I wanted so badly to go back in time and warn him, *Please don't do this*, but then I'd have to give up all the memories I prized that made me feel something other than pain. Those memories were what I had left of the old Chris before he died and this new Chris appeared. I couldn't let go of him. I wouldn't let go.

Eventually, the heaving exhausted me into long, slow breaths. I moved over to the basement loveseat where I planned to sleep for the night, because I didn't want to be upstairs alone. Several minutes of silence passed before I said, "I don't understand why there's only two of us, me and this boy in Florida. It doesn't make sense. Maybe he was trying to stop . . . . Maybe he tried to stop."

Across the room, Ian laid still in the dark, silent.

The next morning, I sent a text to Sergeant Perry:

> I read an article about the new charges against Chris. I couldn't sleep at all. I know I did the right thing by coming forward but everything about this hurts. Everyone sees this monster and I still see a person I care about. I'm trying to come to terms with what actually happened between us. I will do whatever I have to do moving forward for the other victims and because it's the right thing to do. I just needed to get this off my chest.

He responded, and at his request, I called Sergeant Perry around noon.

"We almost had a confession," he said.

"What happened?"

"We caught him coming out of his place. He agreed to talk to us, he even got into the police car. He said he only had twenty minutes, though, because he had to leave for an appointment."

"What did he say?"

"He admitted there was a relationship between you two, but he said it was when you were in college. He said he kissed you on the cheek in high school. He couldn't remember dates."

I was shocked he had not only agreed to talk to the police, but he admitted to our relationship. Sure, he was lying about the details, but still, he acknowledged me. He acknowledged there was an *us*.

"What else?" I asked.

"When we asked him why he would date someone your age, he made a comment about how you were 'thirteen going on thirty.'"

My skin was tingling. I pictured the scene the sergeant was describing. I wanted every detail. I wanted to imagine I was in the car with them. I couldn't believe they were actually in his presence. They'd seen him in the flesh. He was alive and breathing. He was thinking about me. My name was in his mouth. "What was he like?" I asked.

"He was a gentleman."

The sergeant's description of Chris struck a dissonant chord in me. What an odd thing to say, to give my abuser such a flattering title. The trouble was, that's exactly how I would've described him. "What happens now?" I asked.

"We go back and continue to prepare the report for the prosecutor's office. When it's done, they'll make a decision whether or not to arrest him and press charges."

When we hung up the phone, I took deep breaths, trying hard to get my pulse to slow down. Chris, the *gentleman*. Chris, the *romantic*. Chris, the person I knew in a way no one else did. These were the thoughts I couldn't escape. I saw the best in him when everyone around me wanted to label him as a monster. But they didn't understand. They weren't there. They didn't see what I saw. They didn't feel what I felt.

I was getting dressed for work when Ian entered the bedroom and told me he had just finished watching the new documentary *Athlete A* about Dr. Larry

Nassar, who had abused hundreds of female athletes over the decades he worked at Michigan State University.

"That's probably not good for your mental health," I said.

"Well, I can't stop thinking about this stuff. I might as well try to understand it. I'm trying to understand what you're feeling."

I wanted to feel more gratitude for Ian's gesture, but all I could feel was the gaping hole in my chest as Ian remained on one side of the bedroom and me on the other. He was showing support, but not in the way I needed most. Earlier that week, I had written a note in my journal, addressed to Chris: *My husband won't touch me anymore because of you.*

I couldn't tell if Ian was actually touching me less, or if I was simply more cognizant of the times we passed by each other without touching. And even though my statement was aimed at Chris, my anger was not, because it was impossible to produce physical anger toward him. Instead, the blame fell on Ian. His kisses weren't long enough, weren't passionate enough. The few times he'd hold my hand, he didn't squeeze it tightly enough. It killed me that he didn't look at me the way he used to when we were dating and first married.

"What did you learn from the documentary?" I asked.

Ian slumped into himself a bit. "One woman reminded me of you. The day she testified, she woke up still wondering whose side she was going to be on."

JUNE 12, 2019
7:21 P.M.

Becca,

Sorry to bother you outside of our session time. I'm sure you receive a lot of emails from clients . . . . I'm writing to tell you I had a difficult evening on Saturday (one of several this week). I called Chris's number. It rang twice and I hung up. I don't even know if the number would have worked or what I would have said. I think I just wanted to hear his voice. It feels like he died, and I miss him. After I hung up, I felt scared and paranoid that he might actually see I called and recognize the number. One moment I feel sane, and the next I feel like I could make stupid decisions to selfishly ruin the life I have. Anyway, I wanted to know if this is something I should tell the police. We didn't have contact, and he did not show any signs of reaching out to me.

My husband, Ian, is still planning to attend our session tomorrow. I told him I don't have an agenda in asking him to attend, only to see if it might be helpful for us in some way to get through difficult times and to keep our marriage strong.

JUNE 12, 2019
8:35 P.M.

Hi Megan,

It's totally fine to email me between sessions. I got both of your messages. I understand that Ian doesn't know about the call. Was it something you wanted him to know about? I just need to know if it's something I should or shouldn't bring up tomorrow. Right now I'm assuming I shouldn't.

Reaching out to Chris is something we should talk about the next time we get the opportunity. I want to explore with you reasons for calling him, what you were hoping to accomplish, what you were wanting to say to him, etc. As you also alluded to, there are legal issues that could arise from making contact with him, so we can also discuss what that might look like. In the meantime, it's best not to try and contact him anymore. If you get the urge to talk to him, writing him another letter would be more helpful. Thanks for letting me know what's been going on. I'll see you tomorrow!

JUNE 12, 2019
9:19 P.M.

Becca,

Thank you for responding. Ian does not know about the call, and I feel like it would only confuse and hurt him. I want the feelings I have for Chris to go away, and I think the feelings I have are not seeded in reality but in a fantasy, an idealistic world of how I felt when I was with him as a young person. I feel like I'm 16 and he's still 29 when neither of those things are true and we are both different people. Except I don't feel like a different person on the inside. We can talk more later. I won't call [him] again.

2001

The summer that followed my sixteenth birthday was a summer of loss. Losing Chris wasn't just about losing a boyfriend. I had lost my favorite teacher, my mentor, my friend, the source of my highest high and my lowest low. Still, when I knew it was over between us, I was left with no choice but to move forward.

The start of my junior year kept me busy with honors classes, church, marching band, and my new role as class president. I had papers to write, music to rehearse, homecoming events to plan. On the outside I appeared put together, and I believed I was. As always, I had a foolproof method for overcoming any hardship: whenever I dipped into disappointment or sadness, I reminded myself how fortunate I was to be me, how grateful I was for every blessing in my life, and that everything happened for a reason.

In late September, I was preparing to type up an assignment for Honors English, but first I signed into AOL. I was checking my email when the screen name *Concerto72* appeared on my buddy list. Chris was online again. Several times a week his name would appear. It would stare at me for about ten minutes or so, then he'd be gone. At first, it was paralyzing every time I saw his name. But after two months of no contact, I was starting to regain some sanity.

Suddenly, a small box appeared in the corner of my computer screen, accompanied by a startling *bing*.

CONCERTO72: Hi.

One word. That's all it took to turn my world upside down. My cheeks turned hot, as if I'd just held my head near an open oven. I drew closed fists into my chest and whispered to myself, "No way, no way, no way."

Hands shaking, I typed a response.

JAZZ2MEGGYLU: Hey there. How are you?

We made small talk for a while. *How's school? How's work? Loving the new job?* I hoped my intuition was right, that he wanted more than a conversation. And just like magic, the words appeared on my screen.

CONCERTO72: Would you want to come visit me soon?

He didn't apologize for drum major camp or explain his temporary disappearance from my life, but I didn't care. His desire to see me was all it took to wash away months of pain. From that moment on, it was as if the drum major camp never happened.

I typed *yes* into the box and pressed enter.

Autumn sunshine filled my car on the day I drove to White Lake, Michigan. It was one of the most beautiful days of the season, the early afternoon blanketed in a cloudless blue sky.

I followed a highway down to a small unfinished street that led me back to the place where Chris was staying. As I pulled into the driveway of the modest tri-level house, I saw through the bay window a shadowy figure moving briskly toward the front door.

Chris appeared on the small landing as I exited my car. He greeted me with an easy smile. I moved toward him, striving to put on an air of confidence, all the while reminding my legs and feet how to move in a way that resembled walking.

When I entered the house, I was standing in the living room, an open-concept space with wood flooring. Across from me was the kitchen, and to my left two short stairways leading in opposite directions. Chris invited me to the lower level—the den, whose centerpiece was a couch that was reminiscent of the '80s and a matching oblong coffee table. I sank into the couch, noticing the spread of magazines neatly placed in a row. On one of the magazine covers was a picture-perfect image of singer Celine Dion and her much older manager-husband, cradling their infant child.

We sat sideways on the couch facing each other, making awkward conversation like two teenagers fumbling exchanges at the end of a date. His arm was draped across the back of the couch, his fingers dangling inches from my hair. My temperature rose steadily as he inched his way closer to me, one chuckle at a time, until our knees were touching. By this time, the beating inside my chest was at a fever pitch. One more chuckle was all it would take.

He swooped forward and pressed his lips to mine. In a frenzy, I threw my hands up onto his head, grabbing and combing at his hair like a woman embracing a lover returned from war. He scooped me up from the couch and carried me bridal-style up one short staircase, then the other, to a room just large enough for a bed and a nightstand. He lowered my legs onto the bed, my head onto the pillow. Then he climbed on top of me, pressing me into the mattress with his hips and mouth, his jeans rubbing against the thin cotton of my skirt. I was pinned beneath him, his hands running up and down my body, grabbing, squeezing, pressing, the heat between us melting me onto the bed.

An hour later, after we had thoroughly exhausted ourselves from making out, we laid on our sides, gazing at one another, speaking in low voices and hushed laughter. I watched his eyes wander the edges and curves of my face. He cradled my hand in his, interlacing his fingers with mine. He gave me this look from time to time that said, *I need to kiss you again*, and he'd bring his lips to my mouth or forehead, holding them there for several seconds before releasing them. Entwined inside me was ecstasy and comfort, the thrill of falling while also being held. In those precious few hours, there was no world outside of the one we shared in that tiny bedroom.

The sun was setting when we said our goodbyes and stepped out into the evening air, the sky ablaze with brilliant shades of burnt orange and red.

"I'll see you later," Chris said, smiling at me as I waved to him before climbing into my car and pulling out onto the street. As I drove away, I was filled with an inexplicable calm. I didn't know what *later* meant, but I knew it contained an unspoken promise: a future that included both of us.

On the drive home up I-75, I passed a familiar sign—a 50-foot-tall structure advertising the Dixie Baptist Church. Above the church's name was a giant portrait of Jesus; under the portrait, a question in all caps: "ARE YOU ON THE RIGHT ROAD?"

2019

July—Three months into the investigation

JOURNAL ENTRY
JULY 19, 2019

Today is an irrational "I don't like myself" day. I drank an entire bottle of wine, listened to "Annie's Song," and unloaded all of my thoughts and feelings onto my mom. I need to stop drinking at home. I've said this to myself a million times but I struggle to make it happen for longer than a few days. I continue to grieve and long for something I don't know or understand. There's a hole inside my heart that can't be fixed, no matter how hard I try. I wish I could identify the cause of the ache. Something is wrong with me, and I blame myself for feeling this way. One moment I feel joy, the next emptiness. If I start to feel anything, then I feel too much. What do I do?

There had been an obvious downturn in Ian's attitude the past month, and I felt desperate to make him feel better. Only so much time was left before summer ended and the leaves would begin to fall, so I planned a day where Ian and the boys and I could all work together on landscaping our yard. Ian was always talking about wanting to do more projects as a family. He was so buoyed by my idea, he invited my mom to come spend the day with us.

I had this image in my head of what the day would be like, but when it arrived, Ian stayed inside the house and slept most of the day away while the rest of us trimmed bushes and pulled weeds in the sunshine. Since I suspected Ian was in the throes of a manic low, I tried to be understanding—especially since it was me who had put us in this situation.

Mom had taken me to buy a few hanging baskets for the front porch. We brought them home, and since I knew practically nothing about caring for plants, she walked me through how to prune and feed and water them. "You know what I love about flowers?" she said, picking out the dead stems and discolored leaves. "They can look dead, but if you care for them properly you can revive them."

I watched my mom as she continued to tend to the plant, and for perhaps the first time since Chris's arrest, I felt a touch of hope rising up in me. If only I could find what was dead and poisoning the rest of my life, I could simply remove it and everything would be okay again. I had to believe that my life was just as capable of renewal and regrowth as the tiny roots and stems growing inside the dirt.

In the mid-afternoon, Ian emerged wheeling his motorcycle out of the garage and into the driveway. The boys were sitting in the front flower bed, removing debris while Mom and I stood near the front porch, cutting back the overgrown shrubs by the front door.

"Hey there," I said, trying not to let the confusion in my voice show. "What are you doing?"

In a melancholy tone, Ian said, "I was thinking, maybe I'd go for a ride somewhere. Maybe somewhere with water."

I got the feeling he wasn't talking about a nearby lake. "Yeah. Okay. That sounds nice," I said, masking my disappointment. If I asked him to stay, he would have agreed out of obligation or guilt, and that would only make me feel worse. It certainly wouldn't help our relationship. So I shoved my true feelings down and told them to *shut up*.

After he'd left, my mom said, "Is Ian alright?"

I forced a tight-lipped smile. "If this is what he needs to feel better, then I'm glad he's doing it." I played the understanding wife, but inside I was screaming. It was easy on a typical day to slush through, but this day was supposed to be special. It was supposed to be healing, and all he had to do was show up for it. He failed me. And for a brief second, I hated him for it.

Defeated, I turned back to cut away at the spirea, but I could feel my mom's eyes lingering over me.

"You know," she spoke softly, "you can call me anytime you want to talk."

• • •

My mom had been working on a massive genealogy project that summer, attempting to organize hundreds of family photos and facts so we could identify our relatives and their stories stretching back generations. It had been a long time since she had fully immersed herself in any project, and every time I called she had a new story to share about our family, like how my great-great-grandparents were both blind but gave birth to six sighted children, one of them being my great-grandmother. It was amazing to me to think about everything that had to happen in order for my grandfather to exist, then my mom, then me. The more my mom dug into the past, the more I reflected on how the decisions of earlier generations significantly impacted the generations that followed.

I didn't often think about my mom as a teenage girl. To understand who she was at fifteen, you'd have to exchange her long, flowing locks for pubescent stringy hair, bound tightly in two pigtails. Instead of dresses and heels, a pair of overalls and sneakers. *I looked like a tomboy*, she'd say. She had grown up the middle of three girls, her only brother having been stillborn. Boys were a complete mystery to her, and the first time she French kissed one—that is, she and a cute neighborhood boy awkwardly touched the tips of their tongues together in the yard—she convinced herself she was surely going to hell.

It was 1976, and my fifteen-year-old mom had spent the evening babysitting the children of close family friends, Rick and Linda. Rick had offered to bring her home, and on the way he stopped by a local Flint bar, The Wagon Wheel. She waited patiently in the car, unsure of why they had stopped, while he went inside. Within minutes he returned, no explanation for their detour.

Before leaving the parking lot, he told her had a secret he wanted to share, and he gestured for her to lean in close so she could hear. She half expected him to say something funny, to make a joke, but instead he kissed her. She can't remember the details of the kiss itself, but she recalls feeling awkward and confused. He was much older than she was, a married man with kids and he knew her family well.

The second time he took her home, he drove past her street and parked the car in a large, open field not far from her house. He kissed her again. "I can't get you pregnant. I've had a vasectomy," he said, and waited for her response. Her polite avoidance of the subject convinced him to take her home, and she went immediately to bed without saying a word.

The next morning, my mom told her older sister, Martha, what had happened the night before. Martha was horrified, and knew she needed to tell their mom and dad the truth—but it was my grandparent's wedding anniversary, and she didn't want to ruin their day, so she waited with fearful anticipation until the evening to talk to my grandfather.

After Martha told my grandfather what Rick had done, he went to my mom and asked, "Are you okay?."

She said *yes*. In her mind, nothing significant had happened. It was just a kiss; it didn't go further than that.

It was always my grandfather's goal to protect people, to offer love, compassion, and forgiveness. He thought gossip was sinful, and he didn't want to be responsible for causing pain to others. "I don't want to ruin a man's life for making one mistake," he said. Ultimately, he decided it was best to remain quiet about the incident in order to protect Rick's family.

Ten years later, in 1986, my mom and I were alone in the apartment we shared with my father. I was less than a year old, fast asleep in my crib down the hall from my parent's bedroom. My father said he was working late, and my mom went to bed alone that night thinking she had locked the apartment door. When she woke up, there was a stranger standing at the foot of the bed, and before she knew it he was on top of her, raping her. My mom managed to escape, but she wasn't able to grab me from my nursery. It wasn't until the police arrived that she knew for certain whether I was alive or dead.

As I pieced together the history of these traumatic events, I suddenly understood why my mom couldn't see the truth about Chris twenty years earlier. When I told my mom, "Mr. Blackmer kissed me at school," she didn't think of it as assault. It didn't look like what happened to her at fifteen—confusing, unwanted advances by a married man—and it didn't look like being violently raped in her own apartment, terrified, wondering if her toddler was alive in the next room.

I wasn't terrified of Mr. Blackmer. My mom knew how fond I was of him. Teenage girls were often viewed as young women and not as children, especially her bright, precocious daughter. Based on her lived experiences, it wasn't hard for my mom to justify how Mr. Blackmer could genuinely return my affection. So she did what she knew. She asked if I was okay. And I did what I knew: I said I was. I believed I was okay. But I wasn't. I just didn't know it yet.

At last, the picture became clear. I couldn't see the truth about Chris, and neither could my mom. But for different reasons, based on our own upbringing and experiences, the many ways our society failed to educate and protect us. We didn't know—sexual assault comes in many forms, and the world didn't prepare us for any of them.

2003

"I don't want to wait until I'm married to have sex."

Mom looked up from the kitchen table. Her eyes flashed surprise. "What's changed?"

I shrugged. "I just feel differently about it."

It wasn't a great answer, but it was an honest one. I'm not exactly sure why I announced this to my mom. What was I trying to accomplish? Did I want her to convince me *not* to have sex? Was I desperate to tell her a significant truth since I'd been keeping so many other secrets from her?

"Please hold off a few more months until you're in college," Mom said. "You're going to meet so many new people. I don't want you getting emotionally tied to someone from high school."

I knew what she was afraid of. She didn't want me repeating history. *Her* history. There were already so many parallels between my relationship with Sean and her relationship with my father. Sean and I started dating in middle school. So did my parents. Sean and I had broken up many times only to get back together. So did my parents. The last thing she wanted was for me to get married, be miserable, and have to suffer the pain of divorce. Or, worse, be trapped in a miserable marriage for the rest of my life.

"Please wait to have sex," she said.

I told her I'd think about it, but I couldn't get my mind to cooperate with my words. If there was one thing I knew about myself, it was that when I made up my mind to do something, it was as good as done.

It was March of my senior year, less than three months to high school graduation, and I felt like a stranger in my own body. For those who'd been present during my junior and senior year—parents, teachers, friends, people at church—my life appeared fairly consistent. I worked hard in school, participated in loads of activities, won top awards at summer music camps. But somewhere between my sixteenth and seventeenth birthday, something inside me had begun to shift.

Because I was a high-achieving student, I received privileges other students didn't. The first day of my senior year, one of my teachers told me that I didn't need to be in his class unless there was an exam. "You're class president," he said. "You have more important things to do than sit in this room and listen to me lecture."

I was surprised he didn't care where I was—didn't even ask to know—but I didn't argue with him. I appreciated the extra time. However, as the year went on I stopped using that free time to be productive. I found quiet places to doodle in my notebook, write letters to friends or stare at walls.

By winter, I was skipping school a couple times a month. On those days, I'd wake up with a strange discomfort in my body. I didn't feel well, but not in the traditional sense. I wasn't coughing or sneezing or throwing up. It was a jittery sensation that permeated my insides, trapped beneath the surface of my skin. That, or a feeling of complete disconnectedness and disinterest.

Sometimes, after first or second period, I'd leave school, go home and sleep. Other times, whether we were currently together or not, I'd convince Sean to leave with me. We'd walk around empty malls, fool around in the backseat of his station wagon.

Skipping school was new to me but disconnection was not. Ever since my relationship with Chris began at the end of my sophomore year, I had learned to disconnect from one world while spending time in another. I didn't make a conscious decision to sever myself from reality. I think something might've happened the day I drove away from the White Lake house, wanting so desperately to stay with Chris, knowing I couldn't. I couldn't possibly survive in my world constantly wondering and worrying if I would ever return to the world he and I shared. I had to be certain that world would always be there.

By spring of my senior year, Chris and I had been seeing each other in secret for nearly two years. Every few months, I'd meet up with him in a public place—a mall, a restaurant, a movie theater. Once, we made out in his car after dinner, but our visits in public were never centered on physical affection because of the attention it might draw. He would find inconspicuous moments to hold my hand.

He would walk me to my car and kiss me goodnight. But mostly, we just spent time together. Every once in a while, I'd find an opportunity to spend the night with him at his new apartment in Wixom. That's when we would make out and do *other stuff.* I didn't tell anyone about these visits. I even stopped telling Andi about them because she was clearly uncomfortable with the fact that the relationship was still going on.

As for Sean, our on-again-off-again relationship created windows of time where I could see Chris without cheating. But that meant I only ever had one foot on the ground. There was never any stability, no long-term commitment to any one person.

I didn't intentionally break up with Sean so that I could see Chris, it was just the natural cycle of things. I loved Sean, but it was never long before our relationship turned from good to bad, and bad to worse. Every time Sean and I got back together, I could put Chris completely out of my mind. But something had darkened in Sean during our four years of high school. His once immature and mostly harmless behaviors had turned deeply hurtful. I caught him in lies, discovered inappropriate online conversations between him and other girls. It was unlikely that a special occasion would go by—a school dance or a birthday—without me ending up in tears. He'd always apologize and promise to change, but it wouldn't be long before we were arguing about the same things again. Our highs grew higher and our lows sank lower. One moment we were holding hands and the next we were screaming in a fast-food parking lot. I didn't trust him to be honest and he didn't trust me to not leave him, but we kept trying to make it work.

Aside from my romantic relationships, I appeared put together. I had spent the first seventeen years of my life sure of who I was, what I believed, what I was going to accomplish, and it all lined up with what others wanted for me. But now, there were things I wasn't so sure of. Sex was one of them. I was starting to lose my grip on the control I'd had over my life, and I could feel the temple I had built for myself starting to collapse under its own weight.

A significant portion of my classmates were already having sex, but that wasn't why I had changed my mind. It's hard to explain how you wake up one day and you don't feel the same. You're mostly the same, but pieces of you are missing. Pieces that shaped a part of your identity you no longer desire. Did it happen overnight? Or did the change come slowly without you ever being aware of it?

Whatever reasons I had for waiting until marriage to have sex, I'd lost them, and I didn't even know how to want them back.

Following a band concert at school, I convinced Sean to take me home. I hadn't seen Chris in months. Sean and I weren't together but we had started to flirt in recent weeks. I knew it was only a matter of time before one of us would make the move and we'd be back together.

We parked in the service drive of a closed Harley Davidson dealership and crawled into the backseat of his car, still in our black concert attire.

"You ever had sex with a guy in a tux?" Sean grinned, hovering over me.

The answer was *no*. I had never had sex with *any* guy in *any* kind of outfit.

We started kissing, removing necessary articles of clothing. There was no stopping what was going to happen.

"Ow! That really hurts!" I said, holding my hands against his chest to prevent him from moving too quickly.

"I feel fine," Sean said, trying to lighten the moment.

I didn't think it would be as painful as it was. It didn't help that the looming threat of a cop catching us made it nearly impossible to relax. After thirty minutes or so, we had tried long enough, unsuccessfully. Sean took me home.

The next day, Sean and I skipped the only class we had together—Band—so we could finish what we started. Sean drove us to his brother's house, where we knew no one would be home.

When it was over, excitement turned to nauseating dread. It wasn't anything Sean did; I could tell he wanted it to be special. He was careful and constantly asked if I was okay. It was me I was terrified of, how quickly I'd gone from the girl who was saving herself until marriage to the girl who was skipping school to lose her virginity.

What the hell was wrong with me? Why couldn't I wait until a regular Friday night when most kids were choosing to have sex? And why wasn't I scared enough to make him use a condom? Apparently, it wasn't enough to feel *something*. I had to feel *everything*. I had to drain the thrilling well of risk. Every. Last. Drop.

A bad idea would've been for us to panic and call a friend to ask where we could get a Plan B pill. Another bad idea would've been for me to walk in mysteriously late to a rehearsal of *The Wizard of Oz*, which I was student directing, and cry to the theater teacher about how I just couldn't be there that day when it was clear I was having some kind of crisis.

Unfortunately, this was exactly what happened.

The entire afternoon was spent in a self-destructive spiral. I knew the friend we called wouldn't keep it to herself that we'd had sex. Soon, our secret would no longer be a secret. It would become common knowledge at school that good girl Megan Lucius gave it up when she swore she wouldn't.

Later that day, after we had visited Planned Parenthood, Sean and I sat in his car. After a long measure of silence, Sean looked at me as if he was going to cry. "You *do* want to be with me. Right?"

I didn't know how to explain what I was feeling or why I was feeling it. Everything felt too big, too messy, too overwhelming. I wanted to run away and never come back. "This is a lot for me, okay?" I said. "I need some time to think about it."

A few days later, the high school lost power in the middle of the school day and everyone was sent home early. Sean drove me back to my house. My basement bedroom seemed cold and dreary, so instead we went upstairs to my parents' bedroom. We were already naked when I heard the front door slam.

I stopped breathing. *Oh my God. What is Randy doing home? Shit.*

He'd been working for another business, away from home, but I'd forgotten he was getting a vasectomy that morning and took the day off.

Shit. Shit.

I scrambled to find my clothes, but my brain was on fire. Panicked, I ran into the bathroom, leaving the door wide open, sinking to the cold bathroom floor. I drew my legs to my chest and buried my head between them, as if that would somehow make me invisible.

I heard Sean's voice in the hallway outside of the bathroom. "Hi, Randy."

"Hi, Sean." Randy said, with an air of confusion.

Randy stepped into the bathroom and saw me naked and balled up on the floor. He spoke awkwardly. "Are you okay, Megan?"

I felt like I was five again, and he was making sure I wasn't hurt after falling off the monkeybars. "Yes," I said, shaking, my bare bottom freezing on the tile floor while the rest of my body burned with embarrassment.

"Okay, then," Randy said, awkwardly, seeming unsure of what to do, and left the house.

That night, Sean and I walked shamefully into my parents' bedroom. My mom was sitting on the bed—the sheets had clearly been washed and the bed redressed. Randy was on the floor, legs stretched out in front of him, watching the tiny television perched on their nightstand. He stared at the TV, refusing to make eye contact with us, while my mom glared at the wall ahead of her.

Sean cleared his throat. "If it helps, I would be willing to pay for Megan's birth control."

My mom's head turned toward him, her eyes narrowed into piercing slits. She looked like she was going to jump across the room and strangle him. Randy remained quiet on the floor, hands clasped on his lap, twiddling his thumbs. "That will not be necessary," my mom said in a menacing tone. "I think you should leave."

The next few days, the air inside my house was thick like a tropical rainforest. I walked on eggshells around my parents, speaking to them as politely as possible. A few weeks later, the air had thinned and everyone was back to their usual routines.

I had decided to commit to Sean. Regardless of our past struggles, I believed Sean and I loved each other, and since he was the first person I'd had sex with, it was even more important we tried to make it work.

The weekend of my senior prom, I hoped my mom and I would have an opportunity to make amends. I had recently been selected as a top ten vocalist in the state, and was invited to perform at the Michigan Youth Arts Festival in Kalamazoo on May 10th. The challenge was getting back for prom, an event I had spent months planning with the other class officers.

Mom and I made a plan. If I got my hair done in Kalamazoo that morning before the soloist recital, there'd be just enough time to perform and make it back to Flint before Sean picked me up for dinner.

As we waited backstage for the recital to start, my mom held tightly to her purse and car keys, ready to fetch the vehicle as soon as I had sung my final note. I kept checking the backstage doors, hoping to see a familiar face, but when the first singer stepped out onto the stage, I thought maybe I'd been hoping for too much. I sighed and thought, *I guess he's not coming.*

As soon as I learned I had been chosen as a top ten vocalist, I emailed Chris to tell him the news. I didn't consider this to be cheating on Sean. I was letting Chris know because I wanted him to be proud of me. He had been such an integral part of my musical upbringing, and I knew he'd be at the festival for band events. I thought maybe he'd have time to stop by and say hello.

Halfway through the first singer's set, I had started to let go of any hope of seeing Chris, but my heart leapt when the backstage door opened and he stepped into the room. He was wearing the same blue blazer he'd worn the night of my freshman year jazz band concert. The night he said, *That dress looks nice on you.*

My cheeks turned hot. "Hi," I said.

"Hey Megan. It's good to see you," he said, smiling. "Are you ready? Nervous?"

"Definitely." I blinked. "I mean, I'm definitely nervous. But I'm ready."

"You'll do great. I'll be out there watching. Good luck."

When he left, I stood frozen in a daze, until my mind returned to the room and to my mom who was standing beside me. It was then I realized I hadn't acknowledged her at all when Chris was there. Typically, I would have said something like, *Mr. Blackmer, this is my mom*, or *Mom, you remember Mr. Blackmer?* But I was so focused on him, I'd forgotten about everything else.

The performance went *okay*. I was nervous knowing Chris was somewhere in the audience, and I mixed up some of my lyrics but I kept going. When I left the stage, my mom gave me a big hug. "That was great!" she said. After everything we'd been through the past few months, she was still my biggest fan.

On the way home, my mom was quiet. I could see the wheels in her head turning. She kept whispering something to herself, then she looked over at me and said, "That was weird."

"Huh?" I said, feigning cluelessness.

"Your old band teacher. When he came backstage to talk to you, he didn't say anything to me. He didn't even look at me. That's weird, right?"

"I guess so," I said, continuing to look out the window.

"And after what he did two years ago"—she was referring to the one kiss she knew about—"that man's got some nerve."

Part of me wanted her to stop talking, to forget all about it. But another part of me was thinking, *Keep going, Mom, you're almost there.* I sensed that if she were to pry harder, to bear down relentlessly in a quest for truth, I would crack under the pressure, and all the secrets I'd been storing up for years would come spilling out of me like tiny marbles onto my lap.

When she didn't press the issue further, I decided it was for the best. It was a big day, first with the recital, then prom. And things were good between us again. The last thing I wanted to do was cause more problems.

2019

August—Four months into the investigation

I stared catatonically out the passenger side window as Ian drove me and the boys home from a dinner out. I had barely spoken at the restaurant that evening. My body was there, but my mind was somewhere else. One question kept coming back to me the entire evening: *how is it possible to feel so much and nothing at the same time?*

The sergeant was doing the legwork of gathering information from the school districts in Michigan where Chris had worked. Though I saw an eventual end to the legal process, I wasn't sure I saw an end to the void. I didn't know how to get back to the person I was, the life I was building before Chris's arrest shattered everything. I wanted to feel joy in the presence of my children, my husband, my work—but there was a hole where my joy used to live, vacuumed out of me in an instant. The only thing that mattered was solving the mystery of what had happened to me years ago. If I could do that, maybe I could be happy again.

Pulling into the driveway, I whispered to Ian, "I need to talk to you."

He sighed. *"Really?"*

The irritability in his voice gripped my insides. I shot him a look. "Real nice, Ian."

His eyes fell down to his lap. "I didn't mean it like that. I'm sorry."

Ian had become increasingly frustrated every time we talked about Chris. I was a broken record, and Ian hated the song I was stuck on. *Chris this* and *Chris that. Chris. Chris. Chris.* I knew I was hurting Ian, but I didn't know how to stop, because I didn't know how to stop hurting or how to stop wanting something that was always just out of reach.

"Megan, the things that happened to you weren't romantic," Ian had said to me earlier that summer. "That man cared nothing about you. You were sexually assaulted."

Scenes flashed inside my head, of Chris sitting across from me at a restaurant table, asking about my life, telling me about his work, smiling at me. I saw us walking down a snowy street holding hands. I saw everything playing like a movie in fast forward, and none of what I saw was bad.

I told Ian, "When I think of sexual assault, I think of a child lying in their bed and someone coming into their room at night."

Ian's voice hardened. "I think of a girl being locked in a band room by her teacher."

I felt like Chris had left an imprint on my brain, something that was now a part of me, that I couldn't separate myself from. It was obvious the burden I'd become on my husband. I could see what I was doing to my family. I was a burden on myself.

Once the boys were in bed, Ian and I went into the spare bedroom and shut the door. I took a deep breath and tried to ignore how begrudging Ian looked lying on his back, hands resting on his abdomen as I sat cross-legged facing him.

"Something's wrong," I said. "I'm not happy,"

Ian didn't move. "I know you're not happy."

"I feel like I'm losing you. Like you're becoming a shell of a person. We aren't affectionate like we used to be, and I think you resent me for things that have happened in the past."

Ian had never blamed me for what happened when I was a child. I was referring to a different past—the mistakes I'd made in our marriage; the injuries I had inflicted in our almost eleven years together. Like choosing to leave a job without his consent, or leaving him to take care of the boys *after* he'd had a late night of DJing because I was too hung over to get out of bed.

There are hard times in every marriage, but what was happening now—my trauma, the investigation, Ian's guilt—it was like pouring alcohol into every unhealed wound, a burning reminder of each disappointment and failure.

Ian continued to stare up at the ceiling, eyes fixed and glossy. "You're not wrong about the resentment. I'm trying not to be."

Reluctantly, I asked him, "Why haven't you called a therapist yet?" I didn't want to bring this up again, but it seemed like an obvious point. For months we had talked about the idea of him also going to therapy to help deal with stress, but he hadn't made the move toward finding one. The one time he came with me to a therapy appointment, he wouldn't open up about anything. He said he was angry, but it wasn't something I could fix. He had to do it himself.

"I've been busy. I just haven't found the time for that."

Bullshit, I thought. Here I was, going to therapy every week, reading self-help books, journaling, watching videos about mental health, taking daily walks. What was Ian doing to heal? Why was this all on me to fix us?

I'd always thought our marriage was indestructible, a fortress that could withstand anything. Now, I saw there was a limit to how much our marriage could take. In order to save it, I needed to take drastic action. To fly a distress flag from the highest mast and shout, *Help me! I need a sign that you're there! I'm going to drown soon if you don't come to my rescue!*

The lonelier I felt in my own life, the more I longed for a different one. I needed to be wanted. Touched. Held. I needed to feel something other than sad and miserable.

"I feel like I could screw up in our marriage," I said. "I've fantasized about getting dressed up and going to a bar in some exotic place, just so someone will hit on me."

I was sure this would stir something fierce in Ian. In my head I was screaming, *Go ahead! Get angry! Yell at me! Do something!* I was sure this would stir something fierce in Ian.

But he remained subdued despite my words. Motionless. Blank. He drew in a slow, labored breath and said. "I know I need to take steps toward being in a better place mentally and emotionally. I'll call and make an appointment."

Weeks later, Ian still hadn't called a therapist. Nothing had changed since our talk, except for the anger and resentment that continued to build inside me.

Then, out of nowhere, I got a text from my father. *Hey honey. I hope you're doing okay. I just wanted you to know, I might be leaving Cheryl.*

I stared at the words on my phone screen in disbelief. I was fourteen again, riding with him back to Mom and Randy's, my brother Zach asleep in the backseat, my father saying, *Cheryl and I might be getting a divorce.* I was so upset and confused back then. Now I was just livid. I had been drowning for months, with barely any communication from my father—and no wonder, because he was too busy dealing with his own problems. It seemed like he was always so focused on his own life that he didn't have space to care about mine.

Growing up, my father would say, "No one can love you as much as I do, because you're my blood." Then he wouldn't reach out to me for weeks. And I told myself, it didn't matter that we didn't spend that much time together. I knew he loved me, because fathers are supposed to love their daughters. Why was it I had worked so hard my entire life to be loved and I was still coming up short? All my life, I tried to be the best I could be. To follow the rules. To be good and smart and talented. Where did it get me? Why did these men get to do whatever they wanted?

I couldn't separate the anger I was feeling toward my father from the anger I was feeling toward Ian and, for the first time, Chris. I was angry with all of them. I needed them and where were they?

Fathers are *supposed* to love their daughters . . .

. . . Teachers are *supposed* to care for their students . . .

. . . *I'll call and make an appointment* . . .

I was getting tired of trying to do the right thing. Of constantly struggling when others got to take the easy way out. I told Ian I was unhappy. I told him I could screw up. He promised he would take action and he didn't, which meant he didn't love me enough. He no longer loved me the way he used to.

Somewhere, buried under the trauma and grief, I must have known—the problem wasn't that Ian didn't love me. The problem was the lens through which I viewed love.

2003

I couldn't wait to leave Flint. I was eighteen and preparing to move into my dorm room at Central Michigan University where I'd been accepted as a Music Education Major. My last year of high school, I toured several universities—the University of Michigan, Western Michigan, Michigan State—but in the end, I only auditioned for one school. CMU was ninety minutes from my house, which meant I would be away at college but could easily go home for a weekend or holiday.

Unlike some of the other music buildings I visited, CMU's was brightly lit and fairly new, with windows in almost every room. Also, it was the university Chris had attended during his undergrad. He was far from the only reason I'd chosen CMU, but it made me feel connected to him, to walk the halls he'd walked, to learn from some of the same professors he'd learned from.

Before Sean and I broke up that summer, we fought constantly about what would happen when I went away to a university while he continued living at home attending community college. He was either accusing me of cheating or declaring that I *would* cheat on him once I moved away, which was confusing since he was the one who had gone behind my back multiple times with other girls, sometimes having secret online conversations, sometimes having more.

One evening, Sean and I were on our way to have a dinner date when he said, "Everyone thinks you're this goody-goody Christian girl, but I know the truth."

I stared at him from the passenger seat. It wasn't an angry stare . . . I was in awe of him. How someone who was supposed to love me could so casually break me into a million pieces. I wasn't sure what *truth* he was referring to. All I knew was that this was the cruelest thing Sean had ever said to me. How could I stay with someone who didn't see the best in me? Who believed I was every mistake I'd ever made, every flaw and imperfection that stained my otherwise pristine reputation, as if there was such a thing. When I lashed out in frustration and Sean yelled, "Megan, what do you want from me?!" I began listing off all the qualities I was looking for in a boyfriend and eventual husband: kind, thoughtful, loyal, someone who behaved like a Christian. At the very least, someone who didn't make me jealous constantly.

Sean threw his hands up in the air. "Megan, the guy you're imagining doesn't exist."

For what felt like the hundredth time, I grew tired of feeling like the worst version of myself. I didn't want to be in a relationship defined by constant turmoil and sadness. So, I broke up with Sean. Again.

Not long after, I sent a text to Chris. *Are you free soon?*

CHRIS: Hey, Megan. I'm free next weekend.
MEGAN: Great. Can I come to your place?

"Tonight's the night," I said to myself, as I steered my car into the parking lot of a large apartment complex with multiple floors and wings. I took a right in front of the main entrance to the building and parked in my usual spot. Then I picked up my phone and sent a text: *I'm here.* I checked my purse, grabbed the overnight bag from the back seat and strolled up the sidewalk to the nearest door.

I waited, peering through the slotted window into the apartment stairwell. Like clockwork, I saw Chris striding toward me. He pushed open the heavy door between us. "*Heyyy,* Megan," he said.

Similar to his apartment in Davison, the Wixom apartment was remarkably clean and bare, almost to the point of sterility. There were minimal possessions present, only what was necessary to live. No sentimental hangings or keepsakes of any kind. No framed pictures of friends or family members.

Chris asked if, instead of going to the theater that night, I wanted to watch a movie at his place. I was excited to stay in. I wouldn't have to wonder what the restaurant waiter was thinking while serving us or who we might run into from his school while waiting to buy movie tickets in the theater lobby.

I watched him thumb through his collection of DVDs. "Have you seen *When Harry Met Sally?*"

I hadn't. But I knew that I liked Billy Crystal from the movie *City Slickers*, which my parents had rented multiple times.

He inserted the DVD and sat down beside me—not close enough to be touching, but that was okay. Since we had often met in public places where he couldn't openly hold my hand or kiss me, I was used to waiting for him to make a move. At the Wixom apartment, it wasn't unusual for him to wait until we had gone to bed before he would begin touching me. But the second we were under the covers, he'd instantly morph into Rhett Butler. *You should be kissed, and often, and by someone who knows how.* He knew how to expertly caress and hold me, how to fulfill my craving for freedom and my desire for safety. It was something I anticipated long before we retired to the bedroom.

Chris had built a snow globe world around us, everything perfectly placed, where we could hide together, away from conflict, from the judgment of outsiders. He was the one place I could go where there were only good feelings.

The movie began with a compilation of short scenes, a series of older couples reminiscing about their love stories. Chris and I were just like these couples, or would be someday. One woman said, "We both looked at each other, and it was just as though not a single day had gone by." That's the way it was with us. It could be months between visits, but when we were together, nothing had changed. It didn't matter how much time had passed or how I had tried to live a life without him. It was like not a single day had passed. *He was the same. He was exactly the same.*

When the ending credits played "It Had to Be You," Chris stood up and offered his hand to me.

I shook my head, laughing.

"C'mon," he said. He took my hand and pulled me up from the couch. He brought me to him, one arm wrapped around my back, the other holding tightly to my hand. Cheek to cheek we swayed back and forth to the music—Harry Connick Jr. crooning in one ear, Chris humming a wordless tune in the other. He had never spoken the words "I love you," but he didn't need to. It was obvious to me: *We're dancing like this because he loves me . . . . We continue to see each other because he can't let me go . . . . No one could act this way and not be in love.*

At bedtime, I burrowed into the dark-shaded comforter and waited for Chris to join me. He emerged from the bathroom wearing a fresh T-shirt and boxers. He pulled back the covers from his side and climbed under the sheets, scooting inward until he was close enough to kiss me, starting with my mouth then quickly moving to my ear, jawline and neck. Had this been like any other night together, I could have predicted precisely what would happen and how. But that night, I was determined to change the script.

Straddling him in the lacy, white undergarment set I'd picked out for this exact occasion, I leaned over him, kissing him and bracing myself on his pillow while he ran his hands up and down my body.

"What are you thinking?" I asked in the brief moments our lips were not touching.

"I'm thinking about how hot you are . . . . What are *you* thinking?"

"I'm thinking I want to have sex with you."

There was just enough artificial light coming through the window to see the look of surprise on his face. "Are you sure?" he asked. He pushed the curtain of hair back from my face, as if to get a better look at me. "Are you sure this is what you want?"

Most guys would jump at the opportunity to have sex, no questions asked. Chris's obvious concern for me made me want him that much more. I leaned in and pressed my lips against his. "Yes. I'm sure."

I rolled off of him, dropping onto the bed as he got up, reached into the nightstand drawer, and retrieved a shiny plastic wrapper. He pulled his boxers down, tore open the plastic and rolled back the condom. I had only ever seen sections of his bare body. Whenever we touched, there was always some *skin* and some *clothing*. To see him standing upright and naked made me feel strangely out of place, almost like I should be asking permission to watch. This strangeness did not translate to something being wrong, just different.

What did I expect? Of course sex with Chris was going to be slightly strange. I was eighteen and he was thirty-one. He had been my teacher. I wasn't blind to those facts, but I relegated them to the footnotes section of our story. Yes, he had been my teacher, but more importantly, he was a human being. I knew that better than anyone else.

I kept my body soft as he climbed back into bed. While kissing me, he used his weight to turn me on to my back, rolling with me so he was positioned on top. He guided my underwear down my freshly shaven legs, then he undid the front clasp of my bra and slid the straps down my shoulders, gently pulling the stiff lace away from me and dropping it beside the bed.

Now there was only *skin.*

Pressed beneath him, I found myself drifting somewhere between pleasure and pensiveness. It felt good to be wanted by him, to please him, but my mind was working to make sense of his body, which no longer felt like one entity but a conglomerate of human parts—arms, legs, and torso—moving independently toward one goal. As he continued to rock back and forth, my head fell to my left, where I gazed into the dark cove near the bathroom and vanity. Part of me was in the bed and part of me was in the cove.

When he finished, Chris went to the bathroom to dispose of the condom, taking his T-shirt and boxers with him. A minute later, he emerged in his usual nighttime attire and returned to my side, relaxing onto his back and pulling me in close. "Was that your first time?"

I didn't understand. If he thought it might be my first time, why didn't he act like it when we were having sex? He wasn't rough, but he wasn't careful either. He didn't ask what I was feeling, if it hurt, what he could do to make the experience better for me.

"No," I said.

He tilted his head toward me. "Who was your first?"

"Sean." I said it like he should've known.

Chris chuckled, jostling me in his arms as if wanting me to laugh along. Then he smoothed my hair down and kissed me on the forehead. It was reminiscent of the way a parent might pity a child who'd gotten super glue on their hands and then touched their face.

Was it an odd reaction? Maybe. But doubt was not welcome in that bedroom. Neither was anything else that threatened our snow globe world. So I focused on how it felt to be tucked into his side, molded to him, while we talked about other things until we fell asleep in each other's arms.

In the morning, "Annie's Song" played on the alarm clock. I heard the rustling of sheets as Chris got up to turn off the alarm. He crawled back into bed and nestled behind me.

"Don't. Want. To. Get. Up," he grumbled, punctuating each word like an obstinate child.

"You shower first," I said.

"Why? So you can stay in bed longer?"

I turned my head over my shoulder and smirked. "Exactly."

"*Brat,*" he said, nudging me. As soon as he was up, I closed my eyes and went back to sleep.

Mornings at Chris's were quiet. While I got cleaned up and dressed, he'd be in the kitchen or the living room watching TV, always a news or weather channel. Sometimes I would bring my own shampoo and conditioner, other times I'd use the purple bottle of Aussie he kept in the corner of the shower.

When I emerged from the bedroom, he said, "You want breakfast? I don't have to be at school for another hour or so." It never mattered what day of the week it was. Even if it was a Saturday, Chris usually had something he needed to do at work.

We always went to the same place for breakfast, the Big Boy just down the road from the apartment complex. Like usual, the restaurant was full of people that morning. There was always this fear in the back of my head that someone would recognize Chris while we were together. If they were to come over to our table, what would I say? *Hi! I'm a former student of Mr. Blackmer's . . . . Yep, I was just passing through this morning and thought it'd be nice to catch up . . . . Where am I coming from? Uh, I was visiting a friend in Novi last night.*

I didn't have any friends in Novi—and even if I did, telling someone that I was "just passing through" wouldn't have been an honest response. As much as I didn't want to be a liar, I was required to lie if I wanted to be with Chris. I had spent the last two years lying to my parents, my friends, my sometimes boyfriend, my church family, my grandparents. So it was a relief every time he and I made it out of a public place without being questioned. It was one less lie I had to tell.

The ride back from the restaurant was always my least favorite part of the visit because it meant our time together was ending and it was time for me to return to the real world.

Chris parked his car, then walked me to mine. I knew he wouldn't kiss me, it was too risky in broad daylight where his neighbors might see.

"I had fun. Thank you," I said, resisting the urge to hug him.

He smiled. "I'll see you later, Megan."

Driving home, I passed my old friend, the giant Jesus portrait above the Dixie Baptist Church sign. "ARE YOU ON THE RIGHT ROAD?" Jesus asked, with his deep brown puppy-dog eyes.

I glanced at him through the windshield, gave a salute, and said, "Yes, Jesus. I'm fine. You don't have to worry about me."

2019

September—Five months into the investigation

Memories of Chris were like songs I couldn't get out of my head, a greatest hits album that played in a never ending loop morning, afternoon, and night:

> TRACK 1—It's the winter of my junior year. I meet Chris at a restaurant inside Great Lakes Crossings, a mall on the outskirts of the suburbs of Detroit. I order coconut butterfly shrimp. We walk around for a bit and go to his car, which is parked outside the Bass Pro Shop The Great Outdoors. We make out for two hours while giant, fluffy snowflakes float down from the sky onto the windshield. Eventually, his is the only car in the parking lot. He drives me to my car, helps me brush the snow off the hood and roof. The crinkling of his Columbia jacket in my hands matches the crispness of the winter air, and as we say our goodbyes he holds my face in his hands and says, "When can I see you again?"
>
> TRACK 2—I'm seventeen. It's my second visit to Chris's apartment in Wixom. I arrive in a pastel purple pencil skirt, white slip-on sandals, and a floral spaghetti-strap top that's ruched on the sides of my chest with a small bow in the center. When I enter the apartment, Chris pins me to the wall, the full length of his body pressed against mine. My stomach does somersaults while he kisses me. He pulls away, grabs his keys from the kitchen table, and says, "Are you ready for dinner?"
>
> TRACK 3—Another winter. Chris invites me to meet him at Zehnder's, a restaurant in Frankenmuth, Michigan. At the dinner table, I fiddle with tiny plastic animal toothpicks that are buried in

my ice cream. We stand on a street corner, watching the horsedrawn carriages that pass by. "Maybe we can take a ride in one of those someday," he says.

TRACK 4—We're in Chris's car, on our way to the movie theater when Elton John's "I Guess That's Why They Call It the Blues" comes on the radio. He leans forward and twists the dial slightly to the right. I sit in the passenger seat amused, watching his head sway back and forth in time with the music. He's playful and content, looking like he doesn't have a care in the world.

TRACK 5—I offer to cook dinner at the apartment. I only know how to make one dish: a combination of chicken, peppers, and rice with a side of asparagus. I boil the asparagus because I don't know any better. Chris stays in the kitchen with me the entire time, sharing conversation. Then we sit together on the couch, eating and watching a movie. He never once mentions how rubbery the asparagus is.

TRACK 6—We're waiting in line for movie theater tickets, and Chris points to the poster on the wall advertising the newest Star Wars movie, *Episode III: Revenge of the Sith*. He loves Star Wars and knows I couldn't care less about it. "C'mon," he says, arms crossed and smiling down at me, "it has action, adventure, romaaance." He draws out the last word as he teasingly bumps his shoulder into mine. I smirk, roll my eyes, and shake my head. "Nice try," I say. "But, no."

TRACK 7—We're at a restaurant and Chris orders the only beer I've ever seen him drink—a Guinness, which spurs a conversation about Ireland. I joke that I've only been out of the country once, to Canada, for three hours. He smiles, his walnut brown eyes soft and assuring. He tells me, "You have plenty of time. You'll get a chance to travel someday."

TRACK 8—I make a plan to observe the choir director at Chris's school, Walled Lake Northern, so I drive down the night before and stay at the Wixom apartment. Chris invites me into his home office where he sits down, takes my hand, and gently pulls me onto his lap. He keeps one arm wrapped around me while he shows me pictures on his computer from a recent trip he's taken. The next day, he gives me a tour of the school's auditorium. We're in an enclosed space between two sets of double doors when he surprises me by pressing me to the wall and giving me one long kiss goodbye.

TRACK 9—It's the early hours of the morning. Chris and I are lying awake in his bed. I'm tucked into his side, my head against his chest, his heart beating against my temple. He runs his fingers through my hair as we share stories until we can't keep our eyes open. In the morning, the picking of a mandolin rouses me from sleep. John Denver's voice drifts into my head, accompanied by the scent of Chris's pillow.

When Sergeant Perry called, his voice was hopeful. "I've presented the case to the prosecutors. Before they sign the arrest warrant, they want to meet with you. They'll be reaching out in the next few days."

I couldn't believe it. *They're really going to arrest him.*

Despite Ian and me growing apart, we were hanging on. Even though Ian had still not found a therapist, he made an effort to talk about his feelings instead of trying to ignore them. Chris's arrest would be our saving grace; the only thing more powerful than the grieving and the longing had been the belief that God would use my story for some greater purpose. The past five months had been excruciating, but it would all be worth it because God was going to give me everything my heart desired. The chance to see Chris again. To prove he was never the person I thought he was. A chance to find closure. And then, I'd be free. I'd get my life back.

Two weeks went by with no call from the prosecutor's office.

On September 17th, I received a text from Sergeant Perry. *Call me when you have time to talk.* I couldn't shake the feeling that something was wrong. When the sergeant picked up, his voice was somber, apologetic. "The prosecutors say they aren't going to pursue charges against Christopher."

"They're dropping the case?"

"Yes."

My nose burned as water rose to my eyes. "Why?"

"The prosecutors say the statute of limitations didn't increase to fifteen years until 2018. Before that, it was ten. Too much time has passed. I'm so sorry, Megan."

Of all the reasons not to sign an arrest warrant, this was the last one I expected. The prosecutors had already reviewed the timeline of my abuse before agreeing to pursue an investigation. They had invested time and money into the case, flown the sergeant and his partner down to Florida. There was my testimony, the AIM conversation between me and Chris that supported the allegations, the interview with Chris, the interviews with classmates and family to corroborate my statement. Why would they stop now?

"I don't understand. There's just *nothing*? That's it?"

"I can try to work with the prosecutors in Oakland County where you spent time with Christopher after he moved. Maybe I can get a different answer from them."

"What will that do? These are state laws."

"It might be worth a shot."

"Would we have to start all over?"

He waited a moment, then reluctantly said, "Yes."

I wanted to scream. Go back to the beginning? And for what? Another five months of waiting, just to be told *no* again? My heart couldn't take it. If the Genesee County prosecutors couldn't prosecute, or didn't want to prosecute, why would Oakland County be any different? A place where I didn't attend high school, a place that would have no reason to care about me at all.

"I don't want you to take the case to another county. I can't keep doing this."

"If you change your mind, let me know."

When I hung up, I collapsed onto the bed, sobbing into my hands. My head spun thinking about all the losses I'd been grieving since April: the death of Chris as the person I knew and loved, the life I had before his arrest, disconnection from everyone and everything that used to bring me joy, and now, the final nail in the coffin—the unmistakable rejection of my story as having any real value.

The police had been my only hope for answers, my only channel of control. They had asked for help, and I made the choice to come forward, believing they would help me in return and use my story to help others. With that hope gone, I needed to take control some other way. It was clear to me I was in this alone. No one could help me except me.

Becca's words rang through my aching head. *Two things can be true at the same time*. I wanted to know the truth about my past *and* I wanted the truth to be that Chris loved me. I believed that Chris was the source of my pain *and* I believed he was the antidote that could make it stop. I was devastated the police couldn't arrest Chris *and* relieved that, now, nothing was stopping me from going straight to the source for answers.

I gathered my composure and called the sergeant back. "Since the case is closed, would it be illegal for me to call Chris?"

There was a slant of confusion in his voice. "No. But if he asks you not to contact him, you have to listen."

"That's fine," I said. "I just have some things I need to say."

"Let me know what happens when you try to contact him. I'd be curious to know."

Dizzy with anticipation, I laced up my sneakers, grabbed my phone, and marched down the driveway to the sidewalk. As I strode toward the end of the street, I paused to type several words into the text bar. *Chris, this is Megan. The police are not involved in this conversation. I just want to talk to you. If that's not possible, I'd like to send you a letter.*

I read through the message ten or so times, exhaled my fear, and pressed send.

Lightning pulsed through my veins as I took off down the street again, pounding the pavement as a jumble of thoughts filled my head. *What if he never sees the text? If he sees the text, will he know it's me? Will he recognize my number, after all these years? Is he going to believe me about the police, or will he think it's a trick?*

One minute passed.

Two minutes.

I heard a sound that nearly knocked me to the ground—a single *ding* from my hand. I turned my phone over to look, and felt a rush of adrenaline when I saw the message. *Hey Megan—I'm in between appointments. Can I call you in 10 minutes?*

I stared at the words on the screen, examining the lines and curves of each letter strung together, offering a lifeline between us. *It's really him. It's Chris. He's back from the dead.*

I hurried home and sat down in one of the wicker chairs on the front porch. I tried to take slow breaths as my pulse throbbed in the palms of my hands. When the phone rang and Chris's number appeared on the screen, time slowed. I took a deep breath, slid the answer bar to the right, and pressed the phone to my cheek. "Hello?"

A familiar voice poured into my ear, decadent and drawn out. "Hey, Megan."

He sounded the same. *Exactly the same.* I tried to ignore the aching in my stomach and stay focused on what I came to do. I needed honest answers, so I needed him to know it was safe to talk to me. "Nothing is going to happen to you in Michigan," I said.

"I'm relieved to hear that," he said, his voice deflating like an untied balloon.

I expected him to ask why the investigation ended, but he didn't—which was better, because it meant I didn't have to explain my part in all of it. I saw my opening to seize the moment I'd been praying for, an opportunity to be heard by the person I needed most to listen. I had rehearsed this speech in my head hundreds of times. I was going to tell him everything I'd been wanting to but never thought I'd have the chance to say.

"As you can imagine, the past six months have been very confusing for me. I thought what happened between us was . . ." I wanted to say *real*—what happened between us was *real*, but the words were trapped in my throat. It felt too intimate to be talking like this. As my train of thought derailed, my confidence plummeted. I fumbled around for words, hoping to hear something on the other line—hums of agreement, words of affirmation, *anything*—but all I heard was my voice dropping into a void of silence. I began to wonder if I was making any sense at all, so I panicked and hurried to finish my thoughts, the words snowballing into one jumbled conclusion. I balked at my incompetence. I had sculpted the Michalangelo of speeches for this man, and instead I handed over the crayon scribblings of a small child.

"I don't mean to be melodramatic," Chris said. "It's not like I've thought about Megan Lucius every morning for the past twelve years . . . but I've never forgotten about you."

He used my maiden name. He knew that wasn't my name anymore. But it was the name he had called me by, from the very first day we met. *Megan . . . Lucius, is that right?* he'd said when I walked in for my eighth-grade audition. I liked him right away. I trusted him right away. Clearly, he wanted me to still believe I was special, someone worth remembering. He had dropped a shiny lure into the water—*plop*—and waited for me to bite.

Chris went on. "I have to be careful what I talk about. I can hear my lawyer's voice in my head right now. But I know I can say this to *you* and you'll understand."

I waited then, expecting him to offer up some apology for my pain, but instead he launched into how difficult the past five months had been for *him* . . . and just like that I was on the opposite side of the conversation, lending an ear to his woeful struggles.

He wasn't wrong that I'd be understanding. At least, I was trying to understand. I wanted to understand him. I wanted to understand everything about this situation. So I stayed quiet when I could have spoken. I stepped aside and let him have the floor. Several times he finished a statement with, "Does that make sense?" and I felt backed into a corner. If I challenged him in any way, he might stop talking to me, and I feared what that would do.

"You know those moments when you go left and you should have gone right? That's what moving to Florida was. I never should have moved here and left my friends and family. I was lonely."

Loneliness seemed a poor excuse for breaking the law. Lots of forty-year-olds get lonely. They drink. They get high. They watch movies. They sign up for eHarmony. They don't have sex with teenagers. But was he lying to me? Or was it not a lie, because he believed his own story?

I tried desperately to focus on his words instead of what I was feeling. For the first time in five months, I felt alive. *Really* alive. Chris's voice was soothing, like a warm, weighted blanket wrapped around me on a cool autumn night. It was the same voice that had inspired me to become a music teacher, to believe I was worthy of a love no other person my age could have, the first voice to speak *goodnight* and *good morning* into my ear as I had willingly laid defenseless in his bed.

"You know, the Michigan police came here to talk to me," he said.

This caught me by surprise, that Chris would openly acknowledge being visited by the police.

"They asked me why I would date someone your age. When I told them you were mature, one of the officers held his hands out in front of his chest to imitate someone with a large chest and said, 'She was mature, huh?'"

I shook my head. What a ridiculous tactic to, quote, unquote, "get on his level."

Chris told me he corrected the officer. "That's not what I meant . . . I meant, you could talk to her. Like you weren't talking to a kid." He paused. "Megan—they asked me if you were a *booty call*." I could tell by the tone of his voice he wanted me to be as appalled at this as he was. A *booty call*. What an off-the-wall suggestion. Booty calls didn't look like us. They didn't last for six years. You don't take a booty call to dinner, or cook with them, or dance with them in your living room. You don't hold them for hours and share stories late into the night.

At this point in the conversation, there was too much energy inside me to stay seated. I left the porch and began pacing my front yard.

"Appropriateness aside," he said. "I know in my heart I had genuine feelings for you. You were right in front of me every day. You were so easy to talk to . . ."

I could not stop my body from reacting to every word. When he said '*appropriateness aside*,' my muscles tensed with conflict. I knew he was trying to diminish what he had done—but then he jumped into talking about me and the way he saw me back then, about what his *heart* felt, and my bones seemed to soften.

". . . and I want you to know, I don't blame you for going to the police. You did the right thing."

How did he know this was something I needed to hear? For five long months, I'd been sick with worry over his reaction to me reporting him to the police. But he wasn't mad at all. He was sympathetic to it. Proud of me even, for doing the right thing. The moment I was nestled into the comfort of his approval, he said, "I was surprised to see them, though, because, you know, the situation with you was so different. What happened with this guy and what happened with you—the situations couldn't be more opposite. With him, it was purely physical. Does that make sense?"

My muscles tensed. It was the way he said "this *guy*." Not "this *boy*." It was then I felt a part of me split off from myself. The boy had always seemed more like an abstract idea than a person existing in tangible reality. He didn't have a face or a hair color, a group of friends or a favorite band. He was an out-of-focus image, barely a person. The few times I had gotten close to bringing the image into focus, a flicker of jealousy ignited in my gut, and shame re-blurred the lines.

The situations were different, though. That's what Chris said. Not just different. Complete opposites. With me, his heart was involved.

I could feel myself stepping into dangerous territory. Chris had taken my hand, he was leading me further and further into the forest, and I was gradually losing sight of the path that would lead me back out. I needed to take control, and fast.

"It does make sense," I said, my voice cloaked in trepidation. "But we were both—"

C'mon, Megan, say the word.

Children.

This boy and I . . . we were both children.

"—we were both . . . *young.*"

I was disappointed in myself for taking the easy way out. Why was I tip-toeing around everything? Walking on eggshells?

I don't want to ruin this. I need him to keep talking. I need him to not leave.

"I thought he was older," Chris said. "Not *much* older—but legal."

I was gobsmacked by this response—in complete and utter disbelief. He didn't sound ashamed at all. And I swore I could hear him snicker when he said "*not much older, but legal,*" as if he were laughing at his own private joke.

This should have been enough to make me turn and run in the opposite direction. But it wasn't. The small voice inside that whispered, *You should be afraid*, was quickly silenced by every other part of me that shouted, *I know this man*. I had nothing to be afraid of. He didn't mean what he was saying, he was just trying to make light of this so he could survive.

The longer I listened, the more difficult it was to separate truth from lies, elaboration from fabrication. Somehow, he knew what I wanted to hear and how he should say it, and even when his answers rang disjunct, I'd placate him with murmurs of agreeance and empathy.

I checked the time and realized Ian and the boys would be home any minute. "I have more questions," I said, "but I need some time to process this conversation. Can I call you again in a few weeks?" (A few weeks sounded good. It made me seem less needy.)

"I don't want to get you in trouble with your family, but you're welcome to call or text me anytime, day or night."

Of course it would get me in trouble with my family . . . . Despite his obscene offer, I couldn't help the elation I felt knowing he wanted to have more contact with me. I meant something to him. He wanted to be there for me.

I knew the conversation had to end, and already I was sick with longing. It was like being back on the bus my sophomore year headed home from *Blast!*, wishing I could rewind time and experience it all over again.

"I know this is strange to say, but you have someone in your corner," I said.

I could hear him smiling through the phone. "Thanks, Megan. And thank you for calling."

When we hung up, my final words lingered in the air like sulfur, pungent and rotten. *You have someone in your corner.* Why would I say that? I didn't condone his actions. I didn't condone child abuse. I had called to express how *I* was feeling and I ended up consoling *him.* How did I get so turned around? Desperate to preserve his words, I went into the house, grabbed my journal and jotted down everything I could remember about our conversation.

By early evening, the urge to text Chris began crawling under my skin, filling me with discomfort and dread. These feelings were not new to me. The difference now was that I had found a cure, a place I could go to alleviate my pain. And somehow, knowing this only seemed to intensify the feelings.

I texted Chris to give him an exact date and time I would call. *Thought it would be useful for your type-A brain*, I said, hoping he couldn't sense the desperation I felt to connect.

Haha. Sounds good, he responded. It wasn't much to go off of. Was I hoping he'd say more? What was I hoping he'd say?

My brain could not escape the hamster wheel. My body could not release its grip. But I had already used up every dose of comfort. If I reached out to him again, I might push him away, and that felt like the worst thing that could happen to me.

When he died, a part of me died with him. But now he was back, and losing him again would feel like a second death, one that I might not survive.

When I woke the next morning, it was clear to me I was in over my head. I didn't feel in control of myself, didn't trust what I was thinking or feeling. My gut would tell me one thing—*You shouldn't be talking to Chris. You need to stop this.*—but my mind would spin a web of justification for why I should continue down this path. *I need Chris. He has answers and I need answers or I'll never heal. I'm being a friend to someone who needs it. I'm being a Christian by showing forgiveness to someone who doesn't deserve it.*

What I *needed* to do was tell someone what was happening before things got out of hand. I planned to meet Ian during his lunch break and confess to the phone call. But before that, there was something else I had to do.

"You're calling me sooner than expected," Chris said when he picked up the phone, a hint of smugness to his voice.

My hands were already shaking, my chest balling up into a monstrous knot. "Listen—I really appreciate you talking to me yesterday . . . but I love my family and I don't think we should have any communication with each other."

"It's okay, Megan. I didn't expect you to call anyway. Besides, having secret conversations probably isn't good for either of us right now."

I thought he would be sad or disappointed about not talking to me anymore, but there wasn't an inkling of either. And it killed me. I was terrified we would hang up the phone and he would forget about me forever.

It took everything I had to squeak out the word "goodbye."

"You take care, Megan," he said.

As quickly as he had come back into my life, he was gone again.

I doubled over in my chair, holding clenched fists to my chest and choking out tears. The pressure on my heart was so immense, I thought it might tear in two. Rocking back and forth, I prayed to God, *I'm begging you . . . . Please . . . . Please, take this pain away from me . . . .*

It was a miracle I stopped crying long enough to visit Ian during one of his work breaks. As he exited one of the school buildings, he saw me sitting in the parking lot and climbed into the vehicle.

"Hey there," he said, happy to see me, not yet noticing the redness of my eyes, the blotchiness of my complexion.

"I talked to Chris Blackmer," I said.

Ian's head made a jerking motion. "You *what*?"

"Yes—but I told him we couldn't talk to each other again."

Ian closed his eyes in what looked like an effort to stay calm. With a slight tremor in his voice, he said, "Why would you talk to him?"

"I needed answers. I was so devastated when the investigation ended—"

"What did he say?" Ian interrupted.

"He told me things were different with me, that he really cared about me. He said he didn't want to get me in trouble with my family, but I could call or text him anytime day or night."

"*Asshole*," Ian said, staring angrily out the windshield. "Obviously, he thought he was still talking to sixteen-year-old Megan."

I didn't know what I could safely tell Ian about the conversation, so I left parts out. I worried, *Did Chris tell me things his lawyer wouldn't have allowed? Did I know things I shouldn't*? I censored the things I thought or said that I didn't want Ian to know: *I thought you and I were real.... You have someone in your corner....*

"I need to get to class," he said, still shaken. "We can talk about this more later. I love you."

When I called Sergeant Perry to tell him I had spoken with Chris, he seemed surprised. "What did Christopher say to you?"

"He said things were different with me, that he had genuine feelings for me."

"He sounds like a sociopath."

I agreed with him, hoping if I said the words, my body would absorb them. Sure, Chris displayed characteristics of someone with a personality disorder. Sociopaths are capable of breaking social norms and laws, they don't respect boundaries, they use charm and deception to manipulate others and get what they want. But I also saw how all humans are capable of these characteristics to some degree. I didn't want to label Chris as one specific thing, good or bad.

My thoughts shifted back to the Michigan investigation. As much as it had pained me to think about Chris being arrested and tried for my alleged abuse, the investigation gave me purpose and security. Without it, my purpose shifted to connecting with Chris, getting answers for myself. But the investigation in Florida was ongoing. What if the detectives in Florida reached out to me? What if my purpose was still to tell my story?

"When you were in Florida, did the detectives there say they wanted to use my statement?" I asked the sergeant.

"It's always possible, but they didn't say they were interested in using anything from Michigan."

The point of me coming forward in April was to help the investigators in Florida. The articles had said that anyone with information should call the Michigan State Police, so I did. One article said that if Michigan police received any information about Chris Blackmer, they were ready to assist the police in Florida. Well, I gave them what they wanted. I gave them valuable information. Now they weren't even interested in what I had to say?

I noticed a rapid clicking sound in the background of the phone line. "Are you typing?" I asked the sergeant.

"No," he said flatly.

"Okay, well, I just wondered if you were recording this conversation."

"I'm not." More clicking.

A flurry of paranoia rushed through me. *He's lying*, I thought, and suddenly I felt like I was the one on trial. Was he going to use my words against me in some way? Was he going to tell Chris that I said he was a sociopath? Why wouldn't the sergeant just tell me the truth?

Sergeant Perry said the Genesee County prosecutors would like to offer me some money for therapy and, if I wanted, an opportunity to sit down with them and share my story. It was kind of them to offer something, but compared to real justice, it was a poor consolation prize. If they weren't going to take action, why would I relive all my pain in front of them, especially when they were now contributors to that pain?

I respectfully declined the offer.

"I'm really sorry, Megan. Hey, maybe someday you'll write a book about all this."

The rest of the day was spent alternating between fits of crying and periods of numbness. One moment, I couldn't stop tears from running down my face, and the next I was staring off into the distance with no desire to return. I had been so close to having what I needed, but I couldn't have it because what I wanted was for Chris to make everything better.

Ian and I rode together to pick up the boys from school. On the way, he looked over at me and said, "It's like you're experiencing the heartbreak you should have felt over ten years ago."

How could he be so understanding about this? Either he was suppressing his emotions for my sake, or he didn't care enough to be jealous. In recent years, he had started to joke, "*Well*, if you divorce me . . . " I wondered if somewhere deep down he was preparing for something like that. I wondered if he *wanted* me to divorce him. If it would be a relief to him.

By evening, grief had exhausted me into hopelessness.

My mind and body had been stuck in overdrive for five long months—never resting, always wanting, desperate for relief. I opened my journal and wrote, *The pain in my chest is almost unbearable.* What could I possibly do to get rid of this pain? To free myself of this neverending torture? I had tried everything and nothing was working.

It's Chris. Chris is the key to understanding all of it. What happened back then. What's happening now. Why my life was falling apart. *I'm running out of time.* In a matter of months, Chris could be going to prison and I would lose my chance to get real closure. I had been too brash in cutting off contact. If only I'd stuck to my original plan of waiting a few weeks to call him, everything would have been fine. Instead, I messed everything up.

I can fix this. I can make things right again.

Hastily, I picked up my phone and sent a text: *I'm not ready to stop talking.*

At first, the communication with Chris was sporadic—a few texts here and there about nothing, really. The few times we talked on the phone, he told me how his day was, but there wasn't time for much else. I chose small windows of time to call him, like my drive home from work, so I wouldn't stay on the phone too long. I'd say to myself, *I just need a few minutes*, but then I'd end up driving around the block ten times just to listen to his voice longer.

For three weeks, I vowed each morning to get through the day without talking to Chris, and each day I broke that vow. It felt impossible to function without some communication from him. It was as if a million tiny weights were attached to my fingers, arms, legs, every movement of my body oppressed by crushing anxiety. The second I'd hear from him, the weight would lift and I'd be able to move, for a little while, at least. Then the cycle would start all over again.

Though talking to Chris offered physical relief, I was tormented by the constant paranoia about where my phone was and who could see it. Ian had never been the jealous type nor the kind of husband who'd monitor my calls or texts, but if he happened to look and see a number he didn't recognize and ask who it was, I'd have to lie to his face. To solve this problem, I saved Chris's number in my contacts using Andi, the name of my best friend from high school. Andi and I had reconnected since the arrest, so I knew Ian wouldn't think twice about seeing her name on my phone screen. I didn't realize I was breaking a decades-long promise to her that I'd made when we were sixteen. *Don't use me as your excuse*, she'd said.

One night, I told Ian I needed to stop by the store for a few things. As soon as I was on the road, I called Chris. We talked as I meandered the store searching for the few items on my shopping list. By the time I was leaving, it wasn't enough for me to hear his voice. I needed something more. "I want to be able to see your face so I know you're telling me the truth," I said.

He chuckled. "Yeah, that's fine."

"Okay. I'll call you when I'm back in my car."

When Chris appeared on my phone screen, I was shocked to see a man at least twenty pounds thinner than I'd expected, with a scrabbly salt-and-pepper beard in place of the clean-shaven face I remembered. His hair was short on the sides but longer on the top, strategically tousled, making him look younger than forty-seven, though the patches of silver near his temples gave him away.

"You have facial hair!" I said, laughing.

He smiled, shrugging and allowing his head to tilt toward his shoulder.

What did I look like to *him?* I immediately regretted wearing my glasses that morning instead of my contacts. I hated how glasses aged me and distorted the shape of my face.

In a comedic gesture of vanity, I removed my glasses. "Is that better?"

Chris gestured with his pointer finger for me to hold on while he retrieved an object from the table behind him. When he returned, he charmingly placed a pair of glasses on his face and re-tilted his head. His cheeks, which had maintained some of their roundness, lifted to reveal a knowing smile.

I noticed it was closing in on 10:30. I sent Ian a text. *I'm safe. I'm just taking my time shopping.*

IAN: Okay, have fun. I'm going to bed. Love you.

I was surprised he didn't seem concerned that I was out later than I'd ever been. But what reason would he have to be concerned? I had never lied to him about where I was or what I was doing. I hated lying, but the idea of waking up to a world where I would never speak to Chris again felt like a death sentence. Not a physical death, but death by being forever imprisoned in a wasted, unhappy life of grief and loneliness. Given the choice, I'd have chosen physical death.

"You can ask me anything, and I'll give you an answer," Chris said.

I asked him why he never got married. Who he'd dated over the years. He always answered in a way that at first seemed direct but would detour to another closely related story or topic, and by that time I was unwilling to make him circle back to dive deeper into the original question. I figured, if he wanted to dive deeper into it, he would have. I was thankful to have *any* answers.

"Are you gay?" I said. It felt like a bold question, one I never would have dared ask when I was younger.

"I'm bi. But I prefer women. It's probably 70/30."

I wondered how to phrase the next question, the one I'd been thinking about since the day I found out about his arrest. "Am I the only one?" I could have asked, *Am I the only student you've had a relationship with?* But it felt too pointed. He didn't need me to spell it out for him. And besides, if I left it open-ended, it might reveal something even more valuable.

He leaned in, arms crossed, and spoke slowly. "You are the *first* and the *last*. . . . I told you. It couldn't have been more opposite from what happened with that guy. I haven't even spoken to him in two years."

Two years.

An alarm went off in my head. The timestamp on the original video the police had confiscated was from 2014. If they stopped talking two years ago, it would have been 2017, which meant they would have been in contact for at least three years. *How many years did we spend time together?*

I looked at the clock that now read several minutes past midnight. "I really need to go. This should probably be the last time we talk like this," I said.

"Whatever you want to do, I understand. But I want you to know, I'm here if you ever want to talk. I don't care what my lawyer says. I will never ignore you."

When I pulled into the driveway, the house was dark. I crept into the bedroom, crawled under the covers and tried to think of only good things.

The talking continued, and with it the secrecy. The longer I left my world for Chris's, the more my world unraveled. I didn't want to get out of bed in the morning. I struggled to interact with my children, my husband, or my work with any authenticity. I no longer wanted to read my favorite books or write in my journal. The dishes and the laundry and the mail piled up. I avoided things that reminded me of my old life because I could no longer face them with integrity. I was a fraud. I tried to go through the motions, but it was as if toxic lead was pumping through my bloodstream, poisoning my ability to move, think, or feel.

The only time I felt relief was when Chris was there—in my thoughts, in my text messages, on the phone. But even then, the relief was short-lived. While I physically yearned for Chris's company, I was often lonely in his presence. He was likely to monopolize our conversations, talking for a straight hour without asking me a single question. At first, I thought this was because he'd been alone for so long, he just needed someone to talk to. I was willing to be a listening ear for him. In many ways, I felt responsible for him. Now I wondered if this was just how he was. He never said, *Tell me more about that,* or, *That's really interesting.* When he did grant me an opportunity to speak, I was hypervigilant in gauging his reactions. The exact moment his eyes would lose their luster, I'd search for something clever to say or I'd hurry to finish my thought for fear of boring him. I didn't remember him being this way when I was younger. I remembered feeling like his attention was easy to hold. That I mattered more.

Just as I'd begin to grow tired or impatient, Chris would boost his attentiveness and charm. He'd flatter me, tell me things he knew I wanted to hear. One night when we were on a FaceTime call, he must have noticed how often I checked my own video to see that I was holding my head just right, that my face appeared thin and my hair draped perfectly behind my back. After we'd hung up, he sent me a text. *In case you're doubting it, you looked beautiful tonight.*

At some level, I knew the thing I was depending on to feel alive was the very thing that was killing me. I needed to stop. I'd gotten what I wanted, to talk to Chris again, but I couldn't go on this way forever. I couldn't spend the rest of my life lying.

"Have you gotten what you wanted from him?" Becca asked at our session. She was the only person who knew I'd been talking to Chris.

"Yes. I think so."

"And what did you want from him?"

"I wanted to know who he really was so I could understand what happened to me."

"And do you think you know?"

"I think so. He's not really a mystery to me anymore. In some ways, he's the same as I remember, but he's also different."

"Do you think you see him differently because you're an adult and not a child anymore?"

"I think that's a big part of it."

If this was a test, I was clearly acing it. I had all the right answers, and I believed them just enough to be confident in my ability to end contact with Chris. I told Becca what I was planning to say to him during our next—and hopefully last—conversation. I had written it down in my journal so I wouldn't have to remember it when the time came. *I'm glad we've gotten an opportunity to talk, but this needs to stop. We can still walk away without there being irrevocable damage.*

When Chris and I spoke again, I kept my journal in my lap, my eloquent goodbye written out and ready to go. But after another hour of listening to him and speaking very few words, I didn't feel the need to say the things I'd prepared. There were no ceremonial farewells. I told him goodbye as if we were going to talk again the next day.

Except, I didn't text or call the next day. Or the day after that. I was done.

The weekend of October 4th, I traveled downstate to give a presentation at a college. During my drive home that Monday, the sun was shining brightly. I had gone four days without talking to Chris.

I congratulated myself. *It's over. I did it.* I had climbed a mountain, and, standing tall at its peak, I could see a long way out into the blue skies that were all the possibilities of my life. I saw that my marriage could be healed, that I could be present with my children again. I could dream and grow and live fully and authentically without fear.

On Tuesday, I was unpacking my suitcase from the weekend trip when my phone dinged. It was a text from my father: *Honey, your grandpa had a stroke. I'm on my way to Florida right now to see him.*

I read the text repeatedly, my head spinning in disbelief.

. . . your grandpa had a stroke . . .

. . . I'm on my way to Florida right now . . .

. . . I'm on my way to Florida . . .

. . . Florida . . .

And just like that, every promise I had made to myself about not communicating with Chris was crushed under the weight of serendipity. Every logical thought I had used to battle the illogical longing defeated in an instant. Chris and I had been talking for less than a month, and now my grandpa's life was in jeopardy? My grandpa, who was one of the strongest and healthiest men I knew. Going to see him would be the only conceivable grounds for being in the same state as Chris. I knew Ian's work wasn't going to let him miss several days. If I went to Florida, I would have to go alone.

I fell back onto the bed and looked up at the ceiling as if God were hovering above, and said, "What do you want from me?" If the universe didn't want me to go to Florida, why did it put it right there in front of me? As a cruel test of my endurance?

In my grief-warped brain, the complexities of this situation were so vast, so indescribably lacking in one true north, that it was impossible for me to know what path I was supposed to follow. My body was torturing me, aching and screaming, *If you don't go to Florida, you'll never be happy again. You'll spend the rest of your life regretting the chance you didn't take.*

That night, I sent Chris a text message. *My grandpa in Arcadia had a stroke.*

Seconds later, a response appeared. *Arcadia? That's not far from where I am.*

I stood in the doorway to the bedroom, watching Ian fold and stack clothes on our bed. "I think maybe I should go down to Florida . . . " I said, ". . . to be with my father and my grandpa."

I imagined Ian turning to me and saying, *Are you kidding? I can't let you fly across the country alone.* He knew I hadn't been the same person the past five months. I'd been honest about my feelings for Chris and my worry that I might be capable of putting our marriage in jeopardy. And now I was asking to go to Florida? I was sure this was a step too far and he would stop me. Part of me wanted him to stop me, to hold me down as I kicked and screamed and begged to go. I wanted him to tell me, *I can't let you do this to yourself. I love you too much.*

Ian finished folding a T-shirt, then looked at me earnestly. "I was thinking you probably should do that."

Maybe he thought a state created enough distance to keep me away from Chris. He still didn't understand. An entire country wasn't wide enough. Twelve years wasn't long enough. Whatever Chris had done to me, it superseded space and time.

After everything we'd been through since Chris was arrested, Ian still saw me as the same woman he'd married, someone who could never betray him. For him, the history of our marriage was still intact; the minutes, hours, and days that had gradually built a foundation of love and trust still accounted for. Even if he suspected something might be wrong, he could never fathom what grief had made me capable of.

I didn't want to destroy my life. I wanted to *save* it. Whatever I had been doing the past five months wasn't working. I was a prisoner inside my hollow body, wandering around in the dark unknown, searching for answers of how to be whole again. This was my chance for clarity. For closure. I needed to see Chris. Maybe, once I was in his presence, I would realize how crazy I had been to waste my time thinking about him. I would get back on the plane, come home, and finally be able to move on with my life.

I booked my flight from Flint to Punta Gorda, Florida, for the following Monday. I texted Chris to say I'd be visiting for five days, and I planned to spend at least one of them exploring an area I'd never been to before. *Do you have any recommendations about where to visit?* I asked. *I was thinking Tampa.*

Tampa's nice, he said, *but it wouldn't be a good idea for you to be there alone at night.* He recommended a place called St. Pete Beach, near St. Petersburg, describing it as a beautiful coastal area with boutique shops and restaurants.

I conjured a chimerical fantasy of me standing near an endless shoreline, several feet into the crystal ocean, Chris walking out in the water to greet me. *St. Pete Beach sounds right up my alley,* I said. I stared at the screen, my fingers hovering over the keys while I decided my next move. *You know, I wouldn't mind if you met me there for lunch,* I said. My stomach was twisting in knots. I didn't have a plan B for if he said *no*.

Chris said, *Do you think that's wise? I don't want to cause you more grief.*

Before I could type the words I was thinking—*Of course it isn't wise*—he responded.

CHRIS: But I would love to.

TUESDAY, OCTOBER 22nd

In Michigan, the leaves had already turned and begun to fall, spreading a canvas of reds, yellows and oranges across the front yard. In another life, I would've been home, sitting on the porch, inhaling the aroma of coffee and writing in my journal before work.

"Thank you for letting me borrow your car," I had told my father when he picked me up from the Punta Gorda airport the day before. "I never get time alone. I'm just gonna spend a day at the beach."

He'd raised his eyebrows at me. "Megan, I'm not dumb. I know you're on some sort of mission. But as long as you're safe, I'm going to stay out of your business."

It was a sticky 89 degrees that morning as I left my grandpa's house for St. Pete Beach. The cold air from the vents blew hard against my skin, barely able to oppose the noon-day heat radiating through the glass into the car. As I approached the St. Petersburg area, I came up over a large bridge that unveiled a tropical paradise spanning as far as I could see. Bright-blue sparkling water flanked each side of the bridge, stretching out to meet the cityscape below. I took in a deep, tranquil breath, unable to remember the last time I'd been in such an intoxicating place.

I parked at the end of 8th Avenue and climbed down the crooked wooden steps onto the white sands of Passe-a-Grille Beach. I looked out at the array of people gathered. I wasn't used to seeing the sights and sounds of summer in late October: strangers with over-sized sunglasses lounging under gigantic striped umbrellas, children playing in the sand, couples splashing in the water. I pulled the cell phone from my purse and typed out a short message. *I'll be the one wearing the giant hat.*

A response appeared. *You're in Florida. Everyone is wearing a giant hat!*

Smiling, I returned the phone to my purse and tucked it beneath the steps, assuring myself it would remain safely out of sight. With my hands now freed, I moved steadily across the hot, sugary sand and stepped into the tepid water of the Gulf Coast. I gazed at the clear, blue sky above and the water below, two worlds stitched together by the horizon that lay between them, and I believed, for a brief moment, I was dreaming. I pressed my toes into the soft, silky grains that collected below the waves and welcomed the salty breeze into my lungs. The sun and the sea sank into my body, and for the first time in six months I was filled with something resembling happiness.

I glanced over my right shoulder, scanning the beach for a familiar face. When I turned my gaze in the opposite direction, my chest swelled. Chris was standing at the water's edge, dressed in an orange polo and khaki shorts, wearing dark sunglasses. His lips parted into a wide grin.

I took a step in his direction, but he put his palm in the air, commanding me to stay where I was. I could barely breathe when he reached down, removed the sandals from his feet, and started walking toward me.

I was home less than a week when I booked a flight back to Florida. I told Ian that my father had left me a spare key so I could check in on my grandpa. To my relief, Ian didn't bat an eye.

I messaged Chris to tell him I was returning to Arcadia in November.

CHRIS: Are you serious?? Is it the whole family or just you?
MEGAN: Just me.
CHRIS: Do you think you'll have time to get away?

That's when we started texting each other listings for Airbnbs. I suggested a few in Arcadia where I could stay close to my grandfather, but Chris wanted to book a room in St. Pete Beach.

How many more sunsets do we have? he wrote.

I stared at the words for a while, then typed back, *What happens the next morning?*

CHRIS: We wake up. And we don't feel guilty.

At home, I was always floating somewhere above reality, adrift in my body rather than anchored to it. I tried to block out the guilt. I tried to pretend that living a double life wasn't ripping me apart. It was easier when I stayed in my anger for Ian, when I blamed him for letting this happen, for not fighting harder for us. Deep down I knew the truth. Nothing Ian had or hadn't done made him deserve this. No one deserved this. And yet, I couldn't stop. I couldn't pray it away or journal it away or eat it or drink it or talk it away. Something inside me was convinced I would not survive if I cut contact with Chris, but I feared the life I was living now might also kill me.

Two weeks before my planned second trip, I gathered up the courage to cancel the flight. And to make sure I would stick with my decision, I mailed a handwritten letter to Chris explaining that I cared for him but I wouldn't be coming back.

At work, I thought about calling Chris to tell him I had mailed the letter. It seemed like the kind thing to do, I didn't want him to be surprised when it arrived. But also, I knew I was coming up with excuses to talk to him one last time.

As soon as I was out of the building, I dialed his number.

"It doesn't sound like a good letter," he said.

"I canceled my flight. I can't see you again. If I do, I know what will happen."

I pictured us two weeks earlier, standing on a deserted moonlit beach, heat lightning cutting through the sky behind us. He was holding my face in his hands, and I thought, *If this ends after tonight, I can still live with myself. It's just kissing. It's only kissing.*

"Megan, I don't know what you're expecting, but I just like spending time with you. I'd be perfectly happy listening to you read the phone book."

Why did he have to say things like that? I wanted to hate him. I wanted to not want him. "I can't believe I let any of this happen. And I work for a church."

"You're human," he said. "There's nothing wrong with you."

I had tried so hard to do the right thing by canceling the flight and sending the letter, but hearing his voice made me want to go back and undo those things. I didn't want him to read the letter. I wanted him to leave it in the envelope and burn it.

I started to cry. "This hurts," I said, my chest feeling like it was in a bear trap. I didn't know what else to say, I just didn't want Chris to hang up the phone and be gone forever.

"I don't know what you want from me," he said, a sudden callousness to his voice. "We didn't talk to each other for twelve years, and we were both fine."

My chest was now throbbing, my heart breaking into a thousand tiny pieces. How could I tell him that what I really wanted was to drag him back in time and make him explain everything that happened years ago?

"I just don't want to hurt anymore," I cried.

His voice was soft again. "It's a cruel twist of fate knowing what I know now. I should have done things differently. I should have been there for you."

It was excruciating to hear him go on this way, talking about *if only,* then *we would have . . .*

"What would it even look like for us to be together?" he said. "It's not like I can be around your boys."

I stared at my dashboard, saying nothing for a long time.

"Are you still there?" He said.

I took a deep breath and exhaled slowly. *You have to let him go . . . . You have to let him die . . . .*

"Megan . . . . Are you going to be okay?" he said.

I whimpered, "Yes. I'll be fine . . . . This has to be the end."

When he was gone, I held my phone as if it were an animal that had just died in my hand and sobbed. Eventually, I lifted my eyes to the rearview mirror, staring back at bloodshot eyes. I pried the other hand from the steering wheel and put the car in drive. I drove to the store and bought a bottle of wine. When I got home, I snuck to the kitchen, popped the cork, and filled a stemmed glass to the top. Then I snuck into the bedroom and began to forcefully pour the fizzy liquid down my throat, as if punishing myself. When the glass was empty, I went and poured another before retreating back into the bedroom. I remained hidden, guzzling the wine while Ian and the boys relaxed in the living room, unaware of what was happening on the other side of the wall. We had an hour before we needed to leave for a family trivia night at church. Already dehydrated from crying, I snatched the bottle from the fridge and finished it off, all within thirty minutes.

As I sat alone in the bedroom, it was clear to me I would never be happy again. My whole body was knotted up in unbearable agony that threatened to never leave. There was only one thing that would make the pain stop, and it was the one thing I couldn't have. Who was I now? What did it say about me that I would feel this way about a criminal? A child abuser? I hated myself for it. I believed there was a part of Ian that hated me, too.

A few nights earlier, we were sitting at the dining room table alone. "Do you even like who I am anymore?" I asked.

Ian was doing school work on his computer. He glanced over at me, and with very little expression, said, "I love you, even when you're being a pain in the ass."

When Ian and I got married, I had an idea in my head of what our life would look like, and this wasn't it. Where was the Ian I fell in love with? He was probably thinking the same thing about me. *Where's Megan? Where's my wife?*

The situation with Chris didn't make any sense, but what did sense matter when logic was no longer in the driver's seat? All I knew was that I was in pain without him. And as long as I was in pain, I wouldn't heal.

I texted Chris, *I don't want to stop talking. Please talk to me. Forget what I said earlier.* I felt pain and drunkenness and longing and fear all wrapped up in a ball as I slouched on the bed, staring at the screen, tears cascading down my cheeks.

After what seemed like an eternity, he texted back. *I don't know if we should keep talking.*

Please, I begged.

"Megan!" Ian called from the living room. "We need to get going!"

I clutched my phone all evening, secretly texting back and forth with Chris. He was distant, responding only once in a while. *I never should have canceled my flight. I never should have written the letter. Things will never be the same between us. I've ruined everything. I have nothing. I am nothing.* It took all my concentration to try and act natural. I spoke as little as possible, hoping that would hide the mess I was inside. I should have been more afraid that someone would figure out I was drunk in public, but nothing seemed to matter anymore. My life was already falling apart. What was one more thing?

I began to wish someone *would* find me out, that they'd see something was wrong and be moved to help. Maybe they could put me in some kind of rehabilitation center. At least then, I'd be safe from hurting myself or anyone else.

After going to bed, I woke up around 1:00 a.m. I was surprisingly sober. Clear-headed and calm in a way I hadn't been since I began talking to Chris nearly two months earlier. I *was* doing the right thing by saying goodbye. My relationship with him was clearly destroying me, and I had to let go.

I sent him a text. *When I said this had to be the end, it's the right thing to do. I have to say goodbye.*

The next morning, on Saturday, I received a two-word response: *Goodbye, Megan.*

All day, I kept myself busy with chores. I wrote in my journal. I didn't drink.

On Sunday morning, I could feel the threat of discomfort rising in my body, but I went to church hopeful. By late afternoon, I was in a panic. In an act of pure insanity, I sent Chris a final plea: *I know this is going to sound crazy, but I do want to see you one last time. I understand if you don't want to or you can't. If you say no, I will leave you alone.*

Once more, there was a part of me crying out for someone else to save me. If Chris rejected my offer, I would know for certain he didn't love me. I could heal and move on.

I would meet you anywhere, he said. *Do you want me to rebook the room?*

MEGAN: Yes.
CHRIS: OK, but if you don't show I'll just be sitting alone on a beautiful beach.
MEGAN: I'll be there.

I hadn't told Ian that the flight I'd canceled wasn't refundable and had cost us three hundred dollars. It cost another three hundred to rebook the flight and two hundred for the rental car. I booked an Airbnb next to the one Chris rented so there would be a record of me staying at the place where I told Ian I'd be staying. Also, so Chris would know there was a way for the police to track him if he were to physically harm me. Since our family didn't have money to pay for these things, I put the charges on a credit card and ignored the sting of guilt in my stomach, believing that no pain could be worse than the pain of giving up my last chance to see Chris.

The following week, I packed my bags, said my goodbyes, and got on a plane.

MONDAY, NOVEMBER 25th

10:00 A.M.

I forced my trembling hand to reach for my phone and dial the number to the Evergreen Counseling and Wellness Center. Moments later, I heard Becca's voice in my ear. "Megan? What's going on?"

It took everything I had to force the words from my throat. "I need help."

"I have a block open if you can get here right now," she said.

I put the van in drive. "I'll be there soon."

Earlier that morning, I dropped the boys off at school and drove to the grocery store, thinking maybe I'd make spaghetti and garlic toast for dinner, one of my family's favorites. I could hear Ian's voice in my head, saying, *Make sure you get Prego sauce, that's the only kind you like,* as if I needed reminding. As soon as I put the van in park, I couldn't move. *How can I possibly go in there and buy the Prego sauce? How can I cook one of their favorite meals and pretend that everything is okay when nothing is okay?*

For two hours, I sat paralyzed inside the running van, my gaze fixed on the back wall of the nearby pharmacy building. I prayed, *Help me. Help me. Help me. Help me.* Until I had the strength to pick up the phone.

On the drive to see Becca, I'd worked myself into a frenzy. By the time I was in her office, I was pacing the floor and flinging words at rapid speed. "I went back to Florida. I'm going to tell Ian everything, and I think it needs to be today."

"Okay," she said, keeping her voice even. I could tell she was struggling to remain expressionless. Last she knew, I'd canceled my flight and mailed the letter to Chris saying I wouldn't be going back to Florida.

"There's only three days until Thanksgiving. We're supposed to have our family over. Should I wait?"

"Don't wait," she said, with surprising directness. "If you care about saving your marriage, you need to tell him today."

As soon as I was back in the car, I called Chris. He answered playfully. "I always know something's wrong when you call me early in the day."

"I'm going to tell Ian what happened," I said. This must have come as quite a shock to him. In the whole history of our relationship, Chris had never heard me use the words "I'm going to tell . . . "

His voice darkened. "Can he re-open the case against me in Michigan?"

His question hit me like a punch in the stomach. "No, he can't re-open the case."

"Okay," he said, sounding relieved. "Of course, my first concern is *you*."

Did he think I was stupid? If I was his first concern, I would have been the first thing he mentioned. But how could I be angry at him? I did this to myself. Didn't I know what I was getting into? Didn't I know he might do anything to get me on his side? To silence me? That's what my gut had been saying from the first time I called him two months ago, but I didn't listen. I *couldn't* listen. Because I needed this to be a love story.

"I don't know what's going to happen to me in the next few months," he said.

"I'm not doing this for you. I can't live like this anymore. Ian deserves to know the truth."

I wasn't telling the truth so I could be with Chris. I was telling the truth because it was the only way for me to know what was real. I'd been in the dark for so long. Everything had to be brought into the light so I could see it for what it really was. Then I would know what I needed to do.

"Megan, I wish I would have done things differently when you were in college. I should have spent every weekend with you. I thought I was doing the right thing by giving you space. I didn't want to interfere in your life."

A familiar pain rose to the surface. This was my father's reason for not spending more time with me when I was younger. *I didn't want to interfere in your life. I didn't want to force you to spend time with me.* What had I learned from this? That spending time with me was not a prerequisite for loving me? That little effort could be made and I would remain loyal and trusting?

"You said Ian is a good man. Are you sure he won't hurt you?" Chris said.

"He's not going to hurt me," I said. "I think he'll want to. But he won't."

"What about your boys? They won't be in the house?"

"No. I'm going to find a place for them to be."

"When can I expect to hear from you again?"

"It's Monday. Give me until the end of the week."

"I'm here if you need me, whether you want to talk ten minutes or ten hours."

I brought the boys home from school and helped them pack an overnight bag. I dropped them off with a church family who graciously avoided asking why my children were staying at their house on a school night.

"Love you, Mumma," Evan said, as I bent down to hug them both.

"Yuv you, Mama," echoed Eli.

"I love you both so much," I said, trying not to cry. For the first time since before April 8th, I could actually *feel* how much I loved them. I squeezed them as tightly as I could, knowing the next time I'd see them, everything would be different.

At 6:23 p.m., I stood in the middle of what looked like a war zone. Our house was in complete disarray. Stacks of junk mail and unpaid bills strewn in random areas, dishes piled up in the sink and on the countertops. Boxes in the breezeway. Boxes I had brought into the house and never unpacked. The new living room carpet was supposed to be installed on Wednesday, so Ian had pulled up sections of carpet where the floorboards needed attention prior to re-covering them. Every piece of living room and dining room furniture was in one messy heap, the dim glow of the ceiling lamp shining over it like yellow moonlight over a hastily built barricade.

This was our dream home, where we had planned to host holidays with family and game nights with friends. We imagined someday standing in the driveway, watching our boys leave in overpacked cars to whatever colleges they'd chosen. Later, they would bring their children to stay in the rooms they had once slept and played in. Now, as I stood there among the wreckage, the house just looked like one big broken promise.

At 6:31 p.m. I watched from the living room as a pair of headlights spun slowly from the dark street to face toward the house, shining brightly into the window of the breezeway. I could feel the rumble of the truck engine inside my aching chest.

The engine stopped. Silence.

I waited by the slider that led from the breezeway into the house, watching Ian kick snow from his boots before removing them. When he pushed the slider open, the rush of bitter air stung my face.

"Hi!" he said, his dimples prominent in the middle of his cold, rosy cheeks.

I hugged him tightly, feeling the scratchy wool of his coat against my skin, smelling the sweet beard oil he used every morning. I took in the memory of his familiar body against mine, knowing it may be the last time.

Ian glanced around the room, then back at me. "Where are the boys?"

"I dropped them off with some friends. They're okay. I need to talk to you."

"Okay?" he said, and followed me over to the blue chairs. He slid down into one like he was getting ready to watch Sunday football, like it was just another ordinary day.

When I sat down across from him, he asked again, "What's wrong?"

I paused, the words trapped inside my mouth.

No, I have to do this. This is the only way out.

My lips fell open as I drew in a cold breath. "When I was in Florida, I visited Chris Blackmer."

Ian stiffened, his eyes instantly glassy. "What happened on your visit?" he asked, taking his time with each word.

I started to cry.

"*Megan*," Ian said, nearly choking on my name. He was biting his bottom lip and visibly shaking beneath his heavy wool coat. Anger was building in his voice. "What happened on your visit?"

I gathered up my sobs and held my breath, preparing to speak the words that would inevitably end my marriage. "We kissed and . . . " I drew a breath inward, like pulling back on a slingshot. Then, I let go. I exhaled three words. Three awful words. ". . . we had sex."

Terror flashed in Ian's eyes, as if I'd just driven a knife deep into his chest. He stared at me, silent, petrified, searching my face for any trace of the woman he once knew, but I could see he was drawing a blank. I was a stranger to him now.

Dazed, Ian turned his head toward the collage of photos hanging on the wall. Our love story, proudly displayed in pictures of newborn babies, smiling grandparents, our first dog. He looked back at me, eyes narrowed, and spoke somewhere between subdued rage and utter disbelief. "What do these pictures mean to you?"

I hunched over my lap, one hand gripping the top of my wrist. I couldn't speak. I could only cry, my voice heaving sob after sob.

Ian put his fingers to his temple. "I thought you wanted better for your children than you had. Do you not want to be a mom anymore?"

I wish I could have told him, *That's not it. I love them. I love you. This is more complicated than that.* But I didn't have the words to explain something I didn't understand. Instead, I shook my head in agonizing shame, staring at the floor while tears streamed down my face. My voice quivered as I offered up the only explanation I could. "I needed closure."

Ian's voice cut through the air, razor sharp. "You're a mother and wife now. You don't get to have closure." He stood up and moved to the dining room. Painful silence expanded inside the house as he paced back and forth, staring at me, then the floor. "Did you want a fast ticket out of our marriage?" he said, his anger in full view. "*Jesus,* Megan—well, did you?"

I squeezed my eyes shut. "No."

Ian was quiet again, pacing, looking lost in thought. He stopped again. "Did you speak to him today? *Chris*. Did you speak to Chris? And you'd better not lie to me."

I drew in a jagged breath and whispered, "*Yes*."

"I want you out of this house." The words shot out of his mouth like arrows, striking me in the sternum, reverberating through my chest and into my back. My muscles seized up as if to block the pain. He was shouting now. "Where are you going to live, Megan? With Chris in Florida? In Flint with your parents? 'Cause you sure as hell are not staying here."

I was so tired of fighting against myself, of the constant internal battle between two halves—one belonging to me, the other belonging to Chris. And now, if I was going to try to save my marriage, I would have an even bigger battle to fight. A voice inside me said it would be easier for Ian to end things now, to give me permission to stop fighting. To let the darkness win. But another voice, one that radiated from my very core, challenged me to stand my ground.

Don't let despair swallow you. Just hold on. Hold on for another five minutes.

I closed my eyes and pictured myself overlooking a pile of charred rubble. I saw the hand of a woman buried beneath the debris, trapped under the weight of the wreckage, only the soot-covered tips of her fingers visible. The woman was me, the dying shadow of the person I used to know. I clambered toward her, up the treacherous pile until I reached the top and was able to take hold of her hand, wondering if I was too late. *She's still breathing. She's still alive.* Swiftly, I began to dig her out, pulling the rocks off her one by one, until I could get a firm grasp of her hand. I pulled and pulled, and I knew I wouldn't stop until I got her out of that dark hole.

When I opened my eyes, a strength rose in me. I lifted my head up and forced myself to look directly at Ian, my eyes pleading, *Don't give up on me. I'm still in here.*

"How could you do this? And with *him*? I didn't turn him in years ago because I didn't want to lose you, and I'm going to lose you anyway. Oh my God, Megan. Oh my God." He continued pacing, putting his hands to his brow and pressing upward, as if to push the pain out of his head.

I kept my eyes aimed at him. *Don't give up on me, Ian. Don't give up.*

Ian pointed at me. "Promise me you won't speak to him again. And I mean never again. You can't tell him what happened tonight. You can't tell him how I reacted. Promise, and I'll agree to let you be a partner in raising these boys with me."

The thought of never hearing Chris's voice again caused my gaze to break from Ian. *It's a lie. Your mind is lying to you. You're sick. You need Ian to heal. You need your children to heal.*

"I promise," I said.

Ian's voice was shaking. "Good." He made his way slowly back to the chair and sat down. "I'm speaking to you now not as your husband, but as your friend . . . . That you would fuck a child molester—" He paused, inhaling sharply. "You need to sort your shit out."

We stared at each other for a long time.

"What's the date today?" he asked.

"November 25th."

He took a breath. "November 25th is not the day my boys come back to a broken home. Get your coat on. We're going to get my children. I want them to sleep in their own beds tonight."

2006

It was dark outside when my friends and I pulled up to the two-story apartment overflowing with music majors. We maneuvered our way inside through the back kitchen door, pushing past warm bodies holding red Solo cups and smiling at people they recognized. A white basin of jungle juice took up one corner of the dining room, a communal concoction of whatever liquor people had decided to bring to the party. When I saw someone dip their cup into the basin and scoop out what looked like dirty rainbow sludge, I was glad I had volunteered to be our group's designated driver.

There was an energy about that September night. I must have tried on three or four outfits at my friend's apartment before leaving for the party. I settled on bootcut jeans and an olive-green top with a boat neck that swooped just below my collarbone and stretched out to the corners of my shoulders. In my three years at Central Michigan University, I had attended only a handful of parties like this one. I had never been a big drinker, and I preferred the company of a few close friends to a room full of people I may or may not know. So when I heard the guys in Appian 10 were hosting a back-to-school party, it surprised me how enthusiastic I was about it. *Why not?* I thought. I was single and going into my senior year of college. I had spent the last three years building a community of great friends. One more year, and I'd be interning as a student teacher, the final step before earning my degree and my teaching certificate.

After watching several poorly played rounds of beer pong, I ventured through the spacious living room and out the front door to get some fresh air. Stepping onto the porch, a cool breeze passed by, causing me to shiver. I stood there, hugging myself for warmth, and looked around for someone to talk to.

Straight ahead of me was a guy standing alone, leaning against the hood of a beat-up car, the front giving way to his sturdy frame. I recognized him from the university choir. He was in his mid-twenties—older than most of the undergrad students—and built more like a football coach than an aspiring music teacher. We had been in choir together for three years, but somehow had never spoken to each other.

When I approached him, he was staring up at the sky, looking lost in thought. "Hey, Ian!" I said brightly, breaking his meditation.

He turned his gaze toward me, grinning instantly, revealing the crater-sized dimples that sat inside the center of his pink, stubbly cheeks. His eyes were glossy, and in his hand was a comically large beer mug decorated in Super Mario Brothers, an inch or so of beer sloshing around at the bottom. "Hey! *Megan*, right?" he said.

"Yep. I'm the person you beat out for choir president."

Ian furrowed his brow and smiled, seeming intrigued by my forwardness.

"Oh, I'm not mad!" I said, laughing and waving my arms between us. "I'm glad I got treasurer. Less work, you know." We shared a look. Clearly, we both knew being treasurer wasn't less work. He just got the fancier title.

Ian threw his head back in hearty laughter, eyes returning to the sky. "I'm glad you're not mad," he said, then he held a soft smile as his glossy gaze rested on my face. It looked like he was waiting for me to say something.

"So. I guess we're gonna be working together this year," I said.

"I guess so," he said, warmly, his eyes twinkling under the fluorescent light of the parking lot lamps.

"I'm gonna head back inside, but I'll see you around," I said, waving goodbye.

Ian raised his Super Mario mug. "Looking forward to it."

2019

When my alarm went off at 5:30, I was surprisingly alert. I glanced at Ian's side of the bed, and for a brief second I forgot why it was empty.

Then it came back to me—all the gut-wrenching awfulness of the night before. After I had confessed to Ian about Chris and my betrayal, I rode with him to retrieve the boys from our friends' house. On the way over, I sat dead silent in the passenger seat thinking, *This isn't real life. Things like this don't happen to people like us*. How was it that, in a matter of only seven months, my marriage had fallen into complete ruin? How had I gone from devoted wife to adulteress? From a loving mother to a woman who could barely recognize herself in the mirror?

When we arrived at our friends' house unannounced, it was clear they were confused, but they greeted us kindly and called the boys downstairs, who were already in their pajamas. Ian and I apologized for the inconvenience, helped the boys get their coats and boots on, then drove quietly back to the house. We guided them up the stairs to their bedrooms, and I took turns sitting on each of their beds while Ian stood at the doorway watching from a distance. I tucked the blankets under their arms and told them how much I loved them.

Ian and I made our way down the stairs and turned the corner to the living room where we stood quietly for a while. "I can't sleep in the bedroom," he said. He sounded apologetic. He had no reason to be. This was my fault, not his.

I expected to wake up hopeless and unable to get out of bed. But it was the exact opposite. I was energetic and clear-headed in a way I couldn't remember feeling in a long time.

I went straight to the kitchen, filled a kettle with water, and set it on the burner. As I waited for the water to boil, I gathered the messy piles of mail and stacked them neatly in a designated spot on the counter. I scrubbed dishes and loaded them in the dishwasher. I pulled eggs from the fridge and bread from the pantry, salt, pepper, butter, all the ingredients to make poached eggs on toast, a favorite of Ian's. Standing on tiptoes, I reached high for a bag bearing the Dunkin Donuts logo and poured a small mound of coffee beans into the cheap grinder we had purchased from Walmart a few months before. The sound of the grinder was soothing, the blades splitting the beans, buzzing and whirling around in a mad cycle, until they turned to brown grainy dust. On that morning, everything had a newness about it. All the things that had become so commonplace in life were now a novelty, rare and shiny, under the light of a second chance.

I had just finished making the coffee when a distant beeping rang through the floor. It was the alarm from Ian's phone, coming from the basement. It went off several times before I heard the creaking of the basement steps and the click of the doorknob latch. I couldn't see Ian from the kitchen, but I could hear his every move from the basement door to the nearby bathroom. Once I knew he was dressed, I displayed his breakfast on the counter for him to see on his way out.

Ian walked zombie-like through the kitchen, straight past the plate of food. He took his work keys from the table and left without a word.

I watched out the front window to the driveway, praying for him to come back inside to say goodbye. The truck lit up and backed out of the drive. My gut throbbed as it moved further and further away, rounded the street corner, and then disappeared from sight.

Agony seized my abdomen, gripping and twisting up my insides. I slumped over the counter, holding my fist to my stomach, squeezing my mouth shut to trap the cries radiating from my throat. *The boys can't see me this way. They can't know that their life could be different than what it is right now.*

I willed myself into an upright position, and headed to the bathroom for a tissue, knowing they'd soon be awake and trudging down the steps to the main floor. But when I entered the bathroom, the sight of the countertop startled me. It was covered in coarse hair, scattered about like a nest that'd been violently torn apart by a wild animal. My heart sank when I realized what I was looking at—the remains of Ian's beard.

Last January, Ian had made a vow to grow his beard for one full year. He planned to start on January 1st, see how big the beard could get, then shave it off the following January. I wasn't excited about this plan, considering the last time Ian grew a substantial beard, people mistook him for my uncle. My favorite look was a short, well-kept beard that accentuated his jawline and allowed me to see his face, especially his dimples. But to Ian, the smaller the beard, the less attractive he felt.

As the beard grew, he teased more and more often. "Maybe I'll let it grow out another year," he'd say, just to watch me squirm. By our tenth year of marriage, we'd had as many conversations about beards as we'd had about what to name our children. When he returned to school the previous fall, it had grown well below his chin. His students started calling it his wizard beard, which he took immense pride in, making up for the lack of hair on top of his head. As much as he loved the beard, he knew I couldn't wait for him to shave it off so he could grow it to the length I was most attracted to.

We were one month shy of the full year—and there lay the wizard beard, cut off from its proud owner like a form of self-mutilation. I grabbed small areas of hair, one pinch at a time, and placed them in a plastic Ziploc. I was careful to seal it completely, pushing out any pockets of air, then I hid it in one of my dresser drawers. *You did this,* I said to myself, looking down on the messy bundle of dead hair. *You need to keep this as a reminder of the pain you've caused.*

With two days left until Thanksgiving, I was determined to do with the house what Ian and I had planned—to create beautiful and lasting memories for our family. If we could make believe, even for a day, that none of this was happening, that we were fine, maybe we could make it true.

After taking the boys to school, I drove to the store to buy food and decorations for hosting. The carpet installers would be coming the next day, which meant I could put the furniture back in its place and everything would look perfect when I was done. At the store, I felt like I was floating somewhere above reality, drifting from aisle to aisle in a dreamlike state. I took pictures of different decorations and sent them to Ian. He responded, *That looks great!* or, *You should get one!* And I pretended that my life wasn't on the verge of falling apart.

Ian and I didn't text much in the afternoon. He didn't call on his lunch break like he usually did. I reminded myself not to be discouraged. Healing our marriage would be a marathon, not a sprint. It would require a new kind of patience. Up to that point in my life, I'd been living in minutes, hours, days, weeks. Now I'd learn to live in seasons, possibly stretching years at a time.

According to several of the articles I'd read about infidelity, it would take a minimum of two years before either partner could expect things to go back to normal. Internet forums discussing infidelity were bleaker. *Once a cheater, always a cheater . . . . Your marriage will never recover . . . . You're never going to be able to trust her again . . . . You will hold it against her, even if it's not on purpose. Save yourself (and her) the pain and leave now.* Some of the comments attacked women directly. *You know women . . . they can never be satisfied with what they have . . . . Most women have low self-confidence and need constant attention. Someone else was there to give her attention so the weak-minded slut went for it.* Comment after comment of despair and hopelessness and cruelty, all brought upon by betrayal.

But then there were stories of couples who had survived the worst. More than surviving, they had come out on the other side with a stronger marriage, a deeper understanding of themselves and the ability to communicate their needs in a way they never could before their marriage hit rock bottom. I treated each of these stories like a lucky penny I could stick in my pocket and keep near me at all times. If Ian and I were going to get through this, I had to believe we could, and I had to hold on to that belief every second of every day.

I wasn't naive. I knew things were never going to go back to the way they once were. Our marriage—the one we had grown accustomed to for over ten years—was over. But that didn't mean we couldn't start again and build a better marriage. There were so many ways I could have been more supportive, more patient, more of a partner.

Partner. That's the word Ian used to describe what he had lost. *I feel completely alone*, he said. *I feel like I don't have a partner*.

I instinctively knew marriage was a partnership, but I had never used the label *partner* to define my role. I was Ian's *wife*, his *muse*, the *love of his life*—labels that carried connotations of intensity and romance. "Partner" added a dimension to my perception of marriage that hadn't existed before. It meant something else. That Ian and I were a team of equals, sharing an equal role of responsibility in both the intense and mundane moments of life. I wondered how our lives would have been different had I always thought of myself as a partner, rather than an object of everlasting love and desire. Rather than being so caught up in whether we were going out on enough dates or having enough sex, I could have focused on whether we were acting as a team.

Of course, all these thoughts were in retrospect. I couldn't go back in time and tell myself what I knew now. Even if I could go back, I don't know how much it would have changed me. It's one thing to have knowledge of something; it's another thing to truly *know* it, to have that truth living in your bones, filling your lungs, an inseparable part of who you are and what you believe.

Here's what I knew for certain: God has the power to heal broken things. There was evidence of it in the world around me if I only looked for it. But I couldn't rely on God alone to fix everything. I'd have to work at this every day. I'd have to prove to Ian, and myself, that I was worth not giving up on.

The sky had already turned dark when Ian pulled into the driveway. I made sure the table was set and dinner was kept warm for the moment he arrived. The four of us sat around the table asking how each other's days were, a semblance of normalcy.

After dinner, the boys watched TV while Ian and I stepped into the cold breezeway. Ian closed the slider behind us. "I'm *trying*," he said, in a shaky half-whisper. Tears filled his eyes, then mine. I reached out for him, but I stopped midway, knowing I didn't have the right. "You were already unhappy with me," he said. "I'm scared I'm going to try to make this work, and you're gonna leave six months from now."

"I'm not going to leave you. I love you." Since telling Ian about Chris, I felt like a different person. I was focused and grounded. I could feel attachment to my family again. The thought of leaving them for Chris seemed ludicrous and impossible.

After we called the boys up to bed, Ian invited me to watch *Planes, Trains and Automobiles* with him. Other than us sitting on separate pieces of furniture, it would've been difficult to spot the crisis between us. We laughed and talked about different scenes the way we always had when watching movies together. Afterward, Ian and I finished putting away dishes and leftovers. It was then I realized an entire day had passed without us touching each other. I longed for him so much it hurt. But this was different from the way I had longed for Chris. This felt like a space that, with time, could actually be filled.

We turned the lights off in the living room, then the kitchen. We were getting ready to head to our separate sleeping areas when I said, "Would it be alright if I hugged you?"

Ian lowered his head, moving it left and right. "I'm not ready for that." He left the kitchen for the basement stairs, closing the door behind him.

I remained frozen in the spot where he'd left me, willing myself to move my legs. After several minutes, I broke free and walked slowly to the bedroom. I laid in the darkness, thinking about the last twenty-four hours. It didn't seem real that this was happening. It was like I was living someone else's life. I'd wake up and this would all be a bad dream. As my mind drifted into fantasy, I imagined standing in front of my teenage self, urging her to run far away from Chris. I'd tell her, *You don't know this now, but someday this man is going to ruin your life.*

A lonely thirty minutes passed.

When I heard the slow thudding of steps rising from the basement to the main floor, a hopefulness grew inside me. Soon, Ian was standing in the doorway. "I have to ask," he said, his voice low, his face contorted as if the act of speaking was painful. "Is there any chance you could be pregnant?"

My stomach churned. "No."

"Are you sure?"

"Yes."

Ian's eyes traveled the floor. Then he looked at me and said, "I can't be intimate with you until you see a doctor. You need to get tested."

We weren't talking about pregnancy anymore. White-hot shame rose in me as a horrific thought entered my mind: *I only know what Chris has told me about his sexual experiences.* I didn't even know he was bisexual until six months ago. What else hadn't he told me? What if he'd had sex with dozens of people? With strangers? Could I have HIV? Could I die because of this?

"I'll call the doctor on Monday, after the holidays are over," I said.

"Thank you." Slowly, he turned and left for the hallway, pulling the door closed behind him.

I listened to Ian's thuds moving further away from me, down the basement steps, until the house was silent. I laid down on my side of the bed and pulled my knees into my chest. The clattering of raindrops appeared outside, striking the roof above me, the rapid smacking of water pellets against the plants leaning against the bedroom window. There was a clattering inside me that grew louder as the rain came down harder, until I could no longer lie still.

Thrusting myself upward, I snatched the pillow from my side of the bed and shoved it into my face, pressing it against my eyes, nose, and mouth. I screamed into it with such force, I thought my throat would tear open and bleed out onto the white cotton. I stood from the bed, snatched the van keys from the bowl in the entryway and hurried outside into the pouring rain. I didn't know where I was going, I just knew I couldn't stay there.

Aimlessly I drove around the city. I screamed and screeched and wailed, *Why?!? Why?!? Why?!?* while the rain pounded down so fiercely the windshield wipers struggled to keep the window in front of me clear. An hour later, when my throat burned from grief and I could barely keep my head up, I took the path back home.

Inside the house, nothing had changed. The lights were off. The basement was quiet. Ian hadn't called my cell phone while I was gone. Maybe he didn't notice I was gone, or he noticed and didn't care. I dragged myself back to the bedroom. I peeled off my clothes and crawled into bed, eyes heavy with swelling, and passed out.

When I opened my eyes the next morning and saw light, I was once again filled with a sense of hope. There was still so much to feel shameful about, but I allowed myself a small moment of pride. I had made it through the night. I would make it through another.

I prepared breakfast just as I did the morning before, brewing coffee, setting the poached eggs in clear sight on the counter. Just as he had the morning before, Ian trudged through the kitchen, bleary-eyed, looking only for his keys, then left.

In the early afternoon, the new living room carpet was installed. I moved the furniture out of the dining room back into place and set up the decorations I'd purchased at the store the day before. In the evening, our friend Nick helped set up a bed in the spare room for overnight guests. He had no idea the real reason for the bed was so Ian would have a long-term sleeping solution away from our bedroom. In order to avoid suspicion, Ian offered to sleep in our bedroom on the few nights we'd have relatives staying with us.

That night, Ian and I sat together on the basement couch and watched another movie. When it ended, Ian said, "I don't want it to seem like we're going to have a heavy conversation every night, but I want to talk."

I'd been reading about the trauma experienced by partners who've been betrayed with infidelity. I had to let Ian feel and say whatever he needed to, even if it was painful to hear. I owed him that. "We can talk as much as you want," I said.

Ian's hands began to shake. "I've been so angry, I thought maybe I would just go out and cheat on you. But then I realized, it wouldn't make me feel any better. I don't want to cheat. The problem is, I don't want to be married to anyone but you."

I took a breath. "I know that saying 'I'm sorry' isn't good enough, but I'm so sorry for hurting you. I don't know if you'll ever be able to forgive me, but I'm thankful you're willing to try."

I watched Ian as he thought of what to say next. "You know, I was reading that, in some cultures, they don't throw away a piece of pottery just because it breaks. They pour gold into the cracks, and the piece is even more beautiful than it was before it broke." He turned his head and stared into me. "You broke our marriage. I'm hoping, after all this, we can end up with something beautiful."

The week of Thanksgiving, Ian and I managed to survive for a few reasons: We clung desperately to our children. We found humor in small moments. And there was kindness. So much undeserved kindness.

For three days the house was filled with family and friends. It brought normality and warmth into a desperate and cold situation. At night, when the house was quiet and I'd be putting away dishes, Ian would stand next to me at the kitchen sink. He wouldn't touch me, but he'd say, "Thank you for everything you did today," and I'd feel loved, perhaps in a way I had never felt loved before.

Monday morning, once everyone had gone home and we were back to our regular routine, I got up, made Ian his coffee and breakfast. This time, before grabbing his keys and heading out the door, he stopped to eat.

On Tuesday, I was at work in front of my computer when a message box appeared. A wave of panic rushed through me as I struggled to understand how Chris was sending me messages. *I blocked him on my phone. How is he texting me?* What I didn't realize was that his texts could still come through the computer's iMessage app.

Chris's text contained nothing more than a picture of a *Thorn Birds* DVD case sitting on a store rack. *Look what I saw today*, the message read. Chris knew my mom had named me after the character of Meggie.

A minute passed. Another text appeared with a smiley emoji. *I hope you're OK.*

A third text. A picture of a marquee outside a movie theater entrance that read *When Harry Met Sally*. The film had been put back in theaters to celebrate its thirtieth anniversary. When I was with Chris in St. Pete Beach, he had joked about us sneaking away to see it at the same time, him in Florida and me in Michigan. "We can text each other during our favorite parts," he said.

I had been so focused on Ian the past week, it had been fairly easy to block Chris from my mind. Telling Ian the truth opened a door in me that had been previously closed to everyone I loved, and I felt present with my life and my family in a way I hadn't for years. So while Chris's texts were emotionally jarring, the urge to text him back was minimal. I knew he was the reason I was in this mess, and I'd come too far to let him get back inside my head. I found a way to block his number through the computer's iMessage app and called Ian to share what had just happened.

"Thank you for being honest with me," Ian said. And for the first time in over a week, he spoke the words, "I love you."

2006

IAN: I'm going to see a musical tonight. Want to go with me?

I stared at the text for a while, wondering how to respond. Since Ian and I were both on the choir executive board, we had started spending more time together. Discussion at board meetings turned into casual conversation before and after choir. We had gotten comfortable enough for me to tease him about the number of girls I saw hug him every day. When I called him a "hug whore," he smiled coyly and said, "What? I know how to make people feel better."

He was right, though. He did know how to make people feel better. He was easy to be around. Maybe it was his age; at twenty-seven, he was self-assured in a way many college guys weren't. I never had to guess at what he was thinking or feeling. Unlike me, he didn't grow up in a church, but he acted in a more Christian manner than many of the church people I knew. Always kind. Never a gossiper.

One day in October, our choir director was out sick, so Ian—being choir president—stepped in to lead rehearsal. He was in the middle of conducting one of our fall concert pieces and needed to cue the soprano soloist, but he didn't know I had been given the solo, so he didn't know where to look. When he heard my voice, his stare shifted in my direction. I watched as his eyes grew wide and his jaw fell slack. His hands began to slow, until they had reached a full stop, suspended in the air for several seconds before he seemed to regain consciousness and continue conducting.

I didn't think much about that day until I saw Ian's text. Go to a musical with him? It sounded a lot like a date. Ian and I were becoming good friends, which was why I wanted to say *no*. Sure, he was a great guy, but I wasn't attracted to him in that way. If he had romantic feelings for me, I didn't want to lead him on, make things awkward, and ruin the friendship.

Thankfully, one of my professors needed a sitter for the evening. It was the perfect excuse. When I messaged Ian to tell him I couldn't go, I was worried he would be upset or angry with me, but when I arrived at choir on Monday afternoon, Ian looked at me with the same smile he always did. With an innocent lilt, he said, "I'm sorry you couldn't go to the show because you had something important going on. What was it? Weren't you washing your hair?" He knew I had a real reason—a better reason—for not going. He was having more fun getting a rise out of me.

"I had to babysit," I said, rolling my eyes.

"Right, right. Washing your hair. I get it." Ian smiled as he took off toward the tenor section. "See ya later, Meggylu."

MONDAY, NOVEMBER 12th, 2006
7:56 P.M.

FACEBOOK MESSAGE FROM CHRIS BLACKMER TO MEGAN LUCIUS: Hey, how are you doing?

MEGAN: Doing well. And yourself?

CHRIS: Hey, not too bad. It's been a fairly stressful few weeks, but things are slowing down a bit now through Christmas. Everything just seemed to happen all at once—one of those kind of months. How is school treating you? Are you student teaching this spring or is it still next year?

MEGAN: These past few weeks have been especially stressful as well, but some good news today. I landed a lead in the opera so that was a well-needed pick-me-up. I'm still student teaching in the fall, which is exciting. I can't believe this part of my life is almost over. I hear life just gets harder from here, but I'm determined to prove that wrong. You know me. Going on another Vegas holiday?

CHRIS: Congratulations! That's excellent! No Vegas this year—just a traditional Christmas at home! What about you?

MEGAN: Too bad about Vegas. It's home for me as well. Why so busy the past few weeks?

CHRIS: Haha . . . it's called "I can't say no!"

When I was in high school, Chris and I would either text or talk on AIM. With texting, it was short phrases and one-word responses:

Hi there.

Hey. How are you?

Good.

How's school?

Pretty good. Staying busy.

I'd know exactly where the conversation was leading. My body would buzz, waiting for Chris to invite me to meet him somewhere.

I'm passing through Troy this Saturday. Do you want to meet at Somerset Mall for lunch?

I have some free time next weekend. Movie and dinner?

I didn't mind that our conversations were short, because texting was always a means to an end. An end that I wanted, to see Chris in person.

Once Facebook became popular my sophomore year of college, AOL and Instant Messenger practically faded into obsoletion. Students crowded the School of Music's computer lab to create profiles, add their college friends, search for people they knew from high school whom they'd lost touch with. Eventually, Chris started sending me messages through Facebook. Right away, I noticed a difference in our banter. These messages were usually longer than when we talked through text, but they were oddly formal and stilted, like two acquaintances catching up in a grocery store checkout line. Worse, they didn't always lead to an invitation. If someone were to read these messages, would they have any clue what we were to each other?

What were we, though? We weren't acquaintances, and we weren't really friends. We were two people who, for the past five years, had seen each other on occasion and behaved as if no time had passed between visits, as if we were on one endless first date. We had lots of history and little to show for it.

Chris had come up to CMU for different events over the years. If he was in Mount Pleasant and wasn't with students, we'd go to dinner. When he walked me to my car, he'd kiss me goodbye. He never asked permission to touch me, but he never had to because it didn't matter how much time had passed since we'd last seen each other. The fact that I'd showed up meant that part of me still belonged to him.

Only once did I turn down an opportunity to see him. It was my sophomore year of college, and I was a few months into dating a boy from church who I'd grown up with. We had just started to say *I love you* when Chris reached out to tell me he was coming up to CMU that weekend. *I arrive Friday,* the message said. *I'll be staying at the Super 8 hotel. Are you free that evening?*

I told him I was busy. I didn't tell him that having a boyfriend was the real reason I couldn't see him. It would complicate our relationship, and I didn't want that. Our relationship was simple and care-free. In one world was my college life, in another Chris, and the two didn't interfere with each other. At least, that was my belief.

FRIDAY, NOVEMBER 17, 2006
5:23P.M.

FACEBOOK MESSAGE FROM MEGAN LUCIUS TO CHRIS BLACKMER: Hey doofus, way to tell me you were going to be at CMU today. It's weird because I never come through those doors, so I wouldn't even have seen you on any other occasion. I can't remember if you said you were going to the brass band concert Sunday. If you're here through the evening and stranded, let me know.

CHRIS: No . . . I'll be coming up with the parents of the students in Honors Band, so I'll be bound to leave when they do. I think I meant to say that I would be there today back when I was talking the other night, and then you left and I just forgot! [smiley face emoji]

I had long ago accepted that Chris and I lived separate lives. But this bothered me—that Chris would reach out days before coming to CMU, then say nothing about being in the same town with me. I had to find out accidentally by passing by him in the music building?

Maybe the weekend of Honors Band wasn't an opportune time to be together, but why wouldn't he have at least mentioned it? If I'd have known he was in town, we could've at least said *hi* to each other.

His words remained lodged in my chest. *You left and I just forgot . . . .* Out of sight, out of mind.

Christmas and New Year's were supposed to be a bright spot amidst Michigan's wintery months of bitter cold and darkness—but if I was single, all the holidays did was shine a spotlight on my loneliness. I wanted to be one of the people in those Christmas marathon movies, snuggled up by the fireplace with my true love, kissing under the mistletoe, strolling down an empty snow-blanketed street drinking hot chocolate. But all I felt was emptiness.

That winter, I started to long for Sean again.

By senior year of college, it'd been ten years that Sean and I were locked in a cycle of breakups and reunions. With each passing year, the distance between highs and lows widened—which made it easier to break up when things were bad, but also more difficult to stay away when, after a period of separation, all my body could remember was the way it felt when he held me, or when he smiled his indelible smile, or when it seemed like he was the only person who understood me. Sean was the only person I had more history with than Chris, and at least Sean had told me how much he loved me, even if he didn't always show it.

Sean was in Grand Rapids that winter attending school when we got back together. In some ways, the distance made our relationship better. We had time to miss each other. In his absence, I could imagine him as the sweet, honest, committed boyfriend I wanted him to be because there was little evidence to prove the contrary. Maybe he *was* living out what I was imagining. But just as it'd been the nine years before it, the fantasy never lasted.

I spent a weekend with Sean in the city. On Saturday, we decided to go to a bar for some live music. But our date night turned sour when we started talking about the past.

Before long, I was scream-crying about our freshman year of college, when Sean confessed to cheating on me while we were still in high school. We had just returned from a date night, and before I got out of the car, he said there was something he needed to tell me. When he said her name, I thought I was going to throw up. The girl he cheated with had sat in my presence day after day, pretending to be my friend, and if any of our other friends knew the secret, no one had said a word to me about it. *What an idiot*, they must've thought, watching me dote on Sean every day we sat together at the cafeteria lunch table, or the day we went to prom, or when we took pictures together in our graduation robes.

Sean's news had devastated me, but I thanked him for telling me the truth. And because he had been truthful about something difficult, it made me vulnerable to sharing a difficult truth as well. There was something important he needed to know if we were going to have an open, honest relationship.

"The summer before college, *after* we broke up . . . " I paused, my breath catching in my throat. "I had sex with Chris Blackmer."

Sean became unhinged, flailing wildly and slamming his hands against the car's driver side window and steering wheel. Fear threw me into the corner of the passenger seat, my hands raised to block whatever anger was coming at me. Through a rush of tears, he howled, "How could you be so fucking stupid, Megan?"

I could understand him being upset. But *this* upset? He had just admitted to cheating on me and lying about it for months, and now he was acting like what I did was worse. Way worse. That couldn't possibly have been the last time Sean and I spoke about Chris, but whatever might have been said after that was lost to memory.

Fueled by alcohol and adrenaline, I stumbled blurry-eyed out of the bar and onto the sidewalk where Sean and I continued to scream at each other. I hailed a taxi, leaving him on the street. I slurred at the driver, crying hysterically, trying to understand where I was and how to get to Sean's apartment. It was a miracle I made it back.

When Sean returned, the fighting escalated until I was filled with such rage I shoved him. He shoved me back, sending me to the tiled bathroom floor. I stared up at him in astonishment as he glared back at me, fists clenched. Even in my belligerent drunkenness, I was aware that neither of us deserved to be in a relationship like this. It wasn't the first time our fighting had become physical, but this was a new low.

After the visit to Grand Rapids, I received a message from Chris: *Hey, Happy New Year. Hope you had a good break! So do you know where you're student teaching in the fall?*

When Chris invited me to his apartment, I made a choice—to escape instead of facing what I wasn't ready to face. I didn't know how to let Sean go, and I didn't know how to not want happiness. I knew that Chris's apartment was a safe place. With Chris, aggression and affection did not exist in the same room. In our snow globe world, there would only be good feelings.

I was on my way to class when I passed Ian in the hallway. He must've seen the frustration on my face because he stopped me. "Something's wrong. What is it?"

"It's my stupid car," I said. During my lunch break, I had driven myself to a fast food restaurant not far from the music building. When I had finished eating and gotten back in my vehicle, the engine wouldn't start, so I walked back.

"You mean Blazer, right?" Ian said, his head cocked.

I laughed at this more than I meant to. Ian was always teasing me about my old Blazer, saying I needed a vehicle upgrade. It occurred to me he might be right.

"Do you want me to take a look at it? I have a break," he said.

"Thanks, but I have class. What about after?"

"I'm free now," Ian smiled. He gestured in the direction of my professor. "Tell her what's going on and see what she says."

Sheepishly, I made my way over to the professor, who had just unlocked the classroom door. "Could I *possibly* miss class today? My vehicle is having issues and Ian offered to help me fix it."

She glanced past me and saw Ian waiting in the adjacent hallway. "He did, did he?" she said, winking down at me the way a grandmother would when sneaking you a cookie before dinner time. "That's nice of him. You can miss class this one time."

"Well? What'd she say?" Ian asked when I made my way back to him.

"She was all about letting me miss class because *you* were helping me."

"That's sweet. She must think I'm a pretty good guy."

"Don't let it get to your head."

"Too late," said Ian. He picked up his backpack from the floor and we headed for the parking lot.

Ian drove me back to the Blazer, popped the hood, and quickly diagnosed the problem. Then he took us to a local auto parts store where he knew some of the employees and could get a good deal on a battery. He had the Blazer up and running again in less than an hour.

When I got home that day and called Sean, I didn't tell him that a guy had helped me fix my vehicle. Even though Ian and I were nothing more than good friends, it would have been a fight, and I was tired of fighting.

Later that week, I saw a set of drinking glasses for sale at a local pharmacy. They reminded me of Ian—how the night we first talked, he was holding the giant Super Mario Brothers beer mug. I bought them for him as a thank you gift for fixing my Blazer.

The next day, I ran into him in one of the practice room hallways. "Ian!" I spoke excitedly. "I want to thank you for the other day."

"Yeah?" he said in a pitch slightly higher than what was typical for him.

I dug into my backpack, pulled out the box containing the glasses and presented them to him as if they were a highly coveted award.

When Ian saw the glasses, he laughed.

"What?" I playfully scoffed. "You don't like them?"

He laughed again and shook his head. "It's not that. I like them very much. You just surprised me, that's all."

In late February, Sean came home from school to visit his family, so I drove to Flint for the weekend to be with him.

Our relationship hadn't been the same since our blow-up in Grand Rapids. I didn't have much fight left in me. I was tired. I didn't want to carry a decade's worth of jealousy and hurt anymore, and I didn't want Sean to carry it either. There were still secrets between us. I had never told him the whole truth about my relationship with Chris, and I would never tell him I had spent the night with Chris when Sean thought I was at a friend's house.

Sunday evening, I said goodbye to Sean and started the drive back to my apartment in Mount Pleasant. I kept the radio off, keeping company with only my thoughts.

I had just gotten outside of Flint's city limits when a spirit of peace washed over me. In an instant, I knew it was over between Sean and me. This wasn't like other times. I wasn't angry or sad. It was as if a gentle voice had simply whispered in my ear, *It's okay. You can let go now.*

When I got to the apartment, I went straight to my bedroom and called Sean. "I want to break up," I said.

He spewed at me, "You're fucking retarded. You're making the biggest mistake of your life."

"Goodbye, Sean," I said, and hung up the phone.

2020

JOURNAL ENTRY
JANUARY 8th, 2020

It's been three nights now that Ian has returned to sleeping in our bed. I should feel better (and in some ways I do) but in many ways it deepens the sadness and grief I feel for everything that's been lost. It's as if the more we return to normal, the more I feel pain, regret, hopelessness. I don't let the hopelessness stay too long inside my heart. I know it's a lie. No matter what happens, there is life beyond this. I have to remind myself that there were issues in our marriage before any of this, that it wasn't perfect, that I often felt lonely and confused about what was missing. And even if all of that had nothing to do with Ian, it was a feeling I couldn't free myself from. Now I'm free in new ways, and I'm present, truly present, with my family. I will never regret giving all the love I could to try and save my marriage, and I'll be thankful for the time we have together, even if it comes to an end. I don't want to create expectations, and yet, I don't want to stop hoping and trusting that God will help heal us.

"Mumma, are you okay? I heard you yelling for Daddy."

A shadow of Evan came into focus. He was standing in the doorway to the bedroom. I wiped the tears from my cheeks and tried to slow my gasping. "Yeah, buddy. I'm okay. Just having a bad dream. You can go back to bed."

It was the dead of Michigan winter, and nightmares were almost a nightly occurrence. After a few nights in our bedroom, Ian went back to sleeping in the office. I missed having him next to me. I missed *him*, the person he used to be before I caused this irrevocable harm. He was still kind, gentle, thoughtful, but there was an undeniable sadness behind his eyes. I wanted to reach into his chest and repair the damage, but I couldn't. I knew that nothing I did in the future would ever make up for what happened in the past.

Just when I thought Ian and I were making huge strides, something would happen to remind me how fragile our relationship was. Ian would say, *Megan, I do love you, but if it weren't for the boys I don't know that I'd be here.* This was always hard to hear, that I wasn't enough to make him stay. As painful as it was, I didn't want him to lie to me. I reminded myself how important it was for him to be able to express those hard truths. He had suffered trauma too. If we were going to make it, I'd have to let him heal in his own time.

If it weren't for my therapist, Becca, I'd have had no one to talk to that wasn't the person I betrayed. Even my mom didn't know what had happened. I was so afraid that anyone who heard the story would never be able to look at me the same again, that by speaking the words out loud, it would make it all too real. Keeping quiet meant keeping it contained.

At therapy, Becca helped me work toward radical acceptance, which meant I didn't have to approve or agree with everything that had happened in the past, but I could come to accept it, all of it. Refusing to be buried by shame was never easy. Sometimes I would lock myself in the bathroom and turn on the shower so no one would hear me crying. I had to constantly remind myself that I wasn't a bad person. When possible, I found a quiet place to center myself and pray—pray for the strength to forgive myself, for the courage to keep moving forward, for continued faith that God was present and working in and through my life.

One morning before Ian left for work, he asked me to sit down at the dining room table. "You should start to think about what life would be like in the everyday without me," he said. He told me he'd been browsing apartments online and we needed to discuss where the boys were going to live if we had to separate.

Eli had a fever that day, so I stayed home with him while Ian went to work. I spent the whole day writing Ian a letter. I realized there was still so much we hadn't talked about, so much that Ian didn't understand—and because he didn't understand, he thought there was nothing stopping me from hurting him again.

I ended the letter, saying:

> *I don't want to lose you. I love you. I love Evan and Eli. I don't want our family to break apart. For the two months I was talking to Chris,*

> *I didn't know what to do or what my life was going to be like. I lied to myself about many things, that you didn't think our marriage was going to last, that you would rather be a single dad instead of dealing with me. I couldn't see anything clearly. I am so sorry for hurting you. I told you the truth because it's what you deserve and because I love you. I'm not going to hide who I am or what I've done like I've seen other people in my family do. And I obviously have issues I need to work through, things that I didn't even know existed until this past year. You're a better person than I am. You would never have done this. You didn't deserve the deceit and betrayal of my actions. You have every right to leave me, but I hope you will choose to love me through this and eventually find a way to forgive me.*

Writing the letter wasn't just for Ian's benefit. I needed to find the words to create clarity for myself, to understand why I'd risk throwing everything away for a man who had abused me as a child, and who'd proven that—if given the chance—he'd abuse me again. It seemed nearly impossible to put into words what I was feeling and thinking, but I had to keep trying. My marriage depended on it. My life depended on it.

2007

I parked in my usual spot outside of the apartment complex. I typed out, *I'm here*, and pressed send as I made my way up the sidewalk, a soft duffel slung over one shoulder.

A text from Chris. *Be right there.*

I heard the familiar clicks and creaks of the interior stairwell door, watched as he strode toward me. He greeted me with the same familiar smile, the same tone he always used when speaking my name. Chris's apartment was like a time capsule, and every time I stepped through the door I became one of its many preserved fixtures, reprising my role as the submissive starry-eyed girl, again and again and again.

Except, this visit wasn't like the others. I was happy to see him, but there were no stars in my eyes. Maybe it had something to do with my recent breakup with Sean, how I'd gradually lost interest in wishing for what *could* be instead of what *was*.

When I was sixteen, I fantasized about what my and Chris's life would be like together after I graduated from college. Both music teachers, possibly working at the same school, the envy of the students and faculty. We'd cook meals together, take long walks holding hands, watch all the classic films and lie in bed talking until the early hours of the morning. I pictured us in our fifties and sixties, him with salt and pepper hair, and me, his chic younger wife. Decades of marriage would wash away the gossip, the scandal, the whispers of *she was his student*. It was a life perfectly packaged inside my head.

But I wasn't sixteen anymore. In just over a month, I'd be twenty-two.

In six years, the only thing that had grown in our relationship was the duration of its existence. We had our routine: we ate dinner, we watched a movie, then we'd go to the bedroom. What was I to Chris, really? A blip in the scope of his life, an echo of substance. The *goodnights* and *good mornings* only happened when I was at the apartment. He never called to ask how my day was going. We didn't text each other when something funny or strange or stressful happened. I had never hung out with his friends, never met his parents or attended one of his concerts. In all this, I never blamed him once for his absence. We lived separate lives, but I believed wholeheartedly that we shared the same reality. That we were both good, honest people who had to lie in order to be together. That the reason I was still coming to his apartment after all these years, the reason we were still intimate, the reason he never seriously dated or married, was that he had never stopped loving me.

I was older now. Wiser. Even if he did love me, this wasn't enough to satisfy. I wanted more than this. And now I carried guilt because I could feel myself pulling away from him. The cherished memories of us that had once played and replayed in technicolor were fading to black and white, and I didn't know how to revive them.

When I entered Chris's living room, I was surprised to see that the furniture had been rearranged. The loveseat, which had been flush against the wall for years, was turned to face the slider to the tiny outdoor patio. The blinds were drawn wide open, allowing the dull sunshine of early spring to pour over the plush carpet.

Chris invited me over to the newly positioned loveseat, and we sat next to each other, my hands politely folded in my lap, his hands clasped between his legs. We were in the middle of our routine conversation about school and work when he looked straight at me and said, "I'm ready to give you a commitment, *if* that's what you want."

The words lingered in the air, surreal and vapor-like. I imagined them drifting by me in a speech bubble. I'd reach my pointer finger out and—*pop!*—all the words would spill to the ground in some random order with no less meaning than before. I guess I had dreamed of this day differently. Maybe there'd be flowers, or candles, some grand gesture to fit the occasion. Instead, he asked a question—no, made a *statement*—that sounded like he was prompting me to cosign on a car loan, not to be my boyfriend.

What did a committed relationship look like to him? Did it look so different from what was happening now? Would he call me every day? Would he take care of me if I was sick, or come with me to my family's awkward Thanksgiving dinner? I had a hard time picturing it.

To complicate matters more, graduation was approaching. I knew that being in a public relationship with my former high school band teacher while pursuing a teaching job of my own would not be the best look. Would an administrator think I had skewed opinions on teacher-student relationships? I didn't think it was okay for teachers to date their students. But my relationship with Chris was different. We had always been different. How would I explain that? Would we cover things up? Lie to everyone about how our relationship started? When we had children, would we lie to them too?

Chris looked at me expectantly. I looked back into the eyes of a man I had loved since I was fourteen years old. The man I couldn't seem to explain to anyone, including myself. My gaze traced from the walnut brown eyes down to the curve of his nose, then his mouth. I observed the changing lines of his black hair, the roughening of his skin, tiny creases beginning to develop on his forehead. His birthday was earlier that month. He'd turned thirty-five.

"I think we should keep things the way they are for now," I said.

Chris's expression remained steady. "What are you doing the next few weeks?" he asked.

"I don't know. Why?"

"Do you have any concerts coming up?"

I told him about the annual Opus concert on April 20th, just a few weeks away.

"Would it be okay if I came to the concert?" he said.

My stomach tightened. I couldn't tell if it was due to excitement or fear. Chris had visited CMU many times, but never for the sole purpose of seeing me. If he attended the concert, it was a sure bet we'd be seen together by people he knew. We'd be stepping outside of our protected snow globe and into the real world. I didn't know if I was ready for that. What I did know was that I had come too far to give up that easily. I still cared for Chris, but if this was going to work, he would need to prove himself. He would have to show me he could be what I needed.

"You can come to the concert," I said.

Without missing a beat, he said, "What about May 4th? Are you free then?"

"I can be. Why?"

"I'd like to take you to a Billy Joel concert for your birthday."

This wasn't like him at all—planning ahead, wanting to see me multiple times in a month, celebrating my birthday, coming to one of my concerts. Maybe I'd been wrong to doubt this could actually work. I had already invested so much time into this man. We had history. If he was willing to invest in me more, maybe we could have a future. "I'd love that," I said.

That night, Chris and I were lying in bed, my head resting on his chest, my nose pressed to the cotton of the T-shirt he had just put on. He kept a circular floor fan near his bedroom door, its ambient whirring an ever-present comfort in the silence. For most of my life, I'd had trouble falling asleep. When I was little, I saw part of a scary movie that terrified me, and from that night on I would hide in bed with the blanket wrapped tightly around my tensed body, hyper-aware of every noise in and outside my bedroom. I imagined shadows on the wall, waited for scary things to come and get me. But the very first night I stayed with Chris, I forgot to be afraid. When it was time to sleep, I drifted off with ease, free of all fear.

As I lay there beside him, I thought about how much larger this bedroom was compared to the bedroom I had slept in six years earlier in Davison. The space inside this one made me think there was room for us to grow too.

An alert from my phone lit up a small area of the room.

It was rare anyone called or texted me when I was with Chris. I was especially curious who'd be texting me that time of night. I climbed out of the soft sheets and over to the end of the bed toward my phone that was on the floor plugged in to charge. Sprawled flatly on my stomach, I reached down to pick up the phone. I flipped it open and read the text.

What are you doing? Ian wrote.

I thought for a moment, then typed a response. *At a friend's.*

Is this friend male or female?

The corner of my mouth rose in amusement. *Why does that matter?*

It doesn't. Watching a show with some friends. Would be more fun if you were here.

"Who's that?" Chris said, his voice pouring over my back.

"It's my friend, Ian," I said, my eyes still aimed at the text conversation.

Chris pulled back the covers and repositioned himself so that he was lying next to me on his side. I felt his hand on the small of my back, then the movement of his fingers as they slid across my skin. He leaned in and kissed me, keeping his lips pressed to mine for several seconds before pulling away. The phone screen cast a glow across our faces. I saw his dark eyes searching mine, though I wasn't sure what he was looking for.

Ian picked me up from my apartment and drove us to get snacks and bottled water for an upcoming choir event. Ian always got a kick out of taking me to the store. We'd go to one of those giant warehouse stores that only sold items in bulk. I'd insist on pushing the cart, and Ian would laugh as it became harder and harder to maneuver with each crate of bottled water we stacked into the oversized basket. Wherever we went, people thought we were a couple. *How long have you been together?* they'd say. I would start to correct them (*Oh, we're just friends*) when Ian would jump in with some arbitrary number—six months, two years—then flash me a proud smile.

That day, on the way to the store, the subject of romantic relationships came up. Ian joked that many of his choices in life were made under the influence of a pretty girl, like how in middle school the girl Ian liked told him she played French horn, so Ian asked the band director if he could play the same instrument. "I had no idea what the French horn was," Ian said, glancing at me from the driver's seat, laughing and shaking his head.

Band ended up being his saving grace. An injury forced him off the high school football team, which seemed devastating until he decided to invest more time into music. He made it to first chair in his section, and he became drum major of the marching band. Eventually, Ian decided to follow in the footsteps of his band director and was accepted into the music education program at CMU.

"Then the depression hit," Ian said. "Except, I didn't know it was depression at the time. I just knew I didn't feel the same. I had always been the happy, shiny kid, you know? Then I got to college and everything changed. I ignored my friends. I stopped going to class."

I had trouble imagining the person Ian described. A sad recluse. He was so friendly with everyone, always open to talk, always the one looking out for other people. "I'm sorry that happened to you," I said.

"It wasn't what I planned. But after a few years of working different jobs, I went to a doctor, got on medication. Then I asked to come back to finish my music degree."

"You had to ask to come back?"

"I gave a presentation to a committee about why I should be readmitted. Thankfully, they said *yes*."

The image came into focus. This is why Ian was finishing college at the same time I was. If he hadn't experienced a depressive episode, he would have graduated six years before me.

I almost felt guilty for being glad he had ended up at CMU the same time as me. What was even more interesting about Ian was that we had both come to CMU to be band directors, and both of us had changed our focus to choral music, and for similar reasons. Though we would always love band, there was something special about the combination of poetry and music that spoke to us in a way instrumental music did not.

Ian's vulnerability opened up a vulnerability in me. It was my turn to talk about romantic relationships, and I felt so comfortable with Ian, I started telling him things I had only told a handful of my closest friends. When I hinted at my relationship with Chris, Ian's demeanor changed. An emotion I'd never seen in him rang through the van's cabin like a warning shot—it was anger.

"Hold on—you're telling me that you've been dating your band teacher since you were in high school?" The way he said "dating" suggested he found it an appalling description of the situation. Then, Ian used a word no one had ever used to describe Chris: *molester*.

I shot back. "No, he isn't."

"What do you think he is?" Ian said.

"He made a mistake by starting our relationship earlier than he should have. People make mistakes. He's a good person. He wouldn't hurt anyone. He hasn't hurt me."

Ian looked at me, his eyes wide with worry. "Megan, listen to me—"

"This is why I don't talk about this. You don't understand. No one would understand."

"When was the last time you saw this person?"

I opened my mouth to answer, but hesitated. Saying anything about Chris was clearly a mistake. I'd gotten too comfortable. "I don't know, a while ago."

Silence settled between us.

"I don't think it's healthy for you to be spending time with this person," he said.

I grew cold, staring straight ahead at the road, unwilling to look in his direction. "Can we talk about something else?"

We were quiet the rest of the drive to the store.

In Advanced Conducting, everyone took turns leading a song in front of the class. After each person's turn, a piece of paper was passed around the room with our name on it so others could write comments about our performance.

When I got my paper back, the first thing I noticed was that my last name had been crossed off. Written above it was Ian's last name. I leaned forward, eyeing him from down the row. "Hey!" I whisper-shouted. "Ian!"

He turned his head slowly. I jabbed my finger at the spot where his last name was written. "What is this?"

He raised his shoulders, but the smug look on his face said he knew exactly what I was talking about. I made sure he saw me cross off his last name and rewrite mine above it.

After class, I was sitting on a bench in the main lobby when Ian sat down next to me. "What was all that about?" I said, smiling.

I expected him to make a joke. Instead, he leaned his back against the wall, and we quietly watched people pass through the lobby, perhaps on their way to class or to the student coffee shop. Once we were alone, Ian's head fell softly in my direction. "You know . . . one of the first things I noticed about you is how you treat other people."

"What do you mean?" I said, meeting his gaze.

"I mean, you care about people." He gestured to a nearby bench where, one day earlier, a person from choir had been crying before class. "Yesterday, I saw you stop to talk to someone because they were sad. It's not the first time I've seen you do something like that."

I was speechless. I had never heard any guy talk about me the way Ian was talking about me, as if my character was not a matter of opinion but an unequivocal fact. It was strange, but in the best way possible.

Ian stood from the bench and grabbed his backpack. As he was leaving, he said, "I just wish you could see what *I* see when I think about us being together."

2020

The first week of March, I was scheduled to work with choirs at a high school in the Flint area. I asked Ian if it would be okay to stay the night at my parents' so I'd have a shorter drive the next morning. This was the first solo trip I'd made to Flint since November, when I flew to Florida out of the Flint Bishop Airport.

For three months, it had been fairly easy to block Chris from my mind, but one morning it was as if a switch had been flipped. I woke with a familiar sense of loneliness and dread; memories of Chris that had lay dormant were now waking up, demanding my attention.

I tried to talk sense into my body by thinking of moments in Florida when Chris appeared disingenuous. I recalled a moment in Florida where I was walking behind him on a boardwalk and I stepped on something sharp. "Ow!" I said, grabbing at the sore spot on my foot. He was quick in reminding me to be careful, but he never stopped or even looked back to see if I was okay to keep moving forward. Later, when I was walking beside him in the dark, I told him that one of my former students had attempted suicide. I didn't see his expression, but his silence was almost frightening. Yet whenever I felt a twinge of discomfort or doubt, I'd find him taking my hand and leading the conversation in another direction.

... I can't believe you're actually here, standing in front of me ...

... I haven't felt this way in a long time ...

... You know, I was very much in love with you back then ...

... Did you ever wonder what would've happened if we had stayed together ... ?

... Your hair still smells exactly the same ...

... When I saw you in the water, I wanted so badly to kiss you, right then and there ...

The day I left for my parents', a dangerous urge was brewing inside me. I wanted to hear Chris's voice. I wanted to know he was okay. I told myself it was just to prove I was healing, that I could have a short conversation without it going any further. But I also knew that when it came to Chris, I was capable of justifying almost anything. Something about driving back to Flint triggered feelings that had been buried since the night I confessed to Ian.

As soon as I was on the road, what had begun that morning as an intrusive thought was morphing into a plan of action.

On the highway toward Flint, I held the phone in my hand next to the steering wheel. I had typed his number into my cell, my thumb hovering over the green call circle.

Just before I touched the screen, Ian's name popped up as an incoming call. I answered.

"I know you haven't been gone that long," he said. "But I just wanted to check on you."

Maybe he could sense something about me before I left, or maybe my leaving had triggered something in him as well. "I'm good. Just driving," I said.

"You're okay?"

"Yep."

"Okay, well, I love you."

Ian had only recently started saying *I love you* again. For the last three months, when he and I would say our goodbyes on the phone, I would say, "I love you," and he would gently say, "Goodbye." Though the words were absent, there were other ways he showed love to me. He called or texted to share a story about his day or just to say hello. He noticed when I was out of something at the house, like shampoo or face wash, and bought me another bottle. He'd even let me cuddle up to him for periods of time.

A voice inside me was trying to reason, *Why do you want to call Chris? Why would you risk everything again?*

But another voice was saying, *Just one more time. I can handle it. I'm in control.*

When I called Chris's number, the phone rang several times before going to an automated voicemail message.

I tried again. Same result.

As part of an effort to prove my loyalty to Ian, I had given up the Flint phone number I'd had since I was fifteen for a new, local number. I wondered if Chris wasn't answering because he didn't know who from Midland was calling.

When I got to my parents' house, I sent a text. *It's Megan. Can I call you soon?*

Yes, the reply said.

"I'm hungry," I told my mom. "I'm gonna run out real quick and grab a bite to eat."

"You just got here," she said, her brow squinched. "You sure you don't want me to make you something?"

"Nope. I'm good. I'll do a drive thru and be right back."

When Chris said, "Hello," the buzzing inside my head seemed to go quiet.

"It's been a while," I said.

"I know."

"How are you?"

I relaxed into the lulling tones of his voice as he brought me up to date with the Florida investigation. He said a new judge had been assigned to his case, so certain steps in the litigation process had to be resubmitted. I was always conflicted when we talked about his case. I didn't want him to suffer, but I also wanted him to be remorseful about his actions. I wanted him to prove that, given the chance, he would make different choices.

"I saw something today that reminded me of you," he said. "Hm . . . I can't remember what it was."

My breath caught in my throat. I was working hard every day to put my life back together, trying to forget him. He just *happened* to think of me that day and couldn't remember why?

I felt the familiar pull of wanting to go back to the past, to resurrect all the unfinished business between us. "I'm sorry I didn't call months ago," I said.

"Well, when I texted you and you didn't respond, I just moved on."

This comment was so cold, so unfeeling, that it made me wonder if Chris was downplaying his real feelings and pretending not to care. It was such a shift from the last time we spoke, when he said he would always be there for me, when he reached out after Thanksgiving to make sure I was okay.

"So. You're happy?" he asked.

The pivot between his last comment and this one gave me whiplash. Which was it? Did he care or didn't he?

"I am happy," I said, allowing a breath of doubt. "It's complicated . . . I have to be realistic." I hated hearing myself talk like this. It was complicated, but he didn't need to know that. And what was I even trying to say? Was I just trying to please him? To tell him I still cared for him? Why was it that every time I spoke to him, I had so little control over what I said? Like clockwork, I reverted back to that girl who trusted him and believed he was a safe place. He used to be my escape. Now I was trying to escape *him*. "I have to go. I've already said more than I planned to."

Chris chuckled. "That's pretty typical."

"I need to go."

"Take care, Megan."

The following week, I drove to Indiana to clinic my friend's choirs in the district where Ian and I had worked before moving back to Michigan.

I didn't call Chris on the drive. Just as I'd thought, the conversation we had the week before was enough for me. Ian would never have to know that we spoke to each other. Why would I ever tell him? It would only hurt him and our chances of staying together.

News of a possible pandemic was circulating. My friend said, "You watch, by this time next week we won't be in school."

"Really? You think so?" I said.

"Professional sports teams don't stop their seasons for nothing. This is serious."

That was on a Wednesday. On Sunday, we received an announcement from the school that the boys would not be going back that week. The school treated it like an early start to their spring break, and they hoped to be back in session by early April.

News got around of a church choir rehearsal where COVID-19 spread to most of the singers, killing several. My church suspended in-person activities and moved everything online. When it became clear that the school would not be reopening in the foreseeable future, Ian—and every other music teacher—had to figure out how to teach a music class over Zoom. Every morning and afternoon, I'd hear Ian in the basement playing the piano and singing, but I couldn't hear any of the students because they all had to have their microphones muted. Ian had to assume they were actually participating.

Our family was fortunate to be in a position to keep our jobs and work from home. We decided to try and enjoy the extra time we had together. Ian, who hadn't baked in a long time, started making pies and cookies. We watched a Marvel movie every night until we had seen them all.

By mid-May, my mom was begging to visit. "I miss you and the boys. I'll take the risk." None of us had been sick, and Ian and I were only leaving the house to pick up essential items from the grocery store. I agreed to let her come.

She planned to visit for only two days, but on the second day there was an unusually heavy rainstorm, so she decided not to drive home.

The rain continued through the night.

The next day, my phone made an alarming sound. It was an emergency text. "MIDLAND CITY RESIDENTS WEST OF EASTMAN SOUTH OF US-10 NEED TO EVACUATE DUE TO DAM COLLAPSE."

More alerts came in ordering residents to evactuate, but our house was not in any of the evacuation zones. I stood at the back window and watched as water flooded the nearby park and crept steadily toward us. When all was said and done, the water had stopped only inches from the brick and there was only minor damage to our basement.

Others were not so lucky. Twenty-five hundred homes were either damaged or destroyed by the flooding. Street after street there were housefuls of belongings piled up on curbs. As if the pandemic wasn't enough, now some people had to figure out where they were going to live.

The damage in our basement was enough that Randy offered to lend me his large dehumidifier. Since I had to go to Flint to pick it up, I took the boys with me so they could see their grandparents.

It'd been exactly six months since I'd told Ian the truth about my betrayal with Chris. Instead of feeling further away from everything and proud of how far I'd come, I was infested with dread. I'd noticed, in recent days, I'd been less hopeful, more irritable. It was only later I recognized how my change in mood aligned with the calendar.

For most of my life, the word "anniversary" was only associated with happy things—a birthday, a wedding, holidays. As a child, every Valentine's Day my mom would decorate the kitchen table with candies, gifts, and flowers. She always had a way of making special occasions feel special. I had never acknowledged how the body senses an anniversary—and while anniversaries of celebration arrive like welcomed guests stopping by to brighten your day, anniversaries of grief show up uninvited, threatening to move in and ruin your life.

I watched my mom slicing vegetables on the kitchen counter while the boys played in the other room. I had shared very little with her beyond the investigation ending. If she knew what I'd done, it would make it too real. But in the wake of my recent vulnerability, I knew I couldn't hold it in any longer.

"Can we go for a walk?" I said, already shaking.

She looked up from her cutting board. "What's going on?"

Water welled up in my eyes. "I need my mom."

She yelled to Randy, "Megan and I will be back in a little while, we're going for a walk!"

Randy burst through the door, "Is she okay? Is my Megan okay?"

I hid my face as she shooed him out. "Yes, yes, she's fine. We'll be right back."

When we started down the street, I said, "I hope you'll love me no matter what I tell you."

"You're my daughter," she said. "Of course I'll love you."

I told her about September of the previous year, how I had called Chris after the prosecutors decided not to arrest him. I told her about the secret calls and texts, the trying to stop, the growing conflict between me and Ian, getting the text about my grandfather then going to Florida. As I recounted the details, I noticed myself talking wistfully about my time with Chris, breathing romanticism into each scene.

"So when you were there, there was just kissing?" she said.

"The first time, yes." I hesitated. "When I went back, we slept together."

She stopped abruptly and stood square to me. "You can *never* tell Ian about this."

I shook my head. "It's too late for that. I told him six months ago."

She glared at me with frustration that could fill a canyon. "*Wow,* Megan," she said, her words dripping with disappointment. "I just don't know how you could be so selfish."

"I don't regret it," I said, as if trying to convince us both. Whatever had led me down this path, however destructive, it was easier to shrink her words than to allow myself to feel the full weight of my actions. I knew how complicated this had to be for her—my mom, who didn't have a disloyal bone in her body, standing in front of her daughter, the adultress. Her daughter, who she'd bore from a man who had betrayed her.

When the boys climbed into the vehicle to head home, my mom hugged me. "I will always love you."

What I heard was, *I'll find a way to love you again. But not today. Today, I'm angry.*

The unraveling had begun. Whatever focus I'd been able to maintain for six months was blurred, my internal compass pulling toward an alternative north. I was in pain and I knew only one thing that could take it away. More specifically, one person.

I passed by Ian as he was watching TV in the living room. "I'm going for a walk."

He waved. "Have fun."

As soon as I reached the sidewalk, my phone was ringing, my heart picking up speed.

"Hey, Megan." I could hear his smile over a thousand miles away. "I saw what happened in Midland with the flood. Was your house okay? I tried to think of someone we know mutually who I could send a message through."

I wasn't sure I believed the story about why he couldn't reach out. He wasn't scared to contact me right after I told Ian about us. Why now, six months later? What did he have to lose?

"My house was fine," I said. "We were lucky."

He didn't ask anything more about it, about the people whose homes were decimated. I didn't think he really cared, not about my house or anyone else's. It was lip service, and poor lip service at that. For the first time, I was disappointed in him.

I walked one of my usual paths, listening to him talk about work, the pandemic, unemployment checks. Just two friends catching up, that's what we sounded like, which made little sense to me. I was getting impatient. I wanted to talk about real things. I wanted to talk about us.

Chris told me he had wanted to visit Michigan in March, but then the pandemic happened. Then he told me he'd recently spoken to a former student from Michigan. "He feels bad for everything I've gone through," Chris said. "He told me, '*I wish I could just pack up my car and drive down to Florida to see you,*' so I said, 'Hey, there's plenty of room here.'"

Was he out of his mind? Chris would really have a former male student stay with him at his apartment, with everything going on? Either he was lying to try and make me jealous, or he was an idiot.

"I spoke with my lawyer today," Chris said, his voice easing into the statement. I waited for him to finish the thought but instead there was a pause. "You know what I'm going to say, don't you?"

"No . . ." I had no idea what he was talking about, and I found it strange he would wait this long to bring up something that sounded this important.

"It's just—it's weird you're calling right now. I received an email today from my lawyer saying the prosecutors here want to use you in the trial."

I wanted to vomit on the sidewalk. I had specifically asked Sergeant Perry if the police in Florida were going to use my case, and he said they made no mention of it. Why did they wait to ask for my help eight months after the Michigan investigation closed?

"Why are you telling me this?" I said. The strength in my voice surprised me. I had never spoken to him this way. "Are you using our relationship as some kind of leverage? Because I'm not going to lie about what happened."

"No," he said, smoothing down the edges of the conversation. "I'm not asking you to lie. I just didn't want you to be surprised if they call."

My footsteps grew quick and heavy as I made the turn back onto my street, my home now in view. "I don't know what's wrong with me," I said. "I could lose my children for talking to you."

Chris was silent.

I was talking into a void that projected its emptiness onto me. But this time, instead of reaching for his affection to fill that emptiness, I reached for more answers. "When you first kissed me, I didn't know it was illegal. Did you know it was illegal?"

"No," he said, plainly.

Don't believe him, Megan. How could he not know?

A deep sadness took hold of me. I could hear what my gut was saying, but the truth of it was too awful to grasp. If he knew that kissing me was illegal—not just kissing, but everything else that happened between us—what kind of person would that make him? What would that make me?

"When I saw you last year, I don't know if we were there for the same reasons," I said.

A beat of silence. "Is that what you think now?" Chris said.

My stomach soured as I began to relive the night at the Airbnb apartment in St. Pete Beach.

"When we stayed the night together, I didn't make you do anything you didn't want to, right?" I knew how absurd this question was, to make it seem like he was the victim in this. Part of me wondered if I was saying these things just to test his response, to see if he had any ounce of humanity in him.

"You didn't make me do anything. Why do you ask?"

"Well, it's just . . ." I trailed off, not knowing how to tell him the thoughts that continued to haunt me about Florida. I saw myself in the tiny bedroom, waiting anxiously for what I knew was about to happen. Chris slid into the bed. We were kissing, working at each other's clothes when I asked, "Do you have a condom?"

"No," he said.

"What? Why don't you?"

"I didn't want to be presumptuous," he said.

Presumptuous? He knew this was going to happen. What if he didn't buy a condom because he didn't really want to have sex? But if he didn't want to have sex, why was he still kissing me? Was he doing this only because I wanted to? Did he not want this? Did he not want me? Was he toying with me to see how far I'd go? How reckless I'd become?

He was on top of me, his hands in my hair, his mouth pushing hard against mine. If there was a voice inside me telling me to stop, it was being smothered by a barrage of shouts, crying out in agony, *I need this to happen. I'll die if this doesn't happen.* I grabbed harder at him, pulling him toward me, as if I could make his body swallow mine. I felt giant waves pulling me out to sea, and I had nothing to grab onto to keep myself on shore.

A sudden rush of warmth hit me, and my limbs grew heavy. I was on top of the waves now, rocking back and forth. There was nothing beyond that room. No pain. Just nothingness.

Ten seconds went by . . . . Fifteen seconds . . . . Twenty seconds . . . .

Without warning, I felt Chris retreat. He slid backward on the bed and buried his face in the soft flesh of my hip.

I stared wide-eyed at the ceiling, confusion searing my insides. "What's wrong?"

He made a long groaning sound. "I'm nervous."

I wanted to burst into tears. *No, no, no. This can't be what happens. I've given up everything for this man. I've ruined my life for this?*

Out of shameful desperation, I kept kissing him. I tried to keep going, but it was no use. He had gone soft. He blamed it on drinking too much wine, and for a second I believed him. I tallied up the drinks in my head. *A glass of wine at dinner. Two mixed drinks at another restaurant*. But that was hours before. He didn't seem drunk.

Oh God. Was he drinking because he knew he would have to sleep with me, and it was the only way he could stomach it? I knew I didn't have the body I used to. I had given birth to two children. I had stretch marks and a layer of fat on my stomach. He couldn't pretend anymore that he wanted this.

Even though he wasn't acting embarrassed, I told myself he must be. What man wouldn't be embarrassed in this situation? In a calm, understanding voice, I said, "You know what? It's okay."

I started to back away when he put a gentle hand on me and said, "Come here. Let me hold you." The care in his voice was almost enough to break me. But I wouldn't. I refused to let him see me fall apart. Instead, I let his reality become my reality. It was easier to believe it was the drinking—and not me—that made him stop so I could continue to breathe. So the walls wouldn't close in on me. We were running out of time. Once this night was over, I wouldn't be able to make any more memories. This was all I'd have left to remember of us.

"*Megan,*" Chris assured me through the phone line. "You didn't do anything wrong . . . . I didn't want to get you pregnant."

Why couldn't I just tell him what I was thinking? *You're lying. You're a liar. I'm not an idiot, I know how pregnancy works.* If he was worried about getting me pregnant, why didn't he just ask if I was on birth control? Why didn't he just buy a condom in the first place and avoid the whole ordeal? What if the lie went deeper? What if he had gotten a vasectomy years ago and there was zero chance of getting anyone pregnant? He was almost fifty. He must have known he was never going to have children. What if this was all just some sick game of his? What if he did all this just to see if he could?

Chris had just gotten back from the gym and was making a smoothie. I could hear the sounds of the blender echoing off the walls of his townhouse. "If you want," he said, "I can let you know how things are going here, give you updates about whether or not they plan to include you."

"I'd rather not," I said. "I'll just think about it all the time." What I was really thinking was, *This is just another way for you to monitor me.*

"I don't wanna sound weird about this, but you are deleting our texts, right?" he said.

"Yes, I am."

"Good girl."

"I want to keep talking. I'll just have to figure out a way to balance everything." As I was saying this, I heard how crazy it was. As long as Chris was involved, there was no balance.

"Remember, you have to be the one to call me," Chris said.

"You know, my therapist said you making me be the one to call has something to do with you wanting power over me."

Chris's sigh was clearly audible. "These therapists always think they know what they're talking about."

The next day, I stood in line at the store with a cart full of groceries. I felt like I was in some post-apocalyptic movie. Every person was wearing a blue medical mask and the lines extended way out into the aisles. I had never seen anything like it. Nothing seemed real, not even me.

The line progressed so slowly that most of the time I was at a standstill. I'd fixate on an object, paralyzed by thoughts that looped inside my head: *My family is better off without me. Things will never be the same again. I'm never going to beat this. It's easier to just give up now.*

After six months of progress, I was right back to where I had started—flooded with longing for Chris, wanting to run, to give up the battle and stop the pain. I was consciously aware of my insanity but had no idea how to banish it. There were so many logical reasons to hate Chris, to fear him, to never want to see him again, but I couldn't feel any of them. There was a part of me that craved contact with Chris the same way I craved oxygen when underwater for too long, an urgency to resurface radiating through me.

In therapy, Becca gave me the tool of "playing the tape," where I'd imagine every step of what would happen if I were to take a certain action. As I stood there in line, I played the tape: *I go home and fill a bag with everything that will fit. The boys will cry as I pack, and I'll cry, too. I'll tell them how much I love them but explain that I can't stay. Getting myself out of the house will be the hardest thing, but once I leave I can try to forget the life I had. I fly to Florida. Get off the plane. Breathe in the warm tropical air. I'm free. I take a taxi to Chris's place, walk up to his front door and....*

This is where I got stuck, where the fantasy ended. The thought of arriving at his place, of seeing him open the door, was thrilling. But what happens after that? What would actually happen if I just showed up at Chris's? He may pretend to be happy for a day, but that wouldn't last. A man who had lived alone his entire adult life wasn't going to want someone there, especially me. How would that look to the lawyers? How long before he decided to be done with me? Then I'd have nothing. I'd lose my family and I'd lose him.

I needed help right away, no matter how shameful or embarrassing it might be. The only thing that mattered was making sure I didn't destroy my life and the lives of those who loved me. The healthy parts of me that still existed, though they were constantly fighting against trauma and grief, had never left me. It was up to me whether I wanted to listen to the loudest voice inside me or the truest one.

When I left the store, I got in my vehicle and called my mom. "I talked to him again," I said.

The fear in her voice was palpable. "Please stop. You have to stop. You're going to lose everything."

"I know, Mom. That's why I'm reaching out to you instead of calling him. I need help."

"I should have handled all of this differently from the beginning. I should have been screaming instead of staying quiet."

Her anger toward Chris fueled by her love for me snapped me back to reality. "I'm going to stop this," I told her. "I'm going to hang up with you, send him a message and block him."

"Please call me back once you do," she said. "I love you, Megan."

To Chris: *We can never speak to each other again. Leave me alone. Forget about me. I'm blocking your number.*

2007

It was my night to cook at the apartment. I was in the kitchen stirring a pan of chicken, rice and peppers when I heard a text alert from my phone. I flipped it open and saw a block of text from Ian. It was the lyrics to one of the songs we'd been rehearsing in choir for our spring concert.

> O, my luve's like a red, red rose
> That's newly sprung in June.
> O, my luve's like a melody,
> that's sweetly played in tune.
> As fair, art thou my bonny lass,
> So deep in love am I.
> I will love you still my dear,
> til all the seas gang dry.

I shouted across the apartment to my roommate, Sarah, who was relaxing on her bed watching TV, "Now Ian is sending me love poetry!"

She shouted back, "That sounds like him!"

Without hesitation, I found Ian's name in my contact list and pressed the call button. He answered on the first ring. "Yes?" he said.

"Ian, the message you sent is really nice. But I'm sorry. I'm just never going to feel that way about you."

"Okay," he said. "What are you doing tomorrow?"

I laughed. "I don't know. I'm probably studying for finals."

"Well, if you want to hang out, I'll be around."

CMU's Opus concert was only two days away, and I'd heard nothing from Chris since I left his apartment weeks before. I assumed he was still planning to attend the concert. I hadn't heard otherwise, but I was really hoping after my last visit he would have reached out once or twice.

I wanted to reach out to him and say something, but with Chris I had never felt comfortable expressing my feelings in words. He and I spoke plenty of words to each other when we were together, but the meaning behind them only reached so far below the surface. For six years, the physical part of our relationship was our most intimate expression of affection, and for years it felt like enough to satisfy. But something was missing.

I miss you. I need you. I love you. Those words were non-existent between us. When I would lie in his arms at night, feeling his heartbeat against me, it was almost like hearing words. I interpreted his heartbeat to be some sort of Morse code for his feelings, but maybe I was imagining substance where there was only air.

The difference now was that he had finally used words to express his feelings. "I'm ready to give you a commitment," is what he said. That had to mean something.

Maybe it's me, I thought. I was the one who turned him down. If our relationship was going to have any chance at success, I needed to return the vulnerability

> FACEBOOK MESSAGE FROM MEGAN LUCIUS TO CHRIS BLACKMER:
> Just thinking about you. Hope you had a wonderful day.

I waited all through the next day for Chris's response. Finally, at 8:15 p.m., I got one.

> CHRIS: Hey, thanks! Looking forward to coming up tomorrow. I will have to depart Saturday morning around 9am to get back to Detroit in time for a Tigers game [pensive face emoji]

I let out a long sigh. This was like one of those awkward movie scenes where one person says, "I love you," and the other person doesn't know what to say so they just say, "Thank you." What was he thanking me for, anyway? For hoping he had a wonderful day? Or was he thanking me for thinking about him? It wasn't really clear. Adding to the disappointment was the knowledge that he'd be leaving early the next morning, which meant whatever plans I was imagining for us weren't going to happen.

I guess I hadn't made any solid plans in my mind. It was hard to see us doing anything other than breakfast because we had never done anything else in the morning light. It was either breakfast and goodbyes or just goodbyes.

He had never mentioned liking baseball. Who was he going with? A group of friends, no doubt, a part of his world I knew nothing of. Did he make the plans before or after he knew he was coming to visit me? If he had invited me to the baseball game, would I even have felt comfortable going?

I was growing tired of the questions and the doubting. Relationships shouldn't be this complicated. I wanted being with a boyfriend to feel like being with one of my best friends, where I could relax and be myself fully. After everything, I still held onto some hope that Chris could be that person.

On the night of Opus, I was one of the first performers to arrive at the School of Music. As I made my way down the hallway toward the green room, I saw Ian walking toward me. "I finally watched *Mr. and Mrs. Smith* the other night," I said.

"Oh yeah?" He looked pleasantly surprised I had remembered our conversation from months ago. Ian shook his head. "I still can't believe he left Jen for Angelina. *What. A. Fool.*"

"Hey, it hasn't been proven that he cheated," I said. "But it's possible. I mean, look at that super sexy scene where he has her up against the wall. Do you know what I'm talking about?"

Ian smiled a mischievous grin. "You mean the one where he does this?" He stepped toward me, causing my spine to line the white brick, and placed his hands on the wall above my head, his eyes riveting into mine.

A pretzely-ache lodged in my gut. "Yeeeeaaaah," I said, the word escaping in slow motion, a direct contrast to my heart which was now beating in cut time. I had seen Ian be funny and kind, but I had never seen him act sexy.

His eyes lingered a moment longer, then he pulled away from me and flashed a confident smile that brought out the boyishness in his face. "Good luck tonight," he said, and continued in the direction he was going, humming a tune as he walked away.

I stood there for a while, trying to catch my breath, wondering what had gotten into him. I waited for my pulse to recover, then I went to a practice room to warm up.

Chris said he wouldn't make it in time to see me before the concert started, so I told him I'd meet him in the lobby afterward. Minutes before the first act, I waited nervously backstage, wondering if he was already in the building, if someone had recognized him, if they had asked him his reason for coming. Each time I was on stage and stood under the bright lights, I felt unusually exposed. I peered out into the dark, not knowing which of the shadowy figures was Chris.

When the concert was over, the performers poured out from the greenroom to the main lobby to greet their friends and family. I didn't follow them. I took the far hallway down to another lobby around the corner from where everyone was gathered. When I peeked into the main lobby, I saw Chris talking to one of my professors, a friend of his.

If I walked up to Chris and stood by his side, the professor would probably look at me and say, *I didn't know you two knew each other*. Then he'd realize, *Oh, Chris is here for you?* I'd watch the look behind his eyes as he contemplated our history, calculating our age difference, clicking puzzle pieces together, one by one.

I had dreamed of this day for so long, to be together in public as an actual couple, but now that it was happening I wasn't sure how to feel about it. Everything was easier when we stayed safe inside our snow globe, our perfectly crafted world where no one was allowed to interfere. This felt dangerous and messy.

Instead of meeting Chris, I grabbed the bench nearest to the main lobby. I listened to the conversations taking place not far from where I was—boisterous, echoey voices that carried through the building as I hid in solace around the corner. Eventually, the only voices I could hear were Chris's and the professor's. When they said their goodbyes, I waited a few more seconds, then I emerged to greet him.

"Ready to go?" Chris asked, showing no apparent concern for my late arrival. We headed down the empty hall toward the parking lot.

"Did you talk to anyone you knew?" I tried not to let it sound like an interrogation, although I wanted to know everything. *What did you say? Did you tell anyone about me? What was their reaction?*

"I got to catch up with Mark," he said. It was strange to hear Dr. Kettering's first name. Chris said it so casually, but of course he would. Dr. Kettering—*Mark*—was Chris's friend. They had both attended CMU. I waited for him to go into more detail about their conversation, but he had already moved on. "By the way, good job tonight," he said.

This, for me, was the most disappointing moment since Chris's arrival. I had really wanted him to say something about my performance. I wanted to know he was proud of me. But all he could say was "good job tonight," stated so dispassionately, he might as well have said nothing at all.

Chris and I went to the local Applebee's for dinner, then he followed me in his car back to my apartment. It was strange to see him grabbing the overnight bag from his backseat, for him to be staying at my place for once. When I realized he had never been in any of my bedrooms, I began to worry he wouldn't like the decor. I still used the same bed frame and nightstand Mom and Randy had given me the year I turned eleven. I worried he'd think it looked like a little girl's room. My roommate, Sarah, knew Chris was coming to visit me, so she opted to drive home for the weekend. I didn't blame her. I was sure it'd be uncomfortable hosting your best friend's thirty-five-year-old band-teacher-boyfriend for the night. Still, part of me wished she could be there, that Chris was someone my friends wanted to be around.

Alone at the apartment, Chris and I fell into our usual routine of TV watching and talking. Before long, his hand was on my thigh. He reached over to touch my hair, then pulled me to him and began kissing me. I turned the television off, took his hand, and led him to my room.

The next morning, I relaxed in bed as Chris showered. In the light of day, it was like having some mythical creature inhabiting my space, a larger-than-life being using my puny college bathroom. He'd been such a giant in my life, it was as if he had to shrink himself down to fit inside my apartment.

On his way out the door, he kissed me goodbye. "I'll see you in two weeks."

I forced a half smile, knowing he meant precisely what he said. We would talk no sooner than that. "Two weeks. Sounds good," I said.

On April 30th, ten days after the Opus concert, I emptied my locker and got ready to leave the music building for one of the last times before summer break. It was bittersweet. In the fall, I'd be living with my parents in Flint and interning as a student teacher, which I was really excited about. On the other hand, I was going to miss being at school with my friends.

When I stepped outside and headed for the parking lot, I saw Ian leaving at the exact same time through doors on the opposite side of the building. He noticed me from across the parking lot and shouted, "Hey, Lucius! Your birthday's coming up. Do you wanna get some lunch? It's on me."

We met downtown at Max and Emily's, a quaint deli-style restaurant decked out in sports memorabilia, local art, and menus drawn in colorful chalk on gigantic blackboards. We ordered at the counter, then sat down at a small table near a wall accented by a framed #52 Gutierrez jersey. As Ian and I enjoyed our food, we talked about school and summer. He asked me questions about growing up in Flint, about high school. I asked questions about his family. He wanted to know my favorite movie. I wanted to hear more stories about his fraternity. The conversation was so easy, like gently passing a ball back and forth. I studied his expression as he asked one thoughtful question after another and then listened intently as I spoke, his eyes sparkling with curiosity, an upward turn of his mouth.

I'd been in his company so many times before, but something was different—and as we went on talking and smiling and laughing, I tried to make sense of it. Suddenly, a warm wave of affection washed over me, taking me completely by surprise. I saw Ian through a new lens, one that left me momentarily dazed and breathless. It was like waking from a dream.

Ian was the best part of every person I had ever loved. He was handsome, charming, funny, kind, thoughtful, loyal. I had always known these things in a practical way, but now I knew them in both my head *and* my heart. A thought appeared, as loud and clear as if I were speaking it out loud. *This is the way it's supposed to be.*

When we had finished eating, I said, "What do you want to do now?"

"I don't know. What do *you* want to do?"

"Let's go for a walk," I said.

"Ian and Megan!" someone called out from across the room. It was our friend from choir, Rebecca, seated in the corner near the front window. We walked over to say hello. As we chatted with Rebecca, I noticed the immense pride I felt standing at Ian's side. Like I belonged there.

We left Max & Emily's and strolled down to a furniture store on the corner of Franklin and Broadway, a historical building three-stories high, each floor with its own unique history. As we climbed the staircase to the second floor, I saw a painting on the wall of a woman at a tiny restaurant table, dressed in red, her thick curly brown hair pulled into a ponytail. Her elbows were resting on the table as she admired the flower she was holding in her hand. She looked happy, peaceful.

"I love this," I said, pointing at the painting.

Ian looked at the painting, then back at me. "That is really lovely."

Next, we climbed a narrow curved staircase to a balcony overlooking what used to be a ballroom. We stood at the railing, gazing down at the modern decor that clearly did not fit the era of the room itself. "Can't you see it?" said Ian in a cheesy theatrical tone. "Lord and lady, greeting their many guests." He gestured to the floor below, sweeping an outstretched palm from wall to wall, wanting me to imagine a room filled with esteemed guests instead of overpriced couches and coffee tables.

I laughed and shook my head, taken by his unabashed attempts at romantic banter. We started back down the stairs, and in an effort to help me safely through the narrow passageway, Ian placed his hand on the small of my back. *Zing*. Heat. Desire. Passion. It rushed through my body in one cosmic surge, as if altering the chemistry of my whole being.

I couldn't believe it. I had been adamant to Ian that I would never want more than friendship from him, and he was adamant that I was wrong.

I had never been so happy to be wrong in my entire life.

Our final stop was to the basement level where a sea of La-Z-Boy chairs filled a large open space. We each picked a chair to sit in, facing each other, only a small aisle separating us.

"I want to tell you something," I said.

"Oh yeah?" There was a hint of knowing in his voice.

"Yes, but . . . nevermind."

"No, tell me. You can tell me."

We were completely alone. It would have been a perfect moment to walk over and kiss him. But I didn't want to rush into anything and make a mess of our relationship. Ian wasn't the kind of person you kissed and walked away from. I needed to be sure this was real.

"Nope," I said with attempted finality. "Maybe later."

As we climbed the stairs back up to the main floor, Ian and I kept exchanging looks. "Are you *sure* you don't want to tell me?" he said one last time.

I rolled my eyes, pressed my lips together. It was all I could do to keep from blurting out something ridiculous, pulling him into another room and throwing myself at him. We left the furniture store, and walked back to the diner where we said our goodbyes.

When I got home, Sarah was in her room at her computer. "I almost kissed Ian today," I told her, standing in her bedroom doorway.

She spun her chair around, eyeing me. "Don't hurt that boy. He's *so* in love with you."

"I'm serious!" I said, laughing off her comment. "I think I really like him,"

"Okay," she said with a smirk, and spun back toward her computer.

The next day, Sarah invited a group of friends over for an end-of-the-year get together. I was stuck in my room, furiously typing out the final paper for one of my classes. Thankfully, Ian was there to keep me company. He was sitting on the edge of my bed, alternating between looking at his phone, perusing a book from my bookshelf, or sharing a song with me when I needed a break.

I had almost finished the paper when I heard singing rising up from behind me. My friends entered the bedroom, singing "Happy Birthday" and holding a small, beautifully decorated cake. I had gotten so caught up in schoolwork, I had forgotten that in just a few hours, I would turn twenty-two. As my friends sang to me, my heart felt full in a way it hadn't in a long time. *This is the best birthday ever.*

It was approaching midnight when I was almost finished with my paper. The apartment was quiet. All our friends had left except for Ian, who lay quietly on my bed looking up at the ceiling while I continued to work at my desk. Sarah was in her room, the muffled sounds of her television humming through to my side of the wall.

In the flurry of trying to finish my paper and everything else that needed to be done that day, I was an absolute mess. I was dressed in cheap running shorts and a ratty T-shirt, which didn't complement either half of my body. I hadn't showered that day, and I hadn't shaved my legs in several days . . . and somehow, cactus legs and all, I was completely at home in Ian's presence. More than that, I felt beautiful. I loved how comfortable he looked resting on my bed, gazing up at the ceiling, looking content just to be in the same room as me.

"I'm done!" I said, raising my arms in celebration.

"Congratulations," Ian said with a big grin.

I tried to remain calm as I closed my laptop, got up from the desk and turned off the main light switch, leaving only the soft glow of my nightstand lamp. As I climbed onto the bed, Ian turned to face me, and we both gathered the pillows up under our necks.

"Is it my birthday yet?" I asked.

Ian lifted his wrist to look at his watch. "Just about that time."

My heart raced as we laid there in silence, trying not to smile as we searched each other's eyes for what to do next.

"Come here," Ian murmured. He wrapped his arms around me, drawing me to him. When our lips met, I was both thrilled *and* relieved. Kissing Ian was every bit as wonderful as I'd hoped it would be. His hands trembled as he held me close, carefully caressing my back and shoulders. I knew then what I had started to suspect two days earlier at the restaurant. Ian and I were friends. Then we were best friends. And now, I was in love with him.

We woke the next morning, fully clothed, still holding one another.

"Good morning," he said. "How'd you sleep?"

"Really great," I said. "I wonder what Sarah will think when she wakes up and you're still here."

"She won't be surprised. I've got skills."

I started to laugh, but my heart sank when I remembered what was happening in two days. "I have to tell you something," I said.

"What is it?"

"I promised Chris Blackmer I would go with him to a Billy Joel concert on Friday."

"The Billy Joel concert in Auburn Hills? I'm going too."

I lifted my head from his chest, gawking at him. "You're joking, right?"

"I'm serious. I'm going with some friends."

I rested my head back down on his chest. "The tickets were probably expensive. I don't feel right about backing out."

Ian drew in slow rhythmic breaths, his chest rising and falling beneath me.

"I'm not going to let anything happen," I said.

Ian held me tight. "I trust you."

2020

Within days of blocking Chris, a Florida number appeared on my phone. "Hi, Mrs. Farison, I'm a victim's advocate for Orange County. I'm calling in regard to a case against Mr. Christopher Blackmer. I'd like to bring the prosecutor on the line. Is that okay with you?" After a few moments of silence, I heard another woman's voice. She introduced herself and asked if I had been involved in an abuse investigation against Chris in Michigan.

I was certain this phone call was going to be simple and straightforward. In 2019, I had put a lot of time into a victim impact statement that I'd sent to Sergeant Perry, in case it would ever come in handy. I assumed the prosecutor would ask permission to use my statement, I would say *yes*, and then I'd move on with my life.

"Mrs. Farison, would you be willing to testify in person?"

I blinked. *Testify?* I thought they would ask permission to use information from the Michigan investigation, not ask me to be in a room with him. "You have my statement and case files. Can't you just use that?"

"As a William's Rule witness, we would need you to come down here and testify in person if this goes to trial. We wouldn't be asking for your help unless we needed it."

I felt a sudden urge to vomit. "I want to help. But it's complicated."

"How so?"

"I want to know I'm protected," I said. I didn't know what I was asking for exactly, I just kept repeating it. *I want to know I'm protected. I want to know I'm protected.* I must have sounded deranged. How could I get them to understand? I didn't want to hurt my family. I didn't want my words to be used against me. I wanted to trust them, but I'd already been let down by people who said they were going to protect me and didn't.

"Did he give you money not to testify?" the prosecutor asked, fishing for reasons why I was so reluctant.

"No."

"Is there another reason?"

My brain was shouting, *They need to know! Just say it!*

"I had an affair with the defendant." The truth was like jumping into cold water. I began to sob.

With sudden urgency, she asked, "Did he go to Michigan or did you come here?"

"I went down to Florida to see my grandfather who had a stroke."

"I'm so sorry this happened to you, Mrs. Farison. Give me a day to think about the implications of what you've just shared with me. I'll call you back tomorrow."

When I got home, I parked on the street in front of our house. I watched Ian as he moved around the open garage, organizing bins and boxes. I marveled at him. Even the way my husband worked in the garage exuded goodness and honesty.

I couldn't believe I was once again trying to crawl out of some dark hole. If I agreed to testify, I would have to admit to Ian that I had talked to Chris twice in the past eight months. It was sure to come up in questioning with the attorneys. And if the case went to trial, it would also mean flying to Florida and being in a room with Chris. But if I didn't testify, I feared there would be worse consequences.

Ian smiled at me as I walked up the driveway. When he saw I'd been crying, he asked what was wrong. I told him about the phone call, fully expecting him to insist that I say no to the prosecutor, knowing my involvement might mean publicly revealing what had happened in our marriage.

Ian's eyes moved searchingly over my face. "You have to be able to heal from this. Because if you don't, we won't make it. If you have to face him as your abuser to do that, I'll support whatever you decide."

"People will know what happened," I said, struggling to look him in the face. "You know, about our marriage."

"If that happens, we'll figure it out. If you don't do this, I'm afraid it'll be like a door we walk by every day for the rest of our lives pretending it's not there. We'll know it's there, but we can't open it. You need to do whatever it takes to heal."

• • •

When the Florida prosecutor called, she told me that under the circumstances they would not force me to testify. I could choose to be a witness or I could walk away. Thankfully, I had a therapy session scheduled before I needed to give the prosecutor an answer. I sat under the maple tree in our backyard and explained the dilemma to Becca over the phone.

"What do you think Ian will do when you tell him?" she said.

"I don't know. I don't want him to leave me. But if I hide this, I won't heal, and I'll lose him. If not now, then later."

I didn't believe it was a coincidence that I had called Chris the same day his attorney had emailed him about me. If I was looking for a sign, this had to be it. It was a bright star hanging in a pitch-black sky, pointing me in the right direction.

Even though I didn't want to believe it—didn't know how to believe it—there was evidence that proved Chris was willing to let me risk everything I love for what he wanted. I thought back to my conversation with him, when I said, "I could lose my boys for talking to you," and he said nothing. Could he really be that unfeeling? A person who cares about you wouldn't do those things. Ian wouldn't do those things. He would do anything to protect me, the boys, his family and friends.

"You know what you need to do," Becca said. "Hold on to your faith that Ian isn't going to give up on you."

I met Ian on the front porch, where together we waited for the prosecutor's call.

"How was your session? What did you decide?" Ian asked.

"I'm going to agree to testify.... But you need to know, I've spoken with Chris twice since last November. I know the words 'I'm sorry' are not good enough, but you have to trust I'm doing everything I can."

As Ian sat looking stunned, my phone rang. It was the prosecutor. I told them I would agree to be a witness. The next question was exactly what I had predicted. "When did you last speak to the defendant?" She asked a few more questions, then briefly explained where they were at in the process and when I should expect to hear from them again. It could be weeks. It could be months.

When the phone call was over, I turned to Ian again. "Please. I love you and the boys. I don't want to lose you."

Ian looked at me, solemn-faced. "I know you love us, but you have to start acting like it all the time."

• • •

I was scheduled to be deposed by Chris's lawyer in September. In preparation, I started to review everything I knew about our relationship and the Michigan investigation. I had no idea what questions were going to be asked, so I needed to be ready for anything. It was then I realized that I had never checked Facebook messenger to see if I could retrieve our conversation history.

I thought we had only talked once or twice after Ian and I started dating, but we had actually spoken many times in the year before Ian and I got married. Nothing that would have violated my relationship with Ian—they were conversations about student teaching and job searches, lighthearted banter about the 2008 election. But the fact was, we were still in communication with each other.

In spring of 2008, after Ian and I had been dating for almost a year, Chris encouraged me to apply for a position in the Grand Ledge school district where he'd be starting in the fall. He insisted on putting in a good word about me to the district's administration.

"Like hell you are going to apply for that job," Ian said on a drive home from visiting my parents.

"It's a great job," I said.

"I don't care if it's the best job in the world. You're not going to work with him or near him."

It was quiet for a while.

"I should tell someone what he did," Ian said, as if speaking to himself in a mirror. "He shouldn't be teaching at all."

"*Stop it.* You're not going to tell anyone."

"And why wouldn't I do that?"

"Because I don't want you to. And besides, it wouldn't be good for me trying to find a job right now."

The volume of Ian's voice lowered, but the intensity remained. "I don't want you to apply for that job. It's a bad idea. And just so you're aware, I have a zero-tolerance policy."

"What does that mean?"

"If you cheat on me, we're done. No questions. That's it."

My stomach dropped ten floors. "You know I would never do that."

In the end, I did not apply for the job in Grand Ledge. And in May of 2008, I posted a status to Facebook that Ian and I were engaged to be married.

That night, Chris sent me a Facebook message. *Wow . . . congrats.*

Once Ian and I were married, I removed Chris from my Facebook friends list and congratulated myself on my stellar performance as a devoted wife—so willing to let go of the past in order to make way for the future.

When I signed into the virtual meeting room, three people were present: the prosecuting attorney, the victim's advocate, and the court reporter, all women. We exchanged friendly *hellos* and waited for Chris's attorney to sign on. It was nice to put faces to the voices of the prosecutor and advocate; both had been kind to me over the phone. I wanted to do what I normally did when being with people, which is get to know them better. *I love your shirt. How's your family been during the pandemic? Do you get to work from home? Do you have kids? A dog?* But I worried my overt friendliness would come across as disingenuous or manipulative. I needed to become a blank slate, to speak only what was necessary to be a credible victim, nothing more, nothing less.

When the defense attorney signed on, everyone stated their name. The court reporter asked me to hold up my ID to the camera, and everyone agreed that I was, in fact, me. I was sworn in, then the questions began. The defense asked for my birthdate, my current occupation, if I'd ever been arrested. Was I married? For how long? What's my husband's name?

"Okay," she said, matter-of-factly, "you have been listed as a witness in the case of the State of Florida vs. Chris Blackmer. Do you know why?"

"Yes, I do."

"Okay, tell me why you think you've been listed as a witness."

"Because after finding out that Chris Blackmer was arrested in April of last year, I went to the Michigan State Police to explain that I had a relationship with him that started when I was a student."

"Okay. Did you do that on your own or at someone else's urging?"

"I did that on my own. But my husband and I had agreed on it together."

"And did you try to open a case in Michigan for what you were alleging was your own abuse?"

"That is correct. In the article we saw it said to contact the police if you had any information, so I contacted the police."

"Okay. Is that an open case still, or did you have steps to abandon it, or did they abandon it on their own?"

"It had to close because of the statute of limitations."

She paused, like this was not the answer she was expecting. "What—how do you feel about that?"

"Can you restate the question?"

"How do you feel about the fact you weren't able to pursue a criminal action against Mr. Blackmer?"

"This entire situation feels very complicated emotionally and that's the best answer I feel I'm able to give."

"Okay. Are you disappointed, angry that you weren't able to do that, or are you relieved?"

There were too many emotions to grab onto just one. "I am not angry. I'm not disappointed. I'm just trying to do the right thing."

"Okay."

"I'm sorry, if I could clarify . . . . When the investigation closed, I felt a lot of grief and I was extremely upset because I felt like I did not have any closure or answers."

"Has that changed?"

"I have had time to work through and process some things so certainly the way that I felt on that day, I feel differently today."

"Tell me how you feel today."

"I feel like I just want to be honest. I want to do the right thing and that's why I'm here."

"Okay, and I know this sounds cryptic, but what is the right thing in your mind?"

"I believe the right thing is to be honest about what happened so that the best decision can be made in the justice system."

"Do you wish for Mr. Blackmer to be prosecuted?"

This question stopped me dead in my tracks. The very complicated answer was *no*. No, I don't wish for him to be prosecuted, because I *wish* none of this had happened in the first place. I *wish* I wasn't being deposed by his lawyer for an awful crime. I *wish* I hadn't been manipulated and abused as a child. I *wish* I had understood what was happening to me decades ago when I could have stopped it. I *wish* I hadn't hurt my parents and friends. I *wish* I hadn't cheated on my husband and hurt my family. I *wish*. I *wish*. I *wish*. But I couldn't say *no*. I knew it would be a mark against me.

I gave myself time to breathe. Eventually, the answer came to me like a mil-dle breeze brushing my skin. "I think that he should be held accountable for his actions."

"And are you referring to your situation or the situation here in Florida?"

"I'm referring to any situation where he's harmed somebody or done something illegal."

"Okay. Alright. Can you tell me when's the last time you had contact with Mr. Blackmer?"

My stomach dropped. I knew this was coming. Before this, I had tried to imagine her conversations with Chris, if he had told her the truth. Would it help his case if he told her? I thought not. "Towards the end of May of this year," I said.

"Okay. So you were having communication with him even after your case in Michigan was closed—you made the allegations to law enforcement?"

"Yes."

"Okay, and why were you doing that?"

"The day I found out the case had ended I called the investigator in Michigan and I asked if it would be illegal for me to call Mr. Blackmer. I was very grief stricken when it all ended and I felt confused. I had no answers. The sergeant said it was not illegal. So on that day I contacted Mr. Blackmer and we had a conversation over the phone."

"That's the only time you had contact with him was May 2019, 20' . . . — this year?"

"No."

"Okay. How many times have you had contact with him since your allegations last year?"

"We spoke to each other several times for a span of about two months in the last year. We saw each other, and this year I spoke to him once in March and then in May as I had indicated."

"And you came down from Michigan and you were here in Florida?"

"That is correct."

"Did he ask you to come down?"

"No. My grandfather had suffered a stroke and I went to be with my grandfather and my father."

"Okay. Did he reach out to you and want to meet up or did you reach out to him?"

"We were already talking at that point and I told him my grandfather in Arcadia, Florida, had a stroke and he said, 'That's not far from where I am.'"

"Okay. Does—did anything happen in those meetings?"

"Yes."

"Okay. What happened?

I could feel the panic rising in me. "Could you rephrase the question or be more specific?"

"Tell me what you did."

"We spent time together . . . . We kissed . . . and we had sex."

"Did he force himself on you?"

This wasn't the first time I'd been asked this question. I knew it was something they had to ask, but I felt like it only scratched at the surface. He never had to use force. He never had to intimidate or threaten me to get me to do what he wanted. "No," I said.

"Did you record him at any time during these meetings?"

"No."

"Okay. Does your husband know?"

"Yes, he does."

"Okay. Let's talk about you back at Kearsley High School. Tell me when you first entered Kearsley High School."

"That would have been 1999."

"August of 1999?"

"September probably."

"Okay. You were a freshman?"

"Yes."

"Ninth grade?"

"Correct."

"Okay. Were you in music class?"

"Yes."

"Were you in Mr. Blackmer's class?"

"Yes."

"How would you categorize your relationship in the 1999 to 2000 school year?"

"He was my teacher and I was his student."

"Okay. Did you ever go anywhere in his car or to his home—"

"No."

"—that year? Did you have his phone number?"

"I don't remember. I don't believe so, not in that year."

"Okay. September of 2000, you're still at Kearsley and he's still your teacher?"

"Yes."

"Okay. Did your relationship change?"

"Yes."

"Okay. Now in May of 1999, how old were you?"

Wait, why did she go back? I tried to do the math quickly in my head. "May of 1999. I would have turned fifteen years old on May 2nd of 1999. Right. I would have turned—sorry. Fourteen. I would have been fourteen."

"And so, 2000, do you think the school year ended in May or June?"

It wasn't clear to me why this was important, I felt like she was trying to talk me in circles. "The school year ended in the beginning of June," I said.

"So when the school year had ended you were fifteen, your freshman year?"

"If I was a freshman, I would have been fifteen at the time."

"Okay. School year starts and you're still fifteen. And then the school year ends and you're now sixteen."

"Correct. In 2001 I turned sixteen."

"Okay, according to what I'm looking at, which is a Michigan incident report, and I'm assuming they got the information from you, it talks about the first incident of many on the day after the last day of school which would have been June of 2001. Is that correct?"

"That is correct."

"Okay, Leading up to that in tenth grade, did you go on any car rides with him prior to the end of school?"

Her question confused me. When she said "leading up to tenth grade," was she referring to ninth grade? Did I already answer this question? "Yes. In tenth grade?"

"Yes."

I repeated her. "Yes."

"Okay. Well, had you been to his home?"

"Yes."

"Okay, and had you been able to get his phone number at this point?"

"I did have his phone number at some point in tenth grade."

"Alright, but during the year you're saying nothing happened until that day after the last day?"

"The first physical act took place, I believe it was the day after school officially ended."

"Okay. And when did you find out that Mr. Blackmer was leaving that school?"

"A few months prior to June."

I didn't realize it then, but I was wrong when I said this. It wasn't a few months prior, it just felt that way. I hadn't yet made the connection that the day I learned Chris was leaving, I ran to my car in tears. I had my driver's license, which meant it would have happened after May 2nd, after my sixteenth birthday.

"A few months prior?" she asked.

"Yes."

"Two or three?"

"I don't remember. I feel like it was maybe April."

"Uh-huh."

"But I'm not sure of the exact timing of that."

"Okay, and I'm assuming at this time, because you've been in the car with him and in his home, you had kind of developed a relationship, not saying a sexual relationship but a type of relationship that is kind of more than just student-teacher."

"Correct."

"Right, and would you say you had a crush on him at that point?"

"Yes."

"Okay. Not uncommon," she said with what appeared to be a rare moment of genuine kindness. "Okay, were you dating anyone?"

"On and off again. A boyfriend that I had been dating as much as you can date, you know, since middle school."

"Right."

"Can't go anywhere." This was a joke I'd heard many times in my life, when you're *dating but can't go anywhere*. This probably wasn't the right time to make that joke, but there it was.

"Were you sexually active at the time?"

"No intercourse."

"Okay. No intercourse but maybe everything else?"

"Some other things."

"Okay, so you have this kind of relationship with [Mr. Blackmer]. You see him every day, right?"

"Uh-huh, yes."

"Do you go to his classroom during the lunch period, or the period you don't have class, that kind of thing?"

"Sometimes I would stay after school, but I did not go down there during the periods I was not in band."

"Okay. And the day after the last day of school, you realize that he's about to leave, right?"

"I knew that he was done at Kearsley. I was aware of that."

"Right, and was his exit kind of imminent, like he had another apartment, he was leaving, like, in just a matter of days, if not hours?"

I couldn't be sure what the intention was behind this question, but it sounded like she was attempting to paint a possible scenario of desperation, that I knew Chris was leaving very shortly and perhaps I was pushing to make something happen between us. Yes, I wanted to spend time with him before he left, and yes, I had imagined something happening between us, but I never would have made a move on him. I never would have put him in that position.

I responded, "I had no idea when he was moving or leaving, all I knew is that he wasn't going to be at Kearsley anymore."

"At the time you were spending this time with him, and you were developing this crush, were you hoping that he would kiss you or do something?"

"I definitely fantasized about things like that. I had a crush on him as a young girl who admired her teacher."

"Okay, and did you ever make that known to him?"

I didn't hesitate in saying *no* to her. *No, I did not make that known to him*. If he knew I had a crush on him, it was because I was a teenage girl who couldn't hide her feelings. It was because, when he talked to me, touched me, or openly flirted with me, he was watching my reaction. It was he who acted in such a way where other people were sure he had a crush on me.

"Would you wear certain clothes for him? If he commented on, you know, your blouse or something that he liked, would you make it a point of wearing something like that often? Or did you do anything like bring him presents or anything to maybe gain his favor?"

Was she asking me this just to get a reaction out of me? Because it seemed so absurd she would be allowed to ask this for any legitimate reason. Even if I did wear something he liked, even if I was wearing the sexiest dress known to mankind and I sauntered to him and begged him to kiss me, I was still the child and he was the adult, and it was his job to draw boundaries. It is an adult's job to teach children how to behave. He did the opposite.

In fact, all of her recent questions had been aimed at shifting the blame to me, to make it look like I asked for this. I was sixteen for God's sake. I dressed in clothes that made me feel attractive to any cute boy who might look at me.

Calmly, I said, "I did not bring him presents and I don't ever remember wearing an outfit to get his attention."

"Okay, did you ask for help with maybe a particular music piece? You maybe wanted him to give you extra time to go over it, where he would be close to you, or one-on-one with you?"

"No, I was taking lessons through the church that I grew up in and I didn't really need to ask him for extra help. I had other people in my life for that."

"Okay. Why are you there the day after school is over?"

"I was selecting music for the following marching band season. So I was in the office and I was searching online for different pieces. I wouldn't have any access over the summer, so I was trying to plan ahead."

"Okay, and why did it need to be you? That sounds like something maybe the band director would do. Why are you doing it?"

"I was the drum major of the marching band and he gave a lot of autonomy or, you know, power to the drum majors to help run rehearsals. So it wasn't unusual that he would also give me the authority to select some music for the following year."

"Were you the only drum major?"

"No."

"Was the other drum major there?"

"No."

"Okay, why not?"

"I don't remember."

"Tell me what led up to what happened."

I took her through the scene in the office, the shoulder rubbing, the kissing, Chris inviting me to his apartment again.

"Is he, at this point, pressuring you to have some kind of sexual encounter with him or is it just hanging out and we're okay with the cuddling and kissing?"

Her words struck me as odd. I thought shoulder rubbing and cuddling and kissing all qualified as sexual encounters. "He was not putting physical pressure or verbal pressure on me to go further at that point."

I tried to remain calm as the questions continued, a back-and-forth about the events of the summer, the drum major camp.

"Are you in therapy right now?"

"Yes."

"Okay. Was it after you began your therapy that you decided to talk to law enforcement?"

"No. It kind of all happened simultaneously. It was a terrible, terrible day. And I decided that I was going to go to law enforcement and my husband said, 'Do you want to think about maybe talking to a therapist?'"

"When you were shown the story by your husband, did you have the details of the allegation? Like did you know if it was a female or a male?"

I told her how Ian had come to the office and showed me the article, how I felt like Chris had died, how it was only after I read the article that I knew it was a boy.

"Okay. So when you read that article you believed that this boy was a student—a music student of his?"

"No."

"What did you believe he was?"

"I believed he was a student from another school in that same area, but not a direct student of Mr. Blackmer's."

"So from that story, you knew he was not a student of Blackmer's? I'm just trying to get your impression of that. I mean, at the time you saw that article, you saw it was a male, and you knew he was not a student of Blackmer's?" She had shifted gears, the energy in her voice heightened.

"It said in the article that the boy was sixteen or seventeen years old at the time, and that he was a student at . . . . It might have actually named that school in the article."

She asked me what news publication it was, but I only had a vague recollection of the name. "The fact it was a male student, does that surprise you?" she asked.

"Absolutely."

"Did it make you feel a certain way?"

"Yes."

"Okay. How did that make you feel?"

I knew whatever answer I gave would be shallow at best. I didn't have the words to speak what was still too complex to understand, and I wasn't going to try unpacking it in a deposition. This woman didn't deserve to watch me attempt to excavate every piece of my heart, to lay it on the table in front of her just so she could poke at it and see if it would bleed.

"I felt devastated about the whole thing. But I was very confused specifically about that part."

"When you say 'felt devastated' . . . " The prosecutor tried to get me to pinpoint the origin of that feeling—was it because I'd been tricked, or the realization that he'd been using me, or the fear that his sexual history meant I could possibly have been exposed to a sexually transmitted disease?

Sexually transmitted diseases were the furthest thing from my mind when I read the article, even when I was in Florida with Chris. It was the breaking apart of my reality that devastated me, the loss of a person who was more significant to my life than I'd realized until I lost him completely.

"It violated everything I thought he was," I said, "and I did not know how to reconcile that. I thought of all the memories I had with this person and I thought, *Dow did I miss that, I didn't see that?* I didn't see that. I felt like he had died."

"And when you met back up with him, did you start having those conversations again?"

"The initial conversation occurred because I wanted to talk to him. I wanted to be able to share how I was feeling. So, yeah. I told him I was really confused. I just wanted to have an opportunity to share those things with him."

"Okay, and you felt a real hurt when you first saw that, I'm assuming."

"Absolutely. I cannot adequately describe it. I would have never believed that was what happened. I thought he was a good person. I trusted him completely. I never saw myself as a victim. I never thought what he was doing to me was abuse."

"Do you still have the belief after reading those articles that Mr. Blackmer kind of sought out this young man who's sixteen or seventeen years old, and he knew he was a student at a high school?"

If I thought about this question too long, I'd talk myself out of what my gut was telling me to say. After everything I knew, how could I *not* believe Chris knew the age of this boy?

"Yes," I said.

"Do you know the way they met, if they were not student and teacher?"

"My understanding is that they met online."

"Do you know how they met online?"

I could've been wrong, but I got the sense the attorney was looking for missing pieces to a puzzle she hadn't completed. I wouldn't have put it past Chris to lie to even his lawyer.

"I don't know who approached who, I just know that they met online specifically to hook up with one another."

"Do you know if it was an application or like a chat room or something?"

"I don't."

"Any kind of information?"

"I don't know."

"Okay. I don't have any more questions."

Chris's trial date had been rescheduled for what felt like ten times in the past nineteen months. It was supposed to be in January. Now it was set for March, which meant two added months of waiting. Every time I thought something was going to happen, the defense would request another extension, and the judge would grant it.

In early December, I started waking up every night around two in the morning. I took long walks in the basement, making one continuous loop between the laundry room and living area for at least an hour, sometimes two, until exhaustion set in and I could go back to bed.

By the end of the first week, I'd already started to lose my footing in reality. Scenes started replaying in my head. Of Florida. The beach.

"Did you see that?" Chris said, pointing to the sky, his finger tracing the line where the light shot across. "It was a shooting star." We were lying on adjacent wooden lawn chairs, part of a permanent set that stretched across the beach, our clasped hands splitting the space between us.

"I've never seen a shooting star before," I said.

He brought my hand to his mouth and kissed it. "You have to make a wish," he said. "You have to keep it a secret though, or it won't come true."

Of all the moments I would see my first shooting star, why did it have to be now? Chris tried to play it off more as a romantic moment, but I saw it as a message from God directly to me: *I'm still here*. I gazed up at the vast constellation of stars and made my wish. *Please God. Help me get through this.*

The longing for Chris was creeping back in, and, with it, justification for reaching out to him.

The next few nights, I'd sit down between laps and type a message into my notes app, practicing what I would say to Chris if I were to send him a text, but I never went to my texts. The following week, it progressed to typing a message into a text box with his number at the top, my thumb hovering over the send button. But I'd put my phone down and forced myself to go to bed.

By the end of that week, I was sitting in the basement at four a.m. staring at an unsent message to Chris that read, *I'm still grieving all of this. I just want the pain to stop.* I was careful about the words I used. I didn't say, *I miss you. I hate that I miss you. Why do I miss you? What's wrong with me?* I just wanted to make the connection; I wanted him to know I was still hurting. I took a deep breath and sent it.

The next morning around ten, Chris's number appeared on my phone screen with a response. *I love you, Megan. I so wish I could go back in time and do things differently.*

My whole body ached. For most of my life, I'd held on to the belief that Chris had loved me when I was younger, even though he had never said it, not once. And now that he was saying it, it was nearly impossible to believe. My eyes raked over the text repeatedly. *I love you, Megan. I love you, Megan*. But I knew. Love doesn't look like this. Love never looks like this.

It all felt like a game Chris was trying to win. *He's desperate and doesn't want me to testify. He wants to maintain control.* These were explanations that made sense to me, but there was still a complete disconnect between my brain and my body. It didn't matter how many times I said something was true—my body held its own set of beliefs, impervious to logic or reason.

I wanted so badly for his words to be true. I wanted him to love me. It was too painful to think I had almost thrown away my marriage for a man who not only didn't love me but was cruel enough to lie and say he did. A man who probably didn't care if I was alive or dead. It was inconceivable to think that every moment with Chris over the course of my entire life had been a lie. That I was nothing more to him than a body he could use and discard . . . . That he didn't see me as a person at all.

I wanted to text back, *What does that mean, you love me?* But I knew better, because he wouldn't have a good answer, and it would ruin the illusion. At least "I love you" would be the last words he ever said to me.

On New Year's Eve, with mere hours left of 2020, I was sitting beside Ian on the couch, polishing off a bottle of wine and wondering what Chris was doing. Was he alone? Was he lonely? What holiday movie was he watching? Did he put up a tree for Christmas? I knew I shouldn't be having these thoughts, but they seemed nearly impossible to control.

What I did have control over was whether or not I would keep consuming alcohol when I knew it was actively getting in the way of my healing. For me, alcohol opened a floodgate of emotions, which led to reminiscing, which led to longing—and with the trial date quickly approaching, I needed to be as prepared as possible.

To stop drinking felt like an insurmountable task. It had become a part of my daily routine beginning my senior year at CMU. I discovered Cosmopolitan martinis that winter. They instantly became my favorite drink because they tasted great and had an almost immediate effect on my body. Each night, I would make myself a martini and a plate of sliced cucumbers with ranch. I'd sit on my bed with only the glow of my bedside table lamp, eating and drinking, and stream episodes of *Grey's Anatomy* on my Dell laptop. This combination of ambience, alcohol, food, and television binging was pure bliss, and it became something I looked forward to hours before I arrived home. There was always a bottle of Skyy vodka and triple sec in the cabinet, cranberry cocktail and artificial lime juice in the fridge. My nightly ritual didn't seem to interfere with my daily life and it offered a level of pleasure and freedom matched only by sex.

Over time, drinking alcohol made it harder and harder to lose weight—and the effect of it, while still pleasurable, had increasingly negative effects on my wellness and mood. Other people would wake up with a hangover that'd be gone by early afternoon, but I would continue to suffer fatigue, irritation, and nausea for days.

The first time I remember wanting to change my drinking habits was in 2013, the year after I'd given birth to Eli. Since that time, I had tried repeatedly to quit, to slow down, to moderate, but I always ended up back where I'd started, drinking practically every night. The only time I successfully stopped was during pregnancy. My desire to drink was squelched by my deeper purpose of growing a human life inside me.

I didn't touch a drop of alcohol when I was pregnant with Evan. After that, I had two miscarriages, and I quickly realized how fragile life was and how little control I actually had. In my third trimester of carrying Eli, I had a small glass of wine on two separate occasions. Both times, I told myself it wasn't a big deal, that it wasn't a big risk.

And therein was the problem. It might not have been a big risk, but it was still a risk. And for what? It wasn't like I could drink enough to feel buzzed or even relaxed. What need was I trying to fill?

As time went on, the drinking escalated. When the boys were still very young and Ian was working on Saturdays as a wedding DJ, I'd put the boys to bed, then binge on food, mixed drinks and Netflix until I passed out. I should have been the one getting up with the boys the next morning, but Ian was the one who had to pull himself out of bed after working a twelve-hour day. What's worse was the potential danger I put the boys in by becoming inebriated when there was no other adult in the house to help in the event of an emergency.

Saturdays of TV watching and alcohol became weeknights, and this pattern went on for years. Every night I would go to bed drunk, wake up in the middle of the night with a terrible stomachache, get up in the morning sober but miserable, and go to work. Every morning I vowed not to drink that night, but every night, while making dinner, I would inevitably be sipping on a glass of moscato, or, if that didn't satisfy, a cranberry vodka, or, if that didn't satisfy, straight bourbon. By the time dinner was served, my insides were toasty. There were only good feelings. I had blocked out any stress from earlier that day or from any day before it.

I didn't see my nightly drinking as a problem. *Lots of people do this*. Nothing was wrong with me. I was normal. It was easy to say everything was fine because I was able to balance my poor habits with excelling in other areas of my life. I was a successful choir director. I went to church and had a social life. But home was a different story. It was Ian and the boys who witnessed my worst moments. Who became victims of my irritability. I couldn't see how my drinking was driving a wedge between me and Ian, and Ian didn't know how to put into words why he felt alone most of the time.

Looking back on 2019 and 2020, it was impossible to deny the damage alcohol was causing. It certainly was not helping me to heal from my illogical longing for Chris. But I didn't know if I was ready to give up something that brought me pleasure at a time when so much was causing me pain. I prayed to God to help give me the strength to do whatever I needed to do in the upcoming months.

On January 1st, 2021, with no preconceived plans of a New Year's resolution, I woke up and said to myself, *I'm going to become a non-drinker.* Something clicked and I just didn't want to drink anymore. I didn't want to play the game of moderation because it had never worked, and I couldn't afford to waste my energy deciding every day if I'd choose to drink or not.

In order to keep myself motivated, I researched videos and literature about sobriety. That's when I discovered the book *Quit Drinking Like a Woman: The Radical Choice to Not Drink in a Culture Obsessed with Alcohol* by Holly Whitaker. I downloaded the audio version and listened to it every day as I showered, brushed my teeth, got my clothes and makeup on, drove to work, drove home from work. The book's message of freedom from alcohol became a mantra that stayed with me throughout my day.

I went thirty days without an inkling of a desire to drink. My desire for Chris was less, too. New doors opened up inside my mind, offering paths to connections and solutions I had never considered in my daily routines and work. At first, it was hard for me to fall asleep, because for so long I had used alcohol to shut my body down. But after a month it was easier. Instead of watching TV and eating before bed, I read, journaled, or talked to a friend on the phone. I woke up refreshed, each new day filled with possibility. I was even surprised to discover I was a morning person.

One day, I was listening to a chapter of the book where Holly describes the physical process of addiction and our body's need for survival, and it hit me. This is exactly what was happening with Chris. For the first time, I started to put words to the feelings I'd been experiencing since Chris was arrested. This wasn't about love . . . . It was about *addiction*. It was about *survival*.

Soon after, I was listening to Holly talk about gathering your army for support, people who aren't afraid to ask the hard questions and be with you in the darkest places. I realized I wanted more people in my life who were emotionally willing to talk about trauma, who wouldn't run when things got uncomfortable. A woman named Gretchen came to mind. It was surprising, because I'd only been in her presence a handful of times, but I knew her through a trusted mutual friend, and the times we had spent together proved to me she was someone who could be vulnerable. Even better, she was studying to be a counselor, so she knew about trauma.

I called Gretchen later that day and said, "This might seem weird, but I've had a really difficult couple of years and I'm looking for a friend who's willing to be an accountability partner. I felt like I needed to call you."

Gretchen started to cry. "Oh my God, Megan. I've been praying for the exact same thing. You calling me is an answer to *my* prayer."

I had shared the full story of Chris with very few people in the last year. It was lonely, but I wasn't ready to talk about it yet. I was still afraid. The shame of it swam around inside my body. The worst thing that could happen, I thought, was for people to know I had cheated on my husband. I had broken my marriage vows. Worse, I'd betrayed him with a child predator. I needed time to process what had happened, and I needed the distance to see that sharing my story wasn't going to be my downfall, it was going to be what saved me.

Gretchen and I talked on the phone for almost two hours. I told her what had happened and she shared her struggles with me. Because of her own life experiences and her educational background in counseling, she was able to understand and relate to me in a way no one else had been able to. She said, "It makes complete sense why someone who was abused the way you were would react in these ways."

It made sense? It was a normal reaction to abuse? No one besides Becca, my therapist, had ever talked to me like this. The way Gretchen said it, with unapologetic authority, was life-giving. Since Chris's arrest almost two years earlier I'd been walking around with hundreds of invisible holes, the parts of me that were missing. Now I felt some of those holes closing, restoring small pieces of my former self.

Not long after my conversation with Gretchen, one of my work colleagues, Katie, invited me over to her house for dinner. I was giddy with excitement. Katie and I had been friends since I arrived at the church, but we had never spent time together outside of work.

After dinner, we were chatting in her living room. When she asked how I was doing, I told her, "I want to share something personal with you, but it's still hard to do, and I'm afraid."

She said, "You don't have to tell me anything you're uncomfortable with, but if you want to share I'm here to listen."

I did want to tell her. Katie and I had built a relationship of trust over a long stretch of time. She was consistently caring and kind, and I had no reason not to trust her. I thought about how it felt to share my story with Gretchen, the power it had to kill some of the shame. I was building my army. I wanted Katie in it, too.

I couldn't stop shaking when I told her what the past two years had been like. She got me a blanket to cover myself. She kept her eyes on my face, aware but tender, and entirely free of judgment. When I got to the most difficult parts, she waited patiently for me to continue, until I was through.

"I had no idea you were going through all of this," she said. "I'm so sorry. You didn't deserve that. And I want you to know, I've always thought you were a great person, and I still think that. I don't look at you any differently."

Her words were a balm of healing inside my wounded heart. "I'm scared I'm going to have to testify at this trial, and everyone's going to know what I did."

"Anyone who knows you and loves you understands the truth about what's happened. They're not going to look at you and see a terrible person. They're going to see a woman who was manipulated by a bad man." She smiled softly and rested her hand on my knee. "And if anyone has a problem, I'll deal with them."

I received a notice from the victim's advocate that there was a plea hearing scheduled for March 10th, the day of Chris's forty-ninth birthday. If, at the hearing,

Chris pleaded guilty or accepted a plea bargain, there'd be no trial; his sentencing would be determined by the judge. But if he pleaded innocent, Ian and I would be on a plane to Florida and I would have to testify.

Forty-four days into sobriety, I couldn't get myself to stop thinking about Chris. Except, I wasn't lost in romantic delusions. I was angry. I wanted answers from him, and with the plea hearing only one month away, time was running out. That night, I sent him a message:

> I wish you would just tell me the truth: that you don't love me, that you never loved me, and that everything that has happened between us was not what I thought it was. All I have ever done was care about you and want good things for your life. I didn't deserve all this pain and I don't deserve to be deceived and manipulated.

Late at night, just as I was falling asleep, I got a text back. *Sorry—I wasn't ignoring you. I just got out of work.*

I didn't respond, and he didn't send anything after. And I thought, *He's not even pretending to care anymore.*

The next day was a Sunday. I was at church, sitting in a sanctuary filled with empty pews. It had been almost one year since we moved our worship services online. The only people in the building were the pastors and a few staff members and volunteers.

That morning, our pastor was preaching on the parable of the lost sheep and the lost coin. In this passage of scripture, Jesus asks a group of tax collectors and Pharisees, "If you had a hundred sheep and one went missing, wouldn't you leave the ninety-nine and go searching for the lost one until you found it?"

As a teenager, my favorite thing in my church's sanctuary was a framed painting titled *The Lost Sheep*. It hung on the back wall above the main doors and depicted a man in a white tunic leaning over the edge of a cliff, his arm outstretched to save a sheep that's trapped below in the dangerous terrain. You can't see the man's face, only the back of his head. I'd often wondered, *is it supposed to be a shepherd or Jesus in the painting?* Now, as an adult, I think that's the point—not to know. Because whatever Jesus would do for us, we should do that for others.

"And this restoration, our being found. It's not just about us," the pastor said. "Maybe our worth to God has something to do with God's ability to see the whole as even more than the sum of its parts. Let's go back to our penny. What can you get for a penny? Even if you had a penny and I had a penny, that's nothing. But what if everyone in the world had a penny? That would be 70 or 80 million dollars. That's worth noticing.... What value has a sheep? No one is making any sweaters from the wool of one lamb, but if you have a hundred—that's another story."

I felt like God was speaking directly through the pastor to me. Everything that had happened in my life, it was never just about me. I couldn't give up, because there were others who were counting on me to make it. My family. My friends. People I hadn't even met yet, who needed to know there was a way out of hell.

With Chris, there was only lies and destruction. With God, there was purpose. I was just one part of a larger picture, and even though I couldn't zoom out and see the whole of it, I could choose to listen to the voice of truth inside me and do what was possible right now.

When the sermon ended, we sang.

> Amazing grace, how sweet the sound,
> that saved a wretch like me.
> I once was lost, but now I'm found,
> was blind but now I see.

I entered into the noonday sun feeling as though a tremendous weight had been lifted off my chest. When I got into my car, I prayed for what to do next.

I picked up my phone and typed out a message to Chris, each word flowing through me without question or hesitation.

> MEGAN: I shouldn't have sent those texts last night. Grief comes in waves, and sometimes it just feels too heavy to keep carrying, to keep pretending like everything's fine. There's so much about all this I don't understand, but demanding answers from you isn't going to satisfy or fix the damage that's been done. You didn't ask for forgiveness, but I will give it to you anyway because I need to be able to move on.

On the drive home, I began listening to *The Betrayal Bond* by Patrick Carnes, a book Gretchen had recommended for me about breaking free of exploitative relationships. Once again, I felt like God was speaking directly to me through the narrator.

> If you are reading this book, a clear betrayal has probably happened in your life. Chances are that you have also bonded with the person

> or persons who have let you down. Now here is the important part: You will never mend the wound without dealing with the betrayal bond. Like gravity, you may defy it for a while, but ultimately it will pull you back. You cannot walk away from it. Time will not heal it. Burying yourself in compulsive and addictive behaviors will bring no relief, just more pain. Being crazy will not make it better. No amount of therapy, long-term or short-term, will help without confronting it. Your ability to have a spiritual experience will be impaired. Any form of conversion or starting over only postpones the inevitable. And there is no credit for feeling sorry for yourself. You must acknowledge, understand, and come to terms with the relationship.

For two years, I'd been trying to process the truth about my relationship with Chris. As long as I was stuck believing that some part of what he did was done out of love, it seemed impossible to label the entire experience as abuse. If the case went to trial and I had to testify, I would tell the truth about my story. The problem was, no matter what story I told on record, another story would continue to live inside my head.

I'd been asking Chris to tell me the truth—"*tell me you don't love me, that you never loved me*." But he was never going to do that. It was up to me to destroy the illusion for myself. I had to do the thing I was most afraid of. I had to confront Chris with the truth. Not just part of it. All of it. I had to take a match to every positive memory I had of him. I had to make it so I could never go back to those memories with the same fondness. Only then would I be able to fully accept the betrayal.

I pulled into a parking lot and typed out a second message:

> MEGAN: As part of moving on, let me say this so you will hear it. I know you abused me. It's why you were able to connect with me so easily in September of 2019. You exploited me again for whatever you could gain from me. You let me risk my family to have some short-lived fantasy romance that wasn't born of real care or love but an effort to deny the truth about what I am to you. Love doesn't look like this, it puts others above yourself and looks out for the best interest of others. It doesn't lie to get its way. You were the adult and I was the child, and you took so much from me for years without question. And I gave it to you because I loved you and trusted you. I was never in a position (including the past two years) to make

> clear-headed decisions because of my unnamed abuse. But I'm trying really hard to get my life back, and I'm naming this for what it is. I believe no one is beyond redemption if they seek it; you are still worthy of love and you don't have to manipulate others to get it.

I tapped the send arrow and watched as a large block of text soared to the top of the phone screen. Then I went home.

"Can we go for a ride?" I said to Ian when I walked through the door. I could tell by the look on his face he was alarmed.

I drove us to a nearby church and pulled into the parking lot. "I did something big today," I said. "I finally called Chris out on the abuse."

"So you talked to him." Ian's eyes were full of disappointment.

"Yes. I know this is hard to understand, but this is something I needed to do."

"Why didn't you talk to me first about it?"

"Do you really think you would have let me talk to him?"

Ian sat quiet. "I don't know how many times I can turn the other cheek here."

Two things were true at that moment. I had violated Ian's expectation that I would never talk to Chris again, and for that I was genuinely sorry. But also, I knew deep down what I needed to do to save myself. No matter what I did, there was risk involved. All I could do was the next right thing.

"Let me read you what I wrote to him," I said.

When I'd finished, Ian's expression had softened. "That's good," he said. "But how am I supposed to trust you won't just turn around and go back to him?"

"I'm asking you to have faith in me. I know this is difficult to understand, and you've been more understanding than most husbands would be. But I need to stand up for myself and say that, considering the circumstances, I'm doing pretty well. Things could be so much worse. I could be on a plane to Florida right now but I'm not. It's been over a year that I've been here, fighting every day, and in that time I've talked to Chris three times. If I was an alcoholic trying to get sober and all I had was three drinks in over a year, I would count that as a success. I know it feels worse because this is a person, but I didn't ask for this to happen." I reached out and put my hand on Ian's. "You didn't deserve this."

"Neither did you," he said.

I nodded. "Neither did I . . . . So please, I'm begging you to forgive me. I'm doing the best I can. I'm going to keep fighting, whether you leave me or not, but it would be easier with you."

My phone made a sound. Chris had responded to my text. *Can we talk on the phone at some point? I think there's some misunderstanding through these text messages.*

A minute later, another text came in. *Sorry—just read the second text message. No need to call.*

2007

On Friday, May 4th, I met Chris two hours before the start of the Billy Joel concert at a restaurant in Clarkston. As was typical of most of our public outings, he maintained his distance from me throughout dinner. Then, we rode together in his car to the venue.

I had no idea where our seats were located until we got to the floor and moved into one of the center rows. "These are great seats," I said.

He smiled at me, proudly. "I got a good deal."

While we were waiting for the lights to go down, I texted Ian. *Where are you? We're on the floor.*

IAN: Look up. I'm straight ahead of you.

Sure enough, Ian's seats were directly behind the stage, way up in the nosebleed section, and even though he was far away, I was able to recognize him by his peach colored shirt.

MEGAN: I see you!
IAN: I can't see you.
MEGAN: Wait a few songs. I'll message you to meet me somewhere.

Aside from a few shoulder nudges, Chris stayed in his own space. "Captain Jack" started, and the crowd went wild, cheering and singing along at the top of their lungs. I didn't know this particular song very well, so it caught me off guard when Chris looked down at me, a huge grin plastered across his face, and sang a lyric with the word "masturbation" in it.

Even in the heat of the arena, I could feel my blood turn cold. I had never heard him use that word before. In fact, he had never used vulgar or obscene language in front of me at all.

I texted Ian. *Are you ready?*

IAN: Yes. I'll find you.

I leaned over and spoke loudly into Chris's ear, "I have to use the restroom! I'll be right back!" I hurried through the floor seating and dashed up the stairs into the lobby that formed one gigantic loop. I wasn't sure which direction to go, so I pointed myself left and started running.

"Allentown" blared through the lobby speakers as I rushed through the crowd, searching for a familiar face. It felt like I had made an entire lap around the stadium when I saw a peach shirt break through a sea of people. Ian was running, too.

We both came to a sudden halt and stared at each other, smiling uncontrollably. Then we bolted toward each other. I jumped into his chest, throwing my arms around his neck. He took my hand, and together we hurried up the nearest stairwell where one of the entrances to the stadium was blocked off by a giant tarp. At the top of the stairs, we turned the corner, now hidden from view, and began kissing wildly.

"I have to go back," I stammered between kisses.

"No, you don't," he said, bringing his lips back to mine, squeezing me tighter.

"Don't worry. I'll call you right away when I get to my car," I said.

A full thirty minutes had passed when I returned to my seat. Chris's eyebrows were skeptical. He shouted down to me, "Is everything okay? You were gone for a while."

I yelled back, "Yeah. Just ran into someone I know."

After the concert, Chris drove us back to the restaurant where we had met for dinner. When he put the car in park, he slid his hand to the passenger side and set it on my thigh. With small tugs of his fingers, he gathered up my white skirt until the length of my bare leg was visible. "We could get a hotel room tonight," he said, stroking my skin with the side of his hand.

He had never once mentioned the prospect of us staying the night together after the concert. Had he been saving this as a surprise, or was this something he decided last minute? I pushed through the awkwardness I felt, and said, "I'm pretty tired, but thank you for taking me to the concert."

Chris's expression was unwavering, as if he was still awaiting a response.

Quickly, I said my goodbyes and got out of the car. When I climbed into my car, his vehicle was still next to mine. I half expected him to wait, to question what had just happened and try to talk me around. But he backed out and drove off.

I exhaled a sigh of relief and called Ian. "I did it. It's over."

Of course it was over. I knew Chris wasn't going to fight for me, and I doubted he would care when I quietly slipped out of his life.

The end of Chris and me should have felt bigger, but it didn't. It was something that happened, and now it was in the past.

2008

It was late morning when my friends and I arrived at the church. We gathered in the lounge, a room with eggshell concrete brick and a cozy fireplace. I stepped out of my black running shorts and undid the collared button-down I'd borrowed from Randy's closet, a convenient choice for having my hair done that morning. Once the corset and underskirt were on, I held my arms straight up while Andi and Sarah teamed up to hold the bottom of my dress open. They slid it over me, carefully, so as not to ruin my semi-beehived hair. Then, since I could no longer bend over, Andi took my feet, one at a time, and guided them into ivory shoes.

My aunt entered, mildly frantic, and crossed the room to give me a hug. "You look beautiful. By the way, it's raining outside."

My mom politely *shooed* her back out into the hallway, then she looked back at me and smiled. "It's fine. Rain is a sign of good luck."

All four of my parents—Mom, Randy, my father and Cheryl—took turns looking me over and offering expressions of joy. The bridesmaids and groomsmen made their way around the corner toward the sanctuary and formed a double line, exchanging whispers, waiting for their cue. I watched them, overwhelmed with gratitude for every life that'd crossed paths with ours, the friendships that encouraged us along the way.

When the music began, the doors to the sanctuary opened. Each pair disappeared through the doors and out of view, the line growing shorter until the only person left in the lobby was me. I stepped up to the doors, face flush with excitement, as a brass arrangement of "I Vow to Thee, My Country" grew to its climactic apex. The doors opened once more and I started my journey down the aisle

There, at the front of the sanctuary, I saw him, Ian, standing tall with his hands at his side, eyes shining. I had never been happier than I was in that moment, and I knew, without a doubt, I was making the best decision of my life.

During the unity candle ceremony, a group of our friends from college stood to sing René Clausen's "O My Luve's like a Red, Red Rose," the same song Ian and I had performed together in our university choir. As the music began, Ian and I positioned ourselves behind the table that held the unity candle. We took our individual lighters and held our flames to the wick.

The candle wasn't lighting . . . .

Shit.

Ian and I had recently attended a wedding where the couple could not get the unity candle lit. When this happened, an old woman in the pew in front of us whispered to her friend, "That's a sign."

"That is not going to happen at our wedding," Ian declared. "Nothing is going to stop me from lighting that damn candle."

But there we were, in front of our friends and family and God, dealing with a situation we were certain would never happen to us. Why couldn't I have bought a candle from some fancy candle place instead of Dollar Tree? We tried again and again, but the candle just sat there, mocking us.

Panic started to set in. There was still a couple minutes left of the song but, so far, we were unsuccessful at getting the candle to show so much as a desire to burn. I glanced at my mom, in the front row, who was covering her mouth with her hand as the music waned and swelled, sonorous voices proclaiming undying love as we struggled with a cheap tower of wax. The contrast of dramatic music against the tense scene at the table felt a lot like a Bugs Bunny cartoon, and people in the pews began to snicker. Though the singers couldn't see what was happening, the choir director's face, contorted in a mixture of horror and hilarity, clued them in that something was terribly awry.

That's when Ian reached into a hidden pocket of his tuxedo jacket and pulled from it a small pocketknife. He carefully unfolded the blade from its handle until it locked into place. Then, he picked up the candle from the table and, with great determination, began whittling away at the top.

Ian could see the problem: There wasn't enough wick exposed to take hold of the flame. The thread was barely visible, suffocated by the waxy material engulfing it.

My mom tried, not so subtly, to wave off Ian's attempts to rescue an unsaveable state of affairs, but he refused defeat and kept whittling. *Scrape, scrape, scrape.*

With only seconds left before the end of the song, Ian, beads of sweat rolling off his temple, had cut away the wax enough to make lighting the candle possible. He returned the candle to its base, took my hand and placed it on the lighter. Then, he wrapped his hand tightly around mine and, together, we held the flame to the wick. I prayed to God it would work.

When hope was almost lost, the wick started to burn.

2021

Chris's plea hearing was only two days away, and out of the blue, Mom sent me a text. *I want the phone number of the prosecutor in Florida.*

I didn't know what to make of the message, so I FaceTimed her. When she answered, her face was blotchy, eyes puffy and red. "What's going on?" I asked.

My mom struggled to speak without gasping for air, her chest heaving in unpredictable jolts. "I just—I just want the number to—to the person in Florida." Her hands were gripping a stack of pictures varying in shape and size. With trembling fingers, she removed a picture from the top of the pile, then turned it to face me. It was a picture of me at age five, posing in a floral dress and white hat. "See?" She sniffled. She turned another picture toward the phone. Then another. They were all of me, at different ages. Eight. Twelve. Fifteen. Seventeen. "They need to see what he did." Another gasp. Another flipping of a picture. "I want to take these to them. They—they need to see. This is someone's daughter."

This was the first time I had seen her cry about what Chris had done to me. To *us*. Me. My mom. Ian. He had taken something from each of us we could never get back.

Mom's eyes dropped to the floor. "They're going to let him walk away. They will, I know it. I have to tell them."

I was certain Chris would go to prison. But for how long? Would Ian and I be leaving for Florida in the next few days, or would Chris be offered a plea bargain?

"I'll get you the number," I said. "You can call if you want."

She was still gripping the pictures. She held them to her chest, and through broken cries, said, "I'm so sorry, Megan. I should have done something."

"Mom. It's okay. *Really.* I'm okay."

• • •

On the morning of the plea hearing, I received an email from the victim's advocate with a letter attached:

> Please be advised the defendant pled Guilty to the following charges: 5 counts of Use of a Child in a Sexual Performance, 5 counts of Possession of Material Depicting the Sexual Performance of a Child.
> The defendant was sentenced to:
> 5 Years Prison (with credit for 2 days time served) followed by 10 Years Probation.

Five Years. The words didn't seem real. I logged into the court website, clicked on Chris's case, and scrolled down the list of charge details.

Charge #1: Use of child in a sexual performance, second degree felony. Guilty.

Charge #2: Use of child in a sexual performance, second degree felony. Guilty.

Charge #3: Guilty.

Guilty.

Guilty.

Guilty.

Until I got to charge #11–Sexual activity with a sixteen-or-seventeen-year-old by a school authority figure, first degree felony. Next to the plea, I saw two words I had never seen before: *Nolle Prosequi*.

Of the thirty-two charges listed, twenty-two of them were labeled *Nolle Prosequi*. I opened a new window on my browser and typed the words into the search bar. It's a Latin phrase meaning "will no longer prosecute."

From what I understood, a person in Florida convicted of unlawful sexual activity with a minor could serve up to fifteen years in prison. There had been physical evidence on Chris's phone that proved he had broken this law at least five times. Possession of child pornography carried its own severe punishment. Chris pleaded guilty to five charges of possession. How did all this add up to a plea bargain and only five years in prison?

I remembered talking to the victim's advocate on the phone months before. She told me, "The plea bargain is always the goal," to save on time and money—limited resources that, I assumed, were needed for the worst of the worst. Clearly, that wasn't Chris.

The justice system was gaslighting me. Was an adult—a *teacher*—raping a child multiple times and filming it worth only the minimum consequence? What about the pictures of naked children he'd sent to another former student? What about my story? I had been painfully honest with the attorneys about the events of 2019: my betrayal, Chris's proclivity to continue to use his power to prey on child victims. Wouldn't the judge have seen the documents, read that he had done something like this before? Wouldn't he have read the deposition? I had come forward because the Michigan State Police asked me to. Because they needed help. But when I needed their help, it wasn't there.

I tried to remain calm throughout the day, but dangerous emotions were starting to swirl, the tumult building. By evening, I was standing in the eye of a hurricane, surrounded by darkness and the debris of memories I'd been trying so hard to avoid. Hopelessness invaded me. I had made so much progress and, still, I had only scratched at the surface of my healing. I needed a quick plan of escape.

I told Ian I was going to get some ice cream from the store. On the way I pulled into a parking lot. I sat still for a few minutes, staring at the lights on the dashboard. Then I picked up my phone and called Chris's number.

What was I even going to say? *Happy Birthday? I'm so sorry?* But why was I apologizing to him? I just needed to hear his voice one last time.

Two rings went by, then I heard the automated voicemail message. There was no other explanation. He had seen my number and sent me to voicemail. I was relieved he didn't pick up the phone. It would've just pulled me back in, and then I'd have further to climb out. But my heart ached as Chris's words ran through my head. *I'll never ignore you.* It was just another lie.

I bought the ice cream and went home. I got in the shower and cried while Ian and the boys enjoyed s'mores outside by the fire.

Once I was showered and dressed, I went out to the fire and asked Ian to meet me in our bedroom. "I called Chris," I said.

There was quiet rage in his eyes. "Did you use going to get ice cream as an excuse to call him?" he said.

"Yes," I said. Ian's mouth tightened. "Listen. He's going to prison in May. He has two months to get everything in order. What if he comes to Michigan to see his family? What if he reaches out to me or tries to see me? I'm afraid I won't be able to say no to him. Please, I need your help. I don't want to cheat on you."

I heard the words as they were leaving my mouth. *I don't want to cheat on you.* What kind of person has to say this to their partner? Certainly one that isn't in their right mind. But I didn't have time for shame. I was too busy trying to do what was necessary to protect myself and my family. I knew how powerful the effects of this trauma were, even if no one else understood it.

"I don't want to be the kind of husband that has to survey you," Ian said. "I would rather not be married than be that kind of person."

"I know you don't want to. It's not forever. It's just for now."

Ian sat still for a while. Quietly, he said, "Give me your phone."

I watched as he opened different screens and applications. He asked me for Chris's number, then he went to my contacts and started typing something. "Here," Ian said, pointing the phone screen at me. He had saved Chris's number using the contact name *Child Molester*. "If he reaches out, you'll know exactly who's calling you. Every night by nine, I want you to leave your phone in the kitchen. Are you still writing your schedule in your calendar book? Every day, I want you to take a photo of your schedule and send it to me."

As much as he hated doing it, I was thankful Ian would be watching me. I would be safe, which meant my family would be too.

The next morning, as Ian was leaving for work, he said, "Did anyone call or text you last night?"

"No," I said.

He told me he loved me and gave me a reluctant kiss goodbye.

A few hours later, I was surprised to see a text message from him. *Keep kicking ass today. Don't let a minor setback (or my inability to deal with it well) screw up all the progress you've made!*

If unconditional love exists, this had to be it. Ian had not only managed to stay, but he was actively loving me through this.

I had said to Ian several times, "I wouldn't blame you if you chose to leave, but I'm hoping you won't." I promised him that even if we weren't together anymore, I would do everything I could to be a good mom to our boys. I'd find a way to protect myself from Chris, to sever every invisible string that tied me to him.

I sent a message back to Ian. *Don't give up on me.*

• • •

On a picture-perfect Saturday in August, Ian and I were making coffee together in the kitchen. "Let's go for a family drive," he said. He was feeling good that day, I could tell. He's always loved family road trips, especially impromptu ones.

"Where do you want to go?" I said.

He smiled. "Somewhere we've never been."

The four of us loaded up into our fuel-efficient minivan. It continued to rust and it needed work more frequently, but as long as it took us places, we would hold onto it.

As Ian drove, we took turns choosing songs, what our family liked to call "being the DJ."

"It's your turn to pick, Daddy," Evan said.

"First Day of My Life—Bright Eyes," Ian said.

"I don't know that one," I said.

He glanced in my direction. "You'll like it."

I leaned back against the headrest and absorbed the endless panorama of trees, the scattered flashes of light glinting through the branches. We took turns sharing about the places we wanted to go camping the following summer and dreamed up locations to visit if we could go anywhere in the world.

In the early afternoon, we arrived at a quaint coastal town at the tip of Michigan's thumb and parked near a beach that was home to a modest lighthouse. Ian held tightly to Eli's hand as we crossed the empty parking lot. I followed closely behind Evan, marveling at how much he'd grown the past year, how fortunate I was to be there to see it.

When we reached the sidewalk, the four of us removed our sandals, preparing to step into the dusty sand. The boys rushed in, Ian not far behind. I started to follow, but a gust of fear gripped my chest. I looked down and stared at the line dividing the pavement and the beach, remembering the last time my feet were touching sand.

"What are you going to do when you get home?" Chris said as we stared out over the ocean, serenaded by the squawking of seagulls, the waves lapping against the shore.

My eyes drifted across the horizon, my palms pressed into the cool sand. "I don't know . . . . Keep trying to live my life, I guess."

I turned to look at Chris. He was peering down at his lap, fingers outstretched. "My hands look old," he said, as if I wasn't sitting right next to him. As if he was completely alone. His voice was so soft, so stripped of pretense—I wondered if it was maybe the only real thing he had ever said in my presence.

"Momma!" Eli's voice pulled me back to reality.

I saw my family standing near the pier, waiting for me. Ian was smiling—a *real* smile—I hadn't seen in years, and for a brief moment the fear vanished. All that remained was love. For Ian. For my boys.

Today, I did more than survive.

And with that thought, I took my next step.

Coda

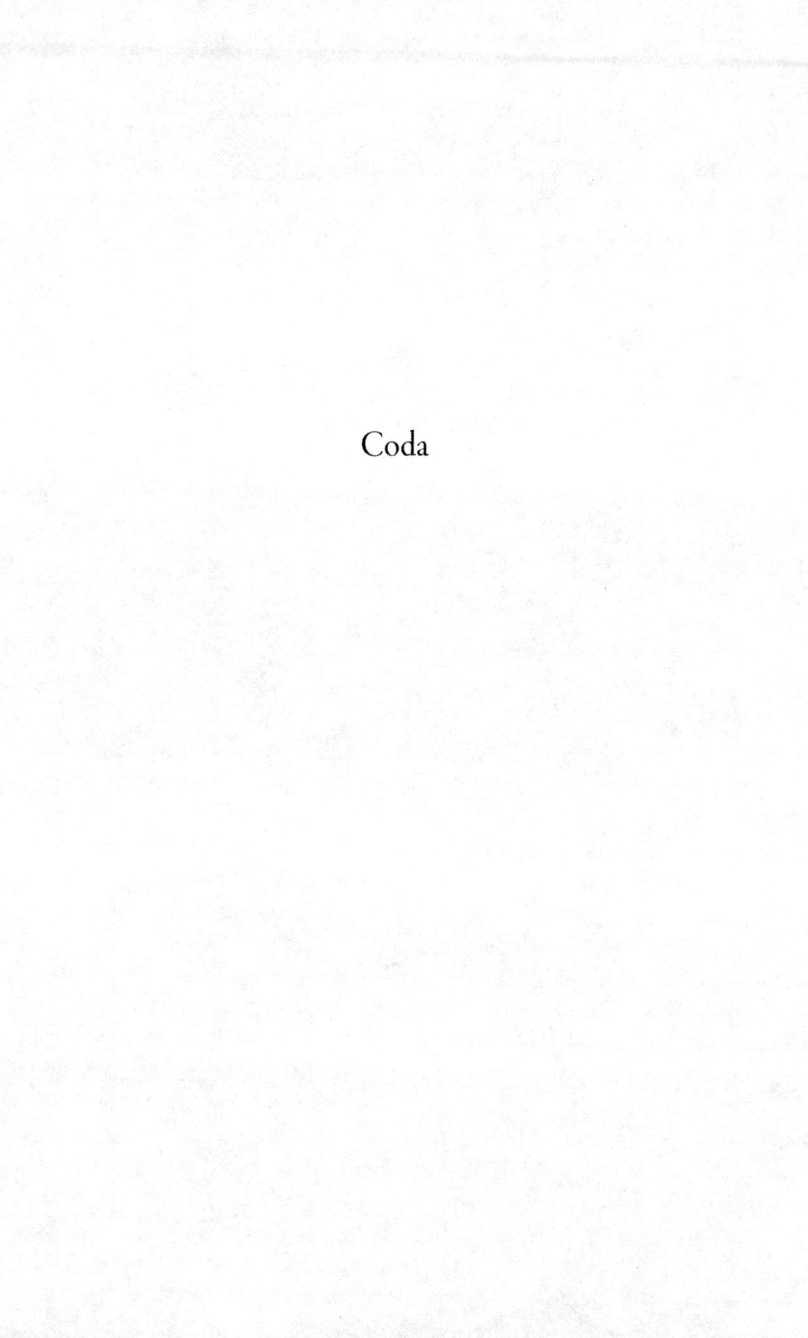

"Everything's as it should be."
—Andy Gullahorn

It's early autumn in Michigan. Some of the most beautiful days of the year happen around this time. Soon, the boys and I will climb into our minivan (now sporting 286,000 miles) and drive to my in-laws, where we'll spend a quiet afternoon. My mother-in-law and I will chat in the kitchen as we prepare dinner and set the table. My father-in-law will be in his living room chair, watching a Western. The boys will be in the back room playing cards. Before we leave, my fifteen-year-old will say, "Hey, Mom, can I drive home?" and I'll get that internal jolt only a parent whose child is starting to drive understands. Later in the evening, Ian will get home from his weekend gig. He'll hug us all, change into comfortable clothes, and send the boys to the basement so he and I can snuggle up on the couch and watch an episode of *Only Murders in the Building*. Tonight, I'll climb into bed, close my eyes, and think, *Today was a great day.*

There was a time not so long ago when a normal life seemed out of reach. Days after Chris's plea hearing in March of 2021, I sat at my computer wondering what was to come of my life. I was afraid. Really afraid. Chris's prison sentence would last only five years, and that's if he served his full sentence. I wondered what would happen once he was released. There was a lingering possibility of him contacting me, though that didn't seem likely. It was me I feared. What if five years wasn't enough time to heal? What if, someday, I reached out to him again, and he was lonely (or bored) enough to respond? What if I sabotaged myself because there was a part of me that still believed I didn't deserve my family? What if I spent the next five years climbing this mountain only to jump off once I reached the top?

In the midst of my despair, a deep calm settled in my chest. A voice emerged from within and told me, "You're going to write your story." It seemed to come out of nowhere. Though I'd been journaling every day, I had no intention of writing something others would read. But once the thought was planted, it instantly took root.

I called Ian. "This is going to sound crazy, but I think I'm going to write a book. I need to share my story. I can't explain it, but I feel like it's what I'm supposed to do."

"Honestly," he said, with an upward inflection, "I'm not surprised."

"I don't want to do this unless you're okay with it. This is your story too."

"Whether people know the story or not.... It's *true*. It happened. You might as well use it to help someone else. As long as it helps you to heal, it'll be worth it."

I knew there was a part of Ian that wished we could dig a hole six feet deep and bury this chapter of our lives, wipe the dirt from our hands, and vow never to tell another soul what we knew. But hiding the damage would not erase it. And secrecy came at too high a cost. Secrecy was what opened the door for Chris to initiate a sexual relationship with me, and for that relationship to contaminate the entire span of my adolescence and young adulthood. Secrecy kept Chris in a classroom, where he had daily contact with vulnerable children, for over twenty years. Secrecy allowed me to get on a plane to Florida, to come within inches of destroying everything that had taken me decades to build. It threatened my marriage, my family, and my very life.

Secrecy was not the answer. Hiding was not the answer. But I feared what was waiting on the other side of the door should I choose to share my story. What if it forever changed the way people looked at me? What if I never again entered a room without at least one person knowing the most private and vulnerable parts of my life? How would Ian's life be affected? What about our children? How would we explain this to them in a way they would understand?

On the other hand, if I didn't face my fear, what kind of example was I setting for others facing a similar choice? How could I tell them to listen to the knowing inside themselves if I was unwilling to listen to mine? What about the victims who didn't feel like they had a choice but to remain voiceless? Who would speak for them?

I was so tired of living in fear. Fear of myself. Fear of Chris. Fear of losing my marriage. Fear that, someday, people might discover the worst things about me. I imagined myself ten, twenty, thirty years in the future, when what seemed so big would eventually seem so small. I would always regret betraying my husband and hurting those who love me, but I'd never regret having done everything I could to make amends and to live a life I could be at peace with at the end of the day. After nearly losing everything, I realized there were things more precious than someone's shallow opinion of me. To be fully known is to be fully loved, and I was through with accepting anything less for myself.

My therapist, Becca, was right: two things can be true at the same time. I wish these painful experiences had never happened, and yet, I would never want to give up the person I've become as a result of those experiences. Continuing to carry shame and fear no longer served any purpose. They would only prevent me from growing into the wife and mother my family needed me to be, the advocate survivors and targets of abuse needed me to be. I had a choice to make: I could let my trauma become the hammer that crushes me, or I could let it be the scalpel I use to carve out a stronger, healthier version of myself. So I opened a blank document on my computer and began writing the story I hoped would save me, and possibly, one day, save others as well.

Writing a memoir was like sitting cross-legged in front of a thousand scattered puzzle pieces, each one representing a snapshot of my life. One by one, I'd pick up each of the pieces, considering their unique intricacies, feeling their corners and edges for clues as to which ones fit together. The more connections I made between my present and past, the more truths I would uncover, and the closer I'd come to forging a path toward healing.

The greatest challenge was needing to spend time with Chris in my mind so that I could get him onto a page, figuring out how to wade into rough waters without being swept away by the undertow. I couldn't prevent the emotional and physical responses to these memories, a constant source of confusion and shame. It would be three more years before I learned, through a Certified Clinical Trauma Professional (CCTP) intensive training course, that these responses were not indicators of voluntary obsession; they were symptoms of post-traumatic stress disorder (I had always believed PTSD felt like *fear*, I had never imagined it could feel like *love*). Until that time, I would continue to struggle with the guilt and shame of having any emotional responses to memories of Chris that manifested in dependency, survival, affection, loyalty and longing.

A few weeks into writing, I was still committed to the sobriety journey I had started that January in preparation for the potential trial in Florida. I was 108 days sober when I began to transcribe the memory of Chris and me on the bus ride back from *Blast!* during the fall of my sophomore year. I had no idea this particular memory would be so painful to write about. There I was, sitting beside him on that green leathery seat, seeing and feeling everything through the lens of my fifteen-year-old self . . . and I felt my insides pulling apart from grief.

When I called Ian, I kept my voice steady to mask the fact that I'd been crying. I asked him to pick up a bottle of my favorite wine. I needed to feel pleasure strong enough to knock out the pain.

"Are you sure that's what you want?" he asked.

I waved off his concern. "It's not a big deal. I'm fine."

Ian brought the bottle home, and I immediately popped the cork. *I'll have just one glass,* I told myself.

The rest of the evening, I sat in front of the TV, drinking steadily until I had finished the bottle. Then I snuck a swig of bourbon from the liquor cabinet, opening and closing the wooden doors quietly so Ian would not hear. Once I was sufficiently numb, I dragged myself to the bedroom and passed out.

The next morning, I experienced the usual regret after a night of drinking, but I didn't wallow in it. I was too focused on getting back to writing, something I now looked forward to every day when I opened my eyes.

My second day writing about the bus scene, the emotions felt less raw. Even less so on the third.

Whenever I took a difficult memory and transcribed it as a scene, bit by bit the memory would lose its original power. It was less upsetting, less disturbing, less shame-inducing . . . because the more I dragged a memory into the light, the better I could see it and understand it, and the less afraid I was to face it. I learned to navigate my grief without resorting to highly self-destructive behaviors. Every day, I took the hand of my younger self and walked with her through valleys of elation and disappointment, embarrassment and fear. I helped her to accept what she couldn't change, and taught her to forgive what she couldn't take back.

I reminded her that, no matter what, she was worthy of love, and that there was reason to believe in a promising future.

Throughout the memoir-writing process, I channeled bravery through other memoirs by women who have boldly laid their stories bare, starting with Cheryl Strayed's *Wild* and Tara Westover's *Educated*. I gathered courage from Brené Brown's *The Wilderness of Belonging* and Glennon Doyle's *Untamed*. I found connection through memoirs written by sexual assault survivors, including Stephen Mill's *Chosen*, Lacy Crawford's *Notes on a Silencing,* Chanel Miller's *Know My Name*, Alisson Wood's *Being Lolita,* Vanessa Springora's *Consent.,* and Daniel Barban Levin's *Slonim Wood's 9*.

Writing and reading inspired me to be creative in other ways. I started a podcast, and an adult women's community choir. I planned an overseas trip for my church's Chancel Choir. I expanded the children's programming at the church to include music classes for all ages. By filling a need or creating an opportunity to improve the lives of others, I started to regain some of the joy I'd lost years earlier. I connected more deeply with the people around me, the way I had before Chris's arrest.

For three years, Ian and I worked diligently to model a happy, healthy marriage in the presence of our children, family members, friends, coworkers, and church community. It wasn't a fake image others were seeing, just an incomplete one. There were countless moments of happiness and laughter between Ian and me, between us and our children. But the shadow of pain was ever present. The longer time ached on, the heavier the shadow grew, and the more fatigued I became dragging the dead weight behind me everywhere I went.

In June of 2022, I woke up to an article about Ghislane Maxwell, who had reportedly received less than the recommended government sentence for assisting Jeffrey Epstien in trafficking and sexually abusing young girls.

I had never written publicly on the topic of child sexual abuse and coercion, but working on my memoir for over a year had helped me to discover language I could use to talk about these complex topics. I took to Facebook and poured my frustration into a post:

> I feel sick. There's such an egregious lack of understanding and accountability when it comes to coercive sexual abuse. It's evil

> to manipulate children to be sexual puppets, to get them to trust you, maybe even love you, so you can use them. It steals from far more than your body. It's something you do not understand unless you've experienced it, which is why we need to listen to victims and believe them. Please, read the testimonies in this article. Women who were groomed and abused as girls—when their brains were forming ideas about themselves, about others, and the world around them—testified to the life-long damage Maxwell caused, yet she was given far less than the recommended sentence. If a child is being abused, go to the authorities, because it's likely the child won't.

The post was more vulnerable than I had intended. Yet, at the far edge of that vulnerability was a margin of relief. Ian's and my marriage had weathered the worst of the storm. We were in a better place now, and it was time to offload some of the dead weight. Speaking out about Ghislaine Maxwell's sentencing was one small thing I could do to lighten the load. It gave me a voice to advocate for victims of child sexual abuse without admitting I was one.

I had just finished rereading my post when the same calming voice that had told me to write my story spoke to me again. This time, it said, *Today is the day you're going to out Chris Blackmer.*

I hadn't planned on sharing anything about my story until the memoir was published. I assumed that, in order for people to understand, I would need to share everything all at once. But that morning, it dawned on me . . . . It was my choice how much I wanted to share and when I wanted to share it. While I had made progress in cognitively processing the reality of my abuse, my mind and body remained disconnected. I would say to myself, *You were raped*, but my body would be unmoved. I would say, *Chris never loved you*, and my body would rebel with disinterest or, worse, longing. If the goal of writing my story was to heal and, through that healing process, build up an impenetrable wall between me and Chris, then I needed to do whatever was necessary, even if it meant surrendering my privacy earlier than I had planned.

All my life, memories of Chris were like a series of rooms no one had been allowed to step foot in except me. As long as I kept people out, I would continue to see what I wanted—what *Chris* wanted—because no one else was there to tell me differently, to point and say, *This was abuse*. I knew that by simply letting people in, it would automatically change the atmosphere of the room, making it impossible to see it the way I once had.

The time had come to trade silence for transparency. I remembered what Pastor William said to me in 2019, that when you love someone you hold them accountable. I loved myself and my family too much to ignore the need for radical accountability. I didn't want these memories anymore; the world could have them. They never should've been mine to keep in the first place.

Around midnight, I published another post:

> When I woke up this morning, I didn't know I'd be writing this. I thought maybe I'd wait a few more years when I could properly share the whole story, but after reading an article reporting that Ghislaine Maxwell received less than the recommended government sentence for coercively sex-trafficking and abusing children, I felt called to offer a glimpse into my own experience with coercive sexual abuse . . . .

I went on to explain that I had been abused by Chris Blackmer for years without any awareness that it was abuse. I gave an overview of the relationship and talked about the state criminal investigation that ended without an arrest. I included the picture from my high school yearbook that showed Chris hovering alarmingly close to me on the football field moments before I conducted the marching band at halftime. (I did not include any information about what happened after the Michigan investigation ended. That would have to wait.)

The comments on the post were overwhelmingly supportive. I received private messages from people I never would've expected—high school classmates, former teachers, people who'd attended college with Chris, all offering their condolences and encouragement.

Then, a tiny miracle arrived in the form of a message from Elizabeth, a college friend two years my senior, who had gone on to become a band director. It said, *I have just the start of a similar story with Chris. I will not share it unless you tell me you want to hear it.*

A pang of betrayal stabbed the center of my gut. Whatever her story, it was going to hurt to hear it. But it didn't matter. I needed to know the truth.

Here's what Elizabeth wrote me after I asked to hear her story:

> ELIZABETH: I hope in the long run this helps you more than it hurts. It's a short story, and I was 18 so it wasn't the same situation, but it was at the same time as yours. In July of 2001, the summer after my freshman year in college, I taught my first band camp. Chris was also an instructor. He flirted heavily with me the entire week, finding lots of excuses to touch me or give me a back rub. I didn't realize how old he was, he looked so young. I don't remember where he was living, but I remember it was like an hour and a half drive to my parents house. He came to my house and took me out to dinner a couple times after camp, and I finally asked him at some point how old he was. When I learned he was 11 years older than me I cut off contact. He technically did nothing wrong. I was 18 so there was nothing to report, and I had no clue who to tell that there was this creepy band director taking 18 year olds out to dinner. I am so sorry this happened to you.

After twenty-one years of not knowing what had happened in the months between drum major camp, where he ignored me, and the White Lake house, where he carried me bridal-style up two flights of stairs, I finally discovered his dirty secret: Chris had tried to seduce another teenage girl.

The major difference between Elizabeth's situation and mine was that he'd held a position of power over me. He had time to groom me from a young age, to carefully build trust over a course of two years. He had known Elizabeth only a week, and aside from him being perceivably older, the two were equals in their paid positions. I never had the opportunity to defend myself the way Elizabeth had after learning his real age. I was only a child when Chris dismantled my ability to see him clearly, an evil exploitative deed that was still harming me well into adulthood.

After Chris's arrest, I was so convinced that the Chris I knew growing up was a different man, a *better* man, than the one I'd read about in the article. I believed I could grieve *that* Chris back into existence. But now I was faced with a sobering thought: maybe there had only ever been one version of Chris. He was an abuser then, and he was an abuser now. As a girl, I'd never considered the possibility that Chris, who acted so romantic and tender, could be so cold-hearted and unfeeling on the inside.

The more people I talked to about him, the more disturbing the picture became. It was as if he was a shapeshifter, becoming whoever he needed to be to win over the people he wanted something from. For some, he was well-composed. For others, like me, he was charming. He played the romantic, because he knew that's what I wanted. And he was able to fool me—not because he was necessarily great at the game, but because he was an adult and I was a child.

A person who can alter their identity at will is a person with no identity at all. It's a person whose behavior has no predictability, and that is a terrifying thing.

Once I stepped forward as a survivor of sexual assault, I was amazed at how quick others were to approach me—either to thank me or to share their own story or a story about a victim they knew. People I knew would stop me at church or in the grocery store parking lot to talk to me or simply give me a hug. I met several women at coffee shops and was privileged enough to be trusted with their stories. More than once, I heard things like, "I've never told anyone this . . . ," or "I always thought it was my fault."

Systems that enable abuse rely on the silence of victims. If every victim felt safe enough to speak out about their experience, they would know that their situation does not exist inside a vacuum. Every account of coercive sexual assault has its own unique characteristics, but there are frequent similarities that reveal the culpability of the person in power and the vulnerability of the person with lesser power. In my many conversations with women who had been violated by a man in authority, physical boundaries were tested when the man offered his target a back massage. If the woman responded positively, he took it as permission to go further. But if the woman appeared uncomfortable or outwardly rejected their advances, the men would play it off like it was an innocuous gesture.

I thought about Chris and me in the band room office, Elizabeth at the band camp she worked with Chris . . . . He used the same technique with us both. Later that year, I would read Jeanette McCurdy's memoir and learn that, when she was a teen, a director at Nickelodeon used a back rub as an excuse to touch her, pretending that it was a caring gesture. I watched a documentary about a corrupted religious organization, where young girls were given back rubs by the organization's leader before the abuse escalated to a criminal level.

Was there some secret handbook these abusers shared that offered time-proven strategies? How did they learn what works best on targets of abuse and what doesn't?

As long as we, the survivors, are too afraid or ashamed to share our stories, it's possible for us to go on believing that our situations are isolated, or that we asked for it—or at the very least, that we were to blame for not stopping it.

Even kind, caring people play a part in these systems because they don't have any awareness of how their beliefs, which have been ingrained in them by society, are directly responsible for perpetuating rape culture. American society, which is still largely in the dark about sexual assault and abuse, continues to victim blame and shame, leading to the silencing of victims—which means society can continue to stroll along, hands in pockets, whistling to the tune of ignorance.

The year 2023 marked a major turning point in my healing process. By this time, I had gone through many front-to-back revisions of my manuscript. The first seven or so were all in chronological order, and it just wasn't where I wanted it to be. I had a vision early on in the writing process that I would alternate between scenes from the past and present so I could tie everything together; I didn't know if it would even work.

Eventually, my writing skills improved enough that I was able to bring that vision to life. I owe a lot of my inspiration to author Kate Elizabeth Russell. In 2021, Ian had discovered her novel, *My Dark Vanessa*, about a precocious teenage girl whose abuse by her high school English teacher significantly impacts her life as a young person and as an adult. Ian waited until he had almost finished the book before he shared its existence with me, because it was too difficult to talk about. He said that every page felt like a punch in the gut, but it also helped him to gain an understanding and empathy for me he didn't have prior to reading the book. *My Dark Vanessa* used an alternating structure, and I knew it was what I needed to do as well.

At a time when I heavily questioned my decision to continue writing this memoir, *My Dark Vanessa*, was the sign I needed to keep going. Aside from the more obvious connections between Vanessa's story and mine, the book was released on March 10, 2020—Chris's forty-eighth birthday—and only one specific date is mentioned in the book—May 2, 2001—the day I turned sixteen years old.

It was also in 2023 that I began making connections with women who had been abused by their high school teachers (several specifically by their band directors). I remembered thinking in high school that my relationship with Chris was a rare case. As it turns out, there are many brilliant women walking around—many with partners and children—whose lives have been significantly impacted by educator abuse. Some who struggle on a daily basis to make sense of the betrayal they experienced at the hand of an adult they cared for deeply, who was supposed to care for them.

During a music education conference, Ian attended a presentation by *The Elephant Alliance*, an organization whose aim is to prevent educator sexual misconduct, actions that range anywhere from dirty jokes and inappropriate texting outside of school to sexual harassment and rape. Ian connected me with the two female founders, who became another source of friendship and support.

In March, I contacted the St. Pete Beach police department in Florida to report a rape—specifically, the sexual encounter between Chris and me at the Airbnb. It wasn't the first time I had thought about that night as being coercive rape, but it'd taken me years to stand firmly in that truth. I needed time to heal, to gather information from mental health professionals, to crawl out from under the weight of shame. I wasn't going to let someone who had no understanding of my trauma and grief tell me what I did or didn't experience.

Early that morning, I had looked up Florida's statutes regarding sexual crimes and read their definition of consent. "'Consent' means intelligent, knowing, and voluntary consent, and does not include coerced submission. "Consent" shall not be deemed or construed to mean the failure by the alleged victim to offer physical resistance to the offender." What interested me even more was the definition of "mentally defective" as it relates to a person's inability to consent: "'Mentally defective' means a mental disease or defect which renders a person temporarily or permanently incapable of appraising the nature of his or her conduct."

Unlike the Michigan statute of limitations, which had long expired for prosecuting my assault and abuse, I was still within the window of reporting a sexual assault in Florida. If it meant that Chris might be held legally accountable for abusing me and he could be sent back to prison where he couldn't hurt me or anyone else, I resolved to leave no stone unturned.

The officer who was taking my report requested that I start at the very beginning. I walked him through the grooming I experienced in high school, the first time Chris sexually assaulted me, the multiple times I was raped in his apartment in Davison, the ongoing sexual interactions throughout high school and college. I told him how traumatized I was the day I saw Chris's arrest article, and how that affected my mental health. I told him about the Michigan investigation, why it ended with no arrest, the grief and desperation that led to contacting Chris, who saw an opportunity to manipulate and use me again. I remembered that, during my official statement to the Michigan State Police, Sergeant Perry asked me to be specific about physical interactions, so I told the Florida officer every shameful detail of my betrayal, every degrading moment at the Airbnb, until I was spent.

Through a fog of exhaustion, I heard the officer say, "I'm sorry—what crime are you reporting?"

My heart skipped a beat. "I'm reporting a rape."

He spoke casually, as if debating with himself about what to order off a restaurant menu. "I'm not the person who makes these decisions, but from what you've said and what I have here, I don't see that any crime was committed . . . . When did the rape happen?"

"He raped me in that bedroom," I said, refering to the AirBnb.

Incredulously, he followed up, "Tell me, how was that rape?"

I tried to steady my breathing. I explained that, in Florida's sexual crime statutes, there's a provision for mental defect as it relates to consent. "I was mentally incapacitated due to the nature of our relationship," I told the officer. I reminded him that this was the man that groomed me and raped me for years when I was a child, that the power imbalance in our relationship had still been intact.

He jeered, "Have you ever been diagnosed? Do you have depression or something?"

I was shaking now. Tears welled up in my eyes. "I'm on medication for anxiety and depression, but that's not what I'm talking about. Do you really think someone in their right mind would leave their family to be with a child abuser?"

He continued to prod until, finally, his apathy was too much to bear. I began to cry openly. I pleaded with him, "You have to believe me."

"I believe that, when you were a child, you had no control over the situation. But you're an adult now . . . . Didn't this all start when *you* contacted *him*?"

"No," I said, with blunt force. "This all started when he groomed and sexually abused me as a child."

"You said you consented at the Airbnb."

"I never said I consented. I said, 'We had sex.' He still had power over me. He was able to manipulate me and warp my reality."

I was shocked by this officer's lack of basic decency and professionalism. The callous disregard he showed for my experience. I didn't fault the man for being confused, especially a man who appeared to have no concept of child sexual grooming and assault. But if he had no concept of these things, why was he the person taking my report? I should have been speaking to someone who was better trained in talking to victims of sexual crimes. Someone who knows that when an adult grooms and sexually assaults a child, they have caused physical harm to that child's cognitive development. Trauma is, after all, a brain *injury*... and unless the wound is acknowledged and tended to properly, there will be lasting implications on a victim's physical, mental, emotional, and spiritual well-being.

Whatever injuries I incurred during my childhood, adolescence, and young adulthood, as a result of Chris's abuse, they were just a prelude to the most devastating injury of all. When I saw Chris's mugshot and read what he had done, it tore through the fabric of my reality, and I had no idea how to stitch it back together. I saw the world through the lens of trauma and grief, where surviving seemed like my only choice.

"You're in Michigan, so our detectives would have to go up there to interview you." The resignation in his voice told me there was no possibility of that happening.

I filed a complaint against the St. Pete Beach officer. A few days later, I was contacted by a sheriff who apologized for the behavior of the officer, explaining—regretfully—that many of the men on the force are young and forget, at times, they are talking to someone on that person's worst day. The sheriff was kind and well-intentioned. He said there probably wasn't anything that could be done because Florida does not provide for coercive rape. "Did you say *no* at any given point?" he asked. "You have to say no."

I didn't want to say no, I thought. *I had never, in the whole of our relationship, wanted to say no.* But that's because of the coercion I'd experienced. The person I was with. Why use force when you can get a person to lie down willingly, and all you have to do is trick them into believing you love them?

The sheriff gave me the phone number of someone I could call to talk to for support. He understood Chris was a threat to me and my family, and he suggested I file a personal protective order (PPO) to ensure no contact between us—no letters to or from the prison, no phone calls. If approved by a judge, the order could be extended after his release. Toward the end of the conversation, he said, "We have to help kids have better self esteem so they can't be taken advantage of so easily."

I didn't have the will to explain to the sheriff: self-esteem is not the problem. I would never hand car keys to a teenager who had never learned to drive, then blame them for crashing the car. How can we expect children to protect themselves from dangerous adults when the safe adults are doing nothing to educate and prepare them for the challenge? Why are we putting the responsibility of protecting children on the children themselves?

Per the sheriff's recommendation, I filed an application in Michigan for a PPO. I included every piece of documentation available to me—the Michigan State Police case file, emails exchanged between me and Sergeant Perry, files from the Orange County Clerk's office that proved Chris's crimes in Florida. On the application, it asked me to identify any unique physical attributes about Chris like piercings, tattoos, or scars. In the blank space I wrote, "Prominent varicose vein on interior of left calf."

A week later, when I hadn't heard back from the courthouse, I called for an answer. The application was denied, citing, "No immediate danger."

In the words of Fred Rogers, "Anything that is human is mentionable, and anything that is mentionable can be more manageable." We live in a society that heaps trauma onto us, then blames us for reacting to that trauma. So we keep secrets. We find places inside ourselves to hide the things we want to forget, because we believe forgetting is the only path to survival and acceptance. We swallow down the words we long to speak. We tell ourselves, *Everything is fine. Everything is fine. Everything is fine.* We do all this in an effort to prevent harm, when, in reality, we continue to be at war with ourselves, and we pass our unresolved trauma down to the next generation.

I dread the day that is quickly approaching when my husband and I will sit down with our oldest child, Evan, and tell him what's happened. (Eli is not yet old enough for the full story.) I can already see the stunned look on Evan's face, the controlled sadness in his voice when he will ask for confirmation. *Mom . . . You cheated on Dad?* And I will feel my heart breaking into a million pieces. I can barely breathe when I think about confessing to my mother-in-law that I hurt her son.

I mourn the loss of my freedom to stand in front of a room of people without them knowing the most vulnerable moments in my life.

I sometimes wonder if this was Chris's plan all along, to purchase my silence with my own fear and shame. When I first contacted him in 2019, he must have sensed my vulnerability. According to the Michigan State Police transcript (which I first read in May of 2022), when Sergeant Perry and his partner spoke to Chris in Florida, they made it sound like my high school—not me—had contacted them about rumors surrounding our relationship. They told Chris I had said that everything between us was consensual, that I had been "head over heels" for him. This was all the information he would've needed to know that I was still living under a cloud of illusion—and if he encouraged communication between us, convinced me to be an ally . . . if something happened between us that I'd want kept secret from the world, then I would never testify against him.

He should have known better. But, then again, he never really knew me. If he did, he would have known I would not only tell the truth, but I would write (and publish) an entire book about it. I would make it my mission to protect other children and their families from the pain my family and I have had to endure. I would make every effort to reach the other children Chris targeted, manipulated, abused—children who are now adults or young adults, so I can tell them that they aren't alone, and I hope they find the love and support they need to forge their own path to healing.

It's difficult to compose an ending to a story that still plays on. As I write this, I am in my ninth month of sobriety. Chris will be released from prison next year, and I have never been less afraid of that fact. Years of therapy and hard work—and by hard work, I mean the practice of choosing what is right over what is easy—have paved pathways for my mind and body to find resolution with one another. While there's still pain and grief to work through, I am no longer at war with myself. As of last year, I have transitioned out of full-time music ministry and am seeking new opportunities to grow and help others. My sister-in-law, (who served as my developmental editor for this memoir) and I have started a business to empower other women to share their stories. I can't wait to see where that journey takes us.

As a girl, I had all these ideas in my head about what true love is. Now I have only one: True love heals. It's a friend that sits with you in your darkest moment, free of judgment. It's a parent that puts your best interest ahead of their own, even when it's difficult. It's a partner who sees the best in you, even when you can't see it in yourself. It's being able to face your past with honesty and compassion, knowing that everything you've experienced has made you who you are today. That's something to celebrate.

If you or someone you know has been sexually assaulted, help is available.
Contact RAINN's National Sexual Assault Hotline:
Confidential 24/7 Support
800-656-4673
Chat online: online.rainn.org

Acknowledgements

Dan, you are the greatest example of love that I know. Your unwavering support has not only made my writing of this memoir possible, but without your presence in my life this story would not be what it is. You are living proof that love can heal unimaginable wounds and bring light into the darkest of places. You have taught me to be a better partner and friend, and I thank God daily for the opportunity to be with you on this grand adventure.

To my boys, who are shining examples of goodness. Someday, you will know the full story, and I hope it serves as a source of strength when you experience dark seasons of life. As your dad and I have told you before, "We're Farisons. We can get through anything."

Thank you, Mom, for greenlighting my telling of this story from day one and for your willingness to face the past with me. I love you.

My deepest gratitude to my sister-in-law, developmental editor, and business partner, Danielle Szabreath, who spent countless hours to ensure this book would be exactly what I dreamed it would be. I couldn't have done this without you.

Max Gorlov and Anna Schechter at First Book Coaching, your invaluable support and expert feedback helped me reach the finish line, and I am forever grateful.

To every friend who gave me a safe space to share my story, and to those who took the time to read my manuscript and offer feedback and encouragement . . . there are no words to describe the love I feel for you. I am the luckiest person alive to be surrounded by such empathetic humans.

Ann Nagley and Molly Clarey, thank you for always advocating for my voice, and giving me the tools I've needed to grow and heal the last five years.

Mackenzie Bufis, thank you for your friendship, trust, and encouragement. You have been a significant part of my healing journey.

To Lisa Cook, I have not forgotten that day in Panera. I thank you (and Ron) for loving us and our boys.

Editor Tenyia Lee, your eye for detail and gift for language helped me to publish this book with confidence.

Editor Jodi Fodor, thank you for pushing me to be a better writer.

I was able to meet my desired publication date thanks to generous backers who invested in this project through Kickstarter: Cynthia and Doug Whitacre, Spencer White, Kori Orlowsi, Randy Kawakita, Dennis Hale, The Saad Family, Robert Dale Pore, Rosanna Dyer, Heather Francisco, and Kate Byrne.

ABOUT THE AUTHOR

Megan Farison is a seasoned educator, musician, and voice coach. She is the Co-Founder of Give Her the Pen, a memoir coaching business that empowers women to own their stories, one page at a time. Megan has interviewed internationally renowned music artists, composers, and educators on her podcast Sing, Coach, Conduct. This is her first book.

Made in United States
Cleveland, OH
04 December 2024

11353464R00182